O1

2011 F

Be book smart. *Why pay* _____ _____ _____ charged by other publishers for the same rules and code! Our annual books are also more current—available in January, just weeks after new rule changes become law. (Other publishers take months to publish!) And our books are compact and portable.

See our website for information on volume discounts and customized covers.

Four easy ways to order:

- *Web:* order on-line at www.legalpub.com.
- *Fax:* this order form to 978-456-9247.
- *Mail:* this order form to the address below.
- *Call:* 888-232-0226.

Order Information:

- ☐ The New United States Patent Law _____ Qty. x $30⁰⁰ ea.............................$ _____
- ☐ Bankruptcy Code & Rules Booklet _____ Qty. x $25⁰⁰ ea............................ _____
- ☐ Federal Civil Rules Booklet _____ Qty. x $23⁰⁰ ea...................................... _____
- ☐ Litigator's Pocket Diary _____ (leather w/Federal Rules) Qty. x $42⁰⁰ ea... _____

Subtotal .... _____
Shipping & handling: Subtotals of $60 or less, $4.80. All others, subtotal x .08................ _____
Sales tax (Massachusetts residents only; subtotal x .0625) .... _____
TOTAL ....$ _____

Payment Method: ☐ Check   ☐ Visa   ☐ Mastercard   ☐ AmEx

Card #: _____ Exp. _____

Printed Name: _____ Signature: _____

Card Billing Address _____
(Street Address & Zip Code only)

Shipping Information:

Name: _____

Firm: _____

Address: _____

City: _____ State: _____ Zip: _____

Phone: _____ Email: _____

LegalPub.com, Inc., 113 East Bare Hill Road, Harvard, MA 01451-1856

The New United States Patent Law

Black Line Edition

Includes:
United States Code Title 35 "Patents"
As amended by
The Leahy-Smith America Invents Act
In Black Line Format

Published by
LegalPub.com, Inc.
Harvard, Massachusetts

Printed and bound in the United States of America. ISBN: 978-1-934852-09-5

Comments and corrections are welcome and may be sent to us via the "contact" page on our website. Corrections, if any, are posted on the "updates" page of our website. The publisher has made every effort to ensure the accuracy of information contained in this product but cannot assume liability for inadvertent errors.

LegalPub.com, Inc.
113 East Bare Hill Rd.
Harvard, MA 01451-1856
Tele: 888-232-0226
Fax: 978-456-9247
Web: www.legalpub.com

Contents

Contents

Preface

On September 16, 2011, President Obama signed into law the Leahy-Smith America Invents Act ("the Reform Act").* The Reform Act imposes the most sweeping changes to the U.S. patent law in nearly 60 years. For example, it moves the U.S. from a "first to invent" to a "first inventor to file" system, provides new post-grant and Inter Partes review procedures, allows third party submissions during the examination of a patent application, limits false marketing suits, excludes tax strategy patents, prohibits use of the best mode requirement for invalidating a patent, limits joinder of defendants in infringement cases, expands the prior commercial use defense, replaces current interference proceedings with derivation proceedings, and provides fee setting authority to the USPTO.

This publication sets forth in black line format each change to Title 35 of the United States Code effected by the America Invents Act. Insertions are identified by underline; deletions are identified by strike-through. Full citation to source legislation follows each code section. The book shows exactly what words in the United States patent law are changed and what words stay the same.

Section 35 of the Reform Act provides that "the provisions of this Act shall take effect upon the expiration of the 1-year period beginning on the date of the enactment of this Act and shall apply to any patent issued on or after that effective date." However, there are numerous exceptions to this general effective date. Many of these exceptions are summarized in the Table that follows.

The publication also includes excerpts from House Judiciary Committee Report 112-98 dated June 1, 2011. The report sets forth the background and need for the legislation and explains many of the changes to the patent law effected by the Reform Act.

This publication does not include all statutory and regulatory provisions which are affected by the Reform Act. Nor does it address those provisions which do not expressly amend the text of existing code (e.g. sense of Congress resolutions, directions to government departments and agencies to prepare reports or establish rules or regulations). Comments and corrections are welcome and may be submitted via the "contact" page of our website *www.legalpub.com*. Corrections, if any, will be posted on the "updates" page of our website.

The Publisher
September 16, 2011

---

*At the time of publication, the Public Law Number for the Reform Act was not yet available.

Table - Effective Date

Table of Exceptions to General Efctive Date*

Affected Code §	Subject	Reform Act §	Reform Act Language Relating to Effective Date/Applicability
28 USC §§ 1295(a)(1), 1338(a), 1454; 35 USC § 299	Jurisdiction and procedural matters.	19e	"The amendments made by this section shall apply to any civil action commenced on or after the date of the enactment of this Act."
35 USC §§ 2b2g, 4h1	prioritized examination	11h4A	"This subsection shall take effect on the date that is 10 days after the date of the enactment of this Act."
35 USC §§ 6, 141	Patent Trial and Appeal Board	7e	"The amendments made by this section shall take effect upon the expiration of the 1-year period beginning on the date of the enactment of this Act and shall apply to proceedings commenced on or after that effective date, except that—[various exceptions listed]"
35 USC § 32	Statute of Limitations	3(k)(3)	"The amendment made by paragraph (1) shall apply in any case in which the time period for instituting a proceeding under section 32 of title 35, United States Code, had not lapsed before the date of the enactment of this Act."
35 USC §§ 32, 145, 146, 154(b)(4)(A), and 293	Venue	9b	"The amendments made by this section shall take effect on the date of the enactment of this Act and shall apply to any civil action commenced on or after that date."
35 USC §§ 41(a), (b), (d)(1), 132(b)	Surcharge	112A-B	"The surcharge provided for in Paragraph (1) -- (A) shall take effect on the date that is 10 days after the date of the enactment of this Act; and (B) shall terminate, with respect to a fee to which paragraph (1)(A) applies, on the effective date of the setting or adjustment of that fee pursuant to the exercise of the authority under section 10 for the first time with respect to that fee."

Statute	Title	Section	Provision
35 USC § 41	Fees for patent services	11j	"Except as otherwise provided in this section, this section and the amendments made by this section shall take effect on the date of the enactment of this Act."
35 USC § 42c	Patent Office funding	22b	"The amendments made by this section shall take effect on October 1, 2011."
35 USC §§ 100, 102-104, 134, 135, 146, 291	First Inventor to File	3(n)(1)A-B	"IN GENERAL.—Except as otherwise provided in this section, the amendments made by this section shall take effect upon the expiration of the 18-month period beginning on the date of the enactment of this Act, and shall apply to any application for patent, and to any patent issuing thereon, that contains or contained at any time—(A) a claim to a claimed invention that has an effective filing date as defined in section 100(i) of title 35, United States Code, that is on or after the effective date described in this paragraph; or (B) a specific reference under section 120, 121, or 365(c) of title 35, United States Code, to any patent or application that contains or contained at any time such a claim"
35 USC §§ 102(g), 135, and 291	Interfering Patents	3(n)(2)A-B	"The provisions of sections 102(g), 135, and 291 of title 35, United States Code, as in effect on the day before the effective date set forth in paragraph (1) of this subsection, shall apply to each claim of an application for patent, and any patent issued thereon, for which the amendments made by this section also apply, if such application or patent contains or contained at any time—(A) a claim to an invention having an effective filing date as defined in section 100(i) of title 35, United States Code, that occurs before the effective date set forth in paragraph (1) of this subsection; or (B) a specific reference under section 120, 121, or 365(c) of title 35, United States Code, to any patent or application that contains or contained at any time such a claim."
35 USC §§ 115, 118	Inventor's Oath or Declaration	4(e)	"The amendments made by this section shall take effect upon the expiration of the 1-year period beginning on the date of the enactment of this Act and shall apply to any patent application that is filed on or after that effective date."
35 USC § 122	Preissuance Submissions by Third Parties	8b	"The amendments made by this section shall take effect upon the expiration of the 1-year period beginning on the date of the enactment of this Act and shall apply to any patent application filed before, on, or after that effective date."

Table - Effective Date

Table of Exceptions to General Effctive Date*

Affected Code §	Subject	Reform Act §	Reform Act Language Relating to Effective Date/Applicability
35 USC §§ 123	Fee Setting Authority	10i1	"Except as provided in subsection (h), this section and the amendments made by this section shall take effect on the date of the enactment of this Act."
35 USC § 157	Repeal of Statutory Invention Registration	3(e)(3)	"The amendments made by this subsection shall take effect upon the expiration of the 18-month period beginning on the date of the enactment of this Act, and shall apply to any request for a statutory invention registration filed on or after that effective date."
35 USC § 202(c)(7) (E)(i)	Funding Agreements	13b	"The amendments made by this section shall take effect on the date of the enactment of this Act and shall apply to any patent issued before, on, or after that date."
35 USC § 257	supplemental examination	12c	"The amendments made by this section shall take effect upon the expiration of the 1-year period beginning on the date of the enactment of this Act and shall apply to any patent issued before, on, or after that effective date."
35 USC § 273	Defense to Infringement Based on Prior Commercial Use	5c	"The amendments made by this section shall apply to any patent issued on or after the date of the enactment of this Act."
35 USC § 282	Best mode requirement	15c	"The amendments made by this section shall take effect upon the date of the enactment of this Act and shall apply to proceedings commenced on or after that date."
35 USC § 287(a)	Virtual Marking	16a2	"The amendment made by this subsection shall apply to any case that is pending on, or commenced on or after, the date of the enactment of this Act."
35 USC § 292	False Marking	16b4	"The amendments made by this subsection shall apply to all cases, without exception, that are pending on, or commenced on or after, the date of the enactment of this Act."

Statute	Topic	Section	Effective Date Provision
35 USC § 301	Citation of Prior Art and Written Statements	6g3	"The amendments made by this subsection shall take effect upon the expiration of the 1-year period beginning on the date of the enactment of this Act and shall apply to any patent issued before, on, or after that effective date."
35 USC § 303(a)	Reexamination	6h1B	"The amendment made by this paragraph shall take effect upon the expiration of the 1-year period beginning on the date of the enactment of this Act and shall apply to any patent issued before, on, or after that effective date."
35 USC § 306	Reexamination Appeal	6h2B	"The amendment made by this paragraph shall take effect on the date of the enactment of this Act and shall apply to any appeal of a reexamination before the Board of Patent Appeals and Interferences or the Patent Trial and Appeal Board that is pending on, or brought on or after, the date of the enactment of this Act."
35 USC §§ 311-319	Inter partes review	6c2A	"IN GENERAL.—The amendments made by subsection (a) shall take effect upon the expiration of the 1-year period beginning on the date of the enactment of this Act and shall apply to any patent issued before, on, or after that effective date."
35 USC §§ 312-313 (transition provisions)	Inter partes review (transition)	6c3Bi-ii, C	"APPLICATION.—The amendments made by this paragraph— (i) shall take effect on the date of the enactment of this Act; and (ii) shall apply to requests for inter partes reexamination that are filed on or after such date of enactment, but before the effective date set forth in paragraph (2)(A) of this subsection. (C) CONTINUED APPLICABILITY OF PRIOR PROVISIONS.—The provisions of chapter 31 of title 35, United States Code, as amended by this paragraph, shall continue to apply to requests for inter partes reexamination that are filed before the effective date set forth in paragraph (2)(A) as if subsection (a) had not been enacted."
35 USC §§ 321-329	Post Grant Review	6f2A	"IN GENERAL.—The amendments made by subsection (d) shall take effect upon the expiration of the 1-year period beginning on the date of the enactment of this Act and, except as provided in section 18 and in paragraph (3), shall apply only to patents described in section 3(n)(1)."
various	Technical amendments	20l	"The amendments made by this section shall take effect upon the expiration of the 1-year period beginning on the date of the enactment of this Act and shall apply to proceedings commenced on or after that effective date."

35 USC Table

UNITED STATES CODE—TITLE 35. PATENTS

Table of Chapters

35 USC Table

§ 103. Conditions for patentability; non-obvious subject matter

§ 104. Invention made abroad

§ 105. Inventions in outer space

CHAPTER 12. EXAMINATION OF APPLICATION

CHAPTER 13. REVIEW OF PATENT AND TRADEMARK OFFICE DECISIONS

CHAPTER 14. ISSUE OF PATENT

35 USC Table

35 USC Table

PART I. UNITED STATES PATENT AND TRADEMARK OFFICE

CHAPTER 1. ESTABLISHMENT, OFFICERS AND EMPLOYEES, FUNCTIONS

§ 1. Establishment

(a) Establishment. The United States Patent and Trademark Office is established as an agency of the United States, within the Department of Commerce. In carrying out its functions, the United States Patent and Trademark Office shall be subject to the policy direction of the Secretary of Commerce, but otherwise shall retain responsibility for decisions regarding the management and administration of its operations and shall exercise independent control of its budget allocations and expenditures, personnel decisions and processes, procurements, and other administrative and management functions in accordance with this title and applicable provisions of law. Those operations designed to grant and issue patents and those operations which are designed to facilitate the registration of trademarks shall be treated as separate operating units within the Office.

(b) Offices. The United States Patent and Trademark Office shall maintain its principal office in the metropolitan Washington, D.C., area, for the service of process and papers and for the purpose of carrying out its functions. The United States Patent and Trademark Office shall be deemed, for purposes of venue in civil actions, to be a resident of the district in which its principal office is located, except where jurisdiction is otherwise provided by law. The United States Patent and Trademark Office may establish satellite offices in such other places in the United States as it considers necessary and appropriate in the conduct of its business.

(c) Reference. For purposes of this title, the United States Patent and Trademark Office shall also be referred to as the "Office" and the "Patent and Trademark Office".

HISTORY:

(July 19, 1952, ch 950, § 1, 66 Stat. 792; Jan. 2, 1975, P.L. 93-596, § 1, 88 Stat. 1949; Nov. 29, 1999, P.L. 106-113, Div B, § 1000(a)(9), 113 Stat. 1536.)

§ 2. Powers and duties

(a) In general. The United States Patent and Trademark Office, subject to the policy direction of the Secretary of Commerce—

(1) shall be responsible for the granting and issuing of patents and the registration of trademarks; and

(2) shall be responsible for disseminating to the public information with respect to patents and trademarks.

(b) Specific powers. The Office—

(1) shall adopt and use a seal of the Office, which shall be judicially noticed and with which letters patent, certificates of trademark registrations, and papers issued by the Office shall be authenticated;

(2) may establish regulations, not inconsistent with law, which—

(A) shall govern the conduct of proceedings in the Office;

(B) shall be made in accordance with section 553 of title 5;

(C) shall facilitate and expedite the processing of patent applications, particularly those which can be filed, stored, processed, searched, and retrieved electronically, subject to the provisions of section 122 [35 USC § 122] relating to the confidential status of applications;

(D) may govern the recognition and conduct of agents, attorneys, or other persons representing applicants or other parties before the Office, and may require them, before being recognized as representatives of applicants or other persons, to show that they are of good moral character and reputation and are possessed of the necessary qualifications to render to applicants or other persons valuable service, advice, and assistance in the presentation or prosecution of their applications or other business before the Office;

(E) shall recognize the public interest in continuing to safeguard broad access to the United States patent system through the reduced fee structure for small entities under section 41(h)(1) of this title [35 USC § 41(h)(1)]; and

(F) provide for the development of a performance-based process that includes quantitative and qualitative measures and standards for evaluating cost-effectiveness and is consistent with the principles of impartiality and competitiveness; and

(G) may, subject to any conditions prescribed by the Director and at the request of the patent applicant, provide for prioritization of examination of applications for products, processes, or technologies that are important to the national economy or national competitiveness without recovering the aggregate extra cost of providing such prioritization, notwithstanding section 41 or any other provision of law;

(3) may acquire, construct, purchase, lease, hold, manage, operate, improve, alter, and renovate any real, personal, or mixed property, or any interest therein, as it considers necessary to carry out its functions;

(4)(A) may make such purchases, contracts for the construction, maintenance, or management and operation of facilities, and contracts for supplies or services, without regard to the provisions of subtitle I and chapter 33 of title 40 [40 USC §§ 101 et seq. and 3301 et seq.], division C (except sections 3302, 3501(b), 3509, 3906, 4710, and 4711) of subtitle I of title 41 [41 USC §§ 3101 et seq. (except 41 USC §§ 3302, 3501(b), 3509, 3906, 4710, and 4711)], and the Stewart B. McKinney Homeless Assistance Act [McKinney-Vento Homeless Assistance Act] (42 U.S.C. 11301 et seq.); and

(B) may enter into and perform such purchases and contracts for printing services, including the process of composition, platemaking, presswork, silk screen processes, binding, microform, and the products of such processes, as it considers necessary to carry out the functions of the Office, without regard to sections 501 through 517 and 1101 through 1123 of title 44;

(5) may use, with their consent, services, equipment, personnel, and facilities of other departments, agencies, and instrumentalities of the Federal Government, on a reimbursable basis, and cooperate with such other departments, agencies, and instrumentalities in the establishment and use of services, equipment, and facilities of the Office;

(6) may, when the Director determines that it is practicable, efficient, and cost-effective to do so, use, with the consent of the United States and the agency, instrumentality, Patent and Trademark Office, or international organization concerned, the services, records, facilities, or personnel of any State or local government agency or instrumentality or foreign patent and trademark office or international organization to perform functions on its behalf;

(7) may retain and use all of its revenues and receipts, including revenues from the sale, lease, or disposal of any real, personal, or mixed property, or any interest therein, of the Office;

(8) shall advise the President, through the Secretary of Commerce, on national and certain international intellectual property policy issues;

(9) shall advise Federal departments and agencies on matters of intellectual property policy in the United States and intellectual property protection in other countries;

(10) shall provide guidance, as appropriate, with respect to proposals by agencies to assist foreign governments and international intergovernmental organizations on matters of intellectual property protection;

(11) may conduct programs, studies, or exchanges of items or services regarding domestic and international intellectual property law and the effectiveness of intellectual property protection domestically and throughout the world, and the Office is authorized to expend funds to cover the subsistence expenses and travel-related expenses, including per diem, lodging costs, and transportation costs, of persons attending such programs who are not Federal employees;

(12)(A) shall advise the Secretary of Commerce on programs and studies relating to intellectual property policy that are conducted, or authorized to be conducted, cooperatively with foreign intellectual property offices and international intergovernmental organizations; and

(B) may conduct programs and studies described in subparagraph (A); and

(13)(A) in coordination with the Department of State, may conduct programs and studies cooperatively with foreign intellectual property offices and international intergovernmental organizations; and

(B) with the concurrence of the Secretary of State, may authorize the transfer of not to exceed $ 100,000 in any year to the Department of State for the purpose of making special payments to international intergovernmental organizations for studies and programs for advancing international cooperation concerning patents, trademarks, and other matters.

(c) Clarification of specific powers.

(1) The special payments under subsection (b)(13)(B) shall be in addition to any other payments or contributions to international organizations described in subsection (b)(13)(B) and shall not be subject to any limitations imposed by law on the amounts of such other payments or contributions by the United States Government.

(2) Nothing in subsection (b) shall derogate from the duties of the Secretary of State or from the duties of the United States Trade Representative as set forth in section 141 of the Trade Act of 1974 (19 U.S.C. 2171).

(3) Nothing in subsection (b) shall derogate from the duties and functions of the Register of Copyrights or otherwise alter current authorities relating to copyright matters.

(4) In exercising the Director's powers under paragraphs (3) and (4)(A) of subsection (b), the Director shall consult with the Administrator of General Services.

(5) In exercising the Director's powers and duties under this section, the Director shall consult with the Register of Copyrights on all copyright and related matters.

(d) Construction. Nothing in this section shall be construed to nullify, void, cancel, or interrupt any pending request-for-proposal let or contract issued by the General Services Administration for the specific purpose of relocating or leasing space to the United States Patent and Trademark Office.

HISTORY:

(July 19, 1952, ch 950, § 1, 66 Stat. 792; Jan. 2, 1975, P.L. 93-596, § 1, 88 Stat. 1949; Nov. 29, 1999, P.L. 106-113, Div B, § 1000(a)(9), 113 Stat. 1536; Nov. 2, 2002, P.L. 107-273, Div C, Title III, Subtitle B, § 13206(a)(1), 116 Stat. 1904; Dec. 15, 2003, P.L. 108-178, § 4(g), 117 Stat. 2641; Jan. 4, 2011, P.L. 111-350, § 5(i)(1), 124 Stat. 3849.)

(America Invents Act §§ 20(j)(1); 21(a); 25(1)-(3).)

§ 3. Officers and employees

(a) Under Secretary and Director.

(1) In general. The powers and duties of the United States Patent and Trademark Office shall be vested in an Under Secretary of Commerce for Intellectual Property and Director of the United States Patent and Trademark Office (in this title referred to as the "Director"), who shall be a citizen of the United States and who shall be appointed by the President, by and with the advice and consent of the Senate. The Director shall be a person who has a professional background and experience in patent or trademark law.

(2) Duties.

(A) In general. The Director shall be responsible for providing policy direction and management supervision for the Office and for the issuance of patents and the registration of trademarks. The Director shall perform these duties in a fair, impartial, and equitable manner.

(B) Consulting with the Public Advisory Committees. The Director shall consult with the Patent Public Advisory Committee established in section 5 [35 USC § 5] on a regular basis on matters relating to the patent operations of the Office, shall consult with the Trademark Public Advisory Committee established in section 5 [35 USC § 5] on a regular basis on matters relating to the trademark operations of the Office, and shall consult with the respective Public Advisory Committee before submitting budgetary proposals to the Office of Management and Budget or changing or proposing to change patent or trademark user fees or patent or trademark regulations which are subject to the requirement to provide notice and opportunity for public comment under section 553 of title 5, as the case may be.

(3) Oath. The Director shall, before taking office, take an oath to discharge faithfully the duties of the Office.

(4) Removal. The Director may be removed from office by the President. The President shall provide notification of any such removal to both Houses of Congress.

(b) Officers and employees of the Office.

(1) Deputy Under Secretary and Deputy Director. The Secretary of Commerce, upon nomination by the Director, shall appoint a Deputy Under Secretary of Commerce for Intellectual Property and Deputy Director of the United States Patent and Trademark Office who shall be vested with the authority to act in the capacity of the Director in the event of the absence or incapacity of the Director. The Deputy Director shall be a citizen of the United States who has a professional background and experience in patent or trademark law.

(2) Commissioners.

(A) Appointment and duties. The Secretary of Commerce shall appoint a Commissioner for Patents and a Commissioner for Trademarks, without regard to chapter 33, 51, or 53 of title 5 [5 USC §§ 3301 et seq., 5101 et seq., or 5301 et seq.]. The Commissioner for Patents shall be a citizen of the United States with demonstrated management ability and professional background and experience in patent law and serve for a term of 5 years. The Commissioner for Trademarks shall be a citizen of the United States with demonstrated management ability and professional background and experience in trademark law and serve for a term of 5 years. The Commissioner for Patents and the Commissioner for Trademarks shall serve as the chief operating officers for the operations of the Office relating to patents and trademarks, respectively, and shall be responsible for the management and direction of all aspects of the activities of the Office that affect the administration of patent and trademark operations, respectively. The Secretary may reappoint a Commissioner to subsequent terms of 5 years as long as the performance of the Commissioner as set forth in the performance agreement in subparagraph (B) is satisfactory.

(B) Salary and performance agreement. The Commissioners shall be paid an annual rate of basic pay not to exceed the maximum rate of basic pay for the Senior Executive

Service established under section 5382 of title 5, including any applicable locality-based comparability payment that may be authorized under section 5304(h)(2)(C) of title 5. The compensation of the Commissioners shall be considered, for purposes of section 207(c) (2)(A) of title 18, to be the equivalent of that described under clause (ii) of section 207(c) (2)(A) of title 18. In addition, the Commissioners may receive a bonus in an amount of up to, but not in excess of, 50 percent of the Commissioners' annual rate of basic pay, based upon an evaluation by the Secretary of Commerce, acting through the Director, of the Commissioners' performance as defined in an annual performance agreement between the Commissioners and the Secretary. The annual performance agreements shall incorporate measurable organization and individual goals in key operational areas as delineated in an annual performance plan agreed to by the Commissioners and the Secretary. Payment of a bonus under this subparagraph may be made to the Commissioners only to the extent that such payment does not cause the Commissioners' total aggregate compensation in a calendar year to equal or exceed the amount of the salary of the Vice President under section 104 of title 3.

(C) **Removal.** The Commissioners may be removed from office by the Secretary for misconduct or nonsatisfactory performance under the performance agreement described in subparagraph (B), without regard to the provisions of title 5. The Secretary shall provide notification of any such removal to both Houses of Congress.

(3) **Other officers and employees.** The Director shall—

(A) appoint such officers, employees (including attorneys), and agents of the Office as the Director considers necessary to carry out the functions of the Office; and

(B) define the title, authority, and duties of such officers and employees and delegate to them such of the powers vested in the Office as the Director may determine.

The Office shall not be subject to any administratively or statutorily imposed limitation on positions or personnel, and no positions or personnel of the Office shall be taken into account for purposes of applying any such limitation.

(4) **Training of examiners.** The Office shall submit to the Congress a proposal to provide an incentive program to retain as employees patent and trademark examiners of the primary examiner grade or higher who are eligible for retirement, for the sole purpose of training patent and trademark examiners.

(5) **National security positions.** The Director, in consultation with the Director of the Office of Personnel Management, shall maintain a program for identifying national security positions and providing for appropriate security clearances, in order to maintain the secrecy of certain inventions, as described in section 181 [35 USC § 181], and to prevent disclosure of sensitive and strategic information in the interest of national security.

(6) **Administrative patent judges and administrative trademark judges.**—The Director may fix the rate of basic pay for the administrative patent judges appointed pursuant to section 6 and the administrative trademark judges appointed pursuant to section 17 of the Trademark Act of 1946 (15 U.S.C. 1067) at not greater than the rate of basic pay payable for level III of the Executive Schedule under section 5314 of title 5. The payment of a rate of basic pay under this paragraph shall not be subject to the pay limitation under section 5306(e) or 5373 of title 5.

(c) **Continued applicability of title 5.** Officers and employees of the Office shall be subject to the provisions of title 5, relating to Federal employees.

(d) **Adoption of existing labor agreements.** The Office shall adopt all labor agreements which are in effect, as of the day before the effective date of the Patent and Trademark Office Efficiency Act, with respect to such Office (as then in effect).

(e) Carryover of personnel.

(1) From PTO. Effective as of the effective date of the Patent and Trademark Office Efficiency Act, all officers and employees of the Patent and Trademark Office on the day before such effective date shall become officers and employees of the Office, without a break in service.

(2) Other personnel. Any individual who, on the day before the effective date of the Patent and Trademark Office Efficiency Act, is an officer or employee of the Department of Commerce (other than an officer or employee under paragraph (1)) shall be transferred to the Office, as necessary to carry out the purposes of this Act, that Act, if—

(A) such individual serves in a position for which a major function is the performance of work reimbursed by the Patent and Trademark Office, as determined by the Secretary of Commerce;

(B) such individual serves in a position that performed work in support of the Patent and Trademark Office during at least half of the incumbent's work time, as determined by the Secretary of Commerce; or

(C) such transfer would be in the interest of the Office, as determined by the Secretary of Commerce in consultation with the Director.

Any transfer under this paragraph shall be effective as of the same effective date as referred to in paragraph (1), and shall be made without a break in service.

(f) Transition provisions.

(1) Interim appointment of Director. On or after the effective date of the Patent and Trademark Office Efficiency Act, the President shall appoint an individual to serve as the Director until the date on which a Director qualifies under subsection (a). The President shall not make more than one such appointment under this subsection.

(2) Continuation in office of certain officers.

(A) The individual serving as the Assistant Commissioner for Patents on the day before the effective date of the Patent and Trademark Office Efficiency Act may serve as the Commissioner for Patents until the date on which a Commissioner for Patents is appointed under subsection (b).

(B) The individual serving as the Assistant Commissioner for Trademarks on the day before the effective date of the Patent and Trademark Office Efficiency Act may serve as the Commissioner for Trademarks until the date on which a Commissioner for Trademarks is appointed under subsection (b).

HISTORY:

(July 19, 1952, ch 950, § 1, 66 Stat. 792; Sept. 6, 1958, P.L. 85-933, § 1, 72 Stat. 1793; Sept. 23, 1959, P.L. 86-370, § 1(a), 73 Stat. 650; Aug. 14, 1964, P.L. 88-426, Title III, § 305(26), 78 Stat. 425; Jan. 2, 1975, P.L. 93-596, § 1, 88 Stat. 1949; Jan. 2, 1975, P.L. 93-601, § 1, 88 Stat. 1956; Aug. 27, 1982, P.L. 97-247, § 4, 96 Stat. 319; Oct. 15, 1982, P.L. 97-366, § 4, 96 Stat. 1760; Nov. 8, 1984, P.L. 98-622, Title IV, § 405, 98 Stat. 3392; Oct. 28, 1998, P.L. 105-304, Title IV, § 401(a)(1), 112 Stat. 2887; Aug. 5, 1999, P.L. 106-44, § 2(c), 113 Stat. 223; Nov. 29, 1999, P.L. 106-113, Div B, § 1000(a)(9), 113 Stat. 1536; Nov. 2, 2002, P.L. 107-273, Div C, Title III, Subtitle B, § 13206(a)(2), 116 Stat. 1904.)

(America Invents Act §§ 20(i)(1); 21(b).)

§ 4. Restrictions on officers and employees as to interest in patents

Officers and employees of the Patent and Trademark Office shall be incapable, during the period of their appointments and for one year thereafter, of applying for a patent and of acquiring, directly or indirectly, except by inheritance or bequest, any patent or any right or interest in any patent, issued or to be issued by the Office. In patents applied for thereafter they shall not be entitled to any priority date earlier than one year after the termination of their appointment.

HISTORY:

(July 19, 1952, ch 950, § 1, 66 Stat. 793; Jan. 2, 1975, P.L. 93-596, § 1, 88 Stat. 1949.)

§ 5. Patent and Trademark Office Public Advisory Committees

(a) Establishment of Public Advisory Committees.

(1) Appointment. The United States Patent and Trademark Office shall have a Patent Public Advisory Committee and a Trademark Public Advisory Committee, each of which shall have nine voting members who shall be appointed by the Secretary of Commerce and serve at the pleasure of the Secretary of Commerce. Members of each Public Advisory Committee shall be appointed for a term of 3 years, except that of the members first appointed, three shall be appointed for a term of 1 year, and three shall be appointed for a term of 2 years. In making appointments to each Committee, the Secretary of Commerce shall consider the risk of loss of competitive advantage in international commerce or other harm to United States companies as a result of such appointments.

(2) Chair. The Secretary shall designate a chair of each Advisory Committee, whose term as chair shall be for 3 years.

(3) Timing of appointments. Initial appointments to each Advisory Committee shall be made within 3 months after the effective date of the Patent and Trademark Office Efficiency Act. Vacancies shall be filled within 3 months after they occur.

(b) Basis for appointments. Members of each Advisory Committee—

(1) shall be citizens of the United States who shall be chosen so as to represent the interests of diverse users of the United States Patent and Trademark Office with respect to patents, in the case of the Patent Public Advisory Committee, and with respect to trademarks, in the case of the Trademark Public Advisory Committee;

(2) shall include members who represent small and large entity applicants located in the United States in proportion to the number of applications filed by such applicants, but in no case shall members who represent small entity patent applicants, including small business concerns, independent inventors, and nonprofit organizations, constitute less than 25 percent of the members of the Patent Public Advisory Committee, and such members shall include at least one independent inventor; and

(3) shall include individuals with substantial background and achievement in finance, management, labor relations, science, technology, and office automation.

In addition to the voting members, each Advisory Committee shall include a representative of each labor organization recognized by the United States Patent and Trademark Office. Such representatives shall be nonvoting members of the Advisory Committee to which they are appointed.

(c) Meetings. Each Advisory Committee shall meet at the call of the chair to consider an agenda set by the chair.

(d) Duties. Each Advisory Committee shall—

(1) review the policies, goals, performance, budget, and user fees of the United States Patent and Trademark Office with respect to patents, in the case of the Patent Public Advisory Committee, and with respect to Trademarks, in the case of the Trademark Public Advisory Committee, and advise the Director on these matters;

(2) within 60 days after the end of each fiscal year—

(A) prepare an annual report on the matters referred to in paragraph (1);

(B) transmit the report to the Secretary of Commerce, the President, and the Committees on the Judiciary of the Senate and the House of Representatives; and

(C) publish the report in the Official Gazette of the United States Patent and Trademark Office.

(e) Compensation. Each member of each Advisory Committee shall be compensated for each day (including travel time) during which such member is attending meetings or conferences of that Advisory Committee or otherwise engaged in the business of that Advisory Committee, at the rate which is the daily equivalent of the annual rate of basic pay in effect for level III of the Executive Schedule under section 5314 of title 5. While away from such member's home or regular place of business such member shall be allowed travel expenses, including per diem in lieu of subsistence, as authorized by section 5703 of title 5.

(f) Access to information. Members of each Advisory Committee shall be provided access to records and information in the United States Patent and Trademark Office, except for personnel or other privileged information and information concerning patent applications required to be kept in confidence by section 122 [35 USC § 122].

(g) Applicability of certain ethics laws. Members of each Advisory Committee shall be special Government employees within the meaning of section 202 of title 18.

(h) Inapplicability of Federal Advisory Committee Act. The Federal Advisory Committee Act (5 U.S.C. App.) shall not apply to each Advisory Committee.

(i) Open meetings. The meetings of each Advisory Committee shall be open to the public, except that each Advisory Committee may by majority vote meet in executive session when considering personnel, privileged, or other confidential information.

(j) Inapplicability of patent prohibition. Section 4 [35 USC § 4] shall not apply to voting members of the Advisory Committees.

HISTORY:

(Added Nov. 29, 1999, P.L. 106-113, Div B, § 1000(a)(9), 113 Stat. 1536; Nov. 2, 2002, P.L. 107-273, Div C, Title V, Subtitle B, §§ 13203(b), 13206(a)(3), 116 Stat. 1902, 1904.)

§ 6. ~~Board of Patent Appeals and Interferences~~

~~(a) Establishment and composition. There shall be in the United States Patent and Trademark Office a Board of Patent Appeals and Interferences. The Director, the Commissioner for Patents, the Commissioner for Trademarks, and the administrative patent judges shall constitute the Board. The administrative patent judges shall be persons of competent legal knowledge and scientific ability who are appointed by the Secretary of Commerce, in consultation with the Director.~~

~~(b) Duties. The Board of Patent Appeals and Interferences shall, on written appeal of an applicant, review adverse decisions of examiners upon applications for patents and shall determine priority and patentability of invention in interferences declared under section 135(a) [35 USC § 135(a)]. Each appeal and interference shall be heard by at least three members of the Board, who shall be designated by the Director. Only the Board of Patent Appeals and Interferences may grant rehearings.~~

~~(c) Authority of the Secretary. The Secretary of Commerce may, in his or her discretion, deem the appointment of an administrative patent judge who, before the date of the enactment of this subsection [enacted Aug. 12, 2008], held office pursuant to an appointment by the Director to take effect on the date on which the Director initially appointed the administrative patent judge.~~

~~(d) Defense to challenge of appointment. It shall be a defense to a challenge to the appointment of an administrative patent judge on the basis of the judge's having been origi-~~

26

~~nally appointed by the Director that the administrative patent judge so appointed was acting as a de facto officer.~~

§ 6. Patent Trial and Appeal Board

(a) In general.—There shall be in the Office a Patent Trial and Appeal Board. The Director, the Deputy Director, the Commissioner for Patents, the Commissioner for Trademarks, and the administrative patent judges shall constitute the Patent Trial and Appeal Board. The administrative patent judges shall be persons of competent legal knowledge and scientific ability who are appointed by the Secretary, in consultation with the Director. Any reference in any Federal law, Executive order, rule, regulation, or delegation of authority, or any document of or pertaining to the Board of Patent Appeals and Interferences is deemed to refer to the Patent Trial and Appeal Board.

(b) Duties.—The Patent Trial and Appeal Board shall—

(1) on written appeal of an applicant, review adverse decisions of examiners upon applications for patents pursuant to section 134(a);

(2) review appeals of reexaminations pursuant to section 134(b);

(3) conduct derivation proceedings pursuant to section 135; and

(4) conduct inter partes reviews and post-grant reviews pursuant to chapters 31 and 32.

(c) 3-Member panels.—Each appeal, derivation proceeding, post-grant review, and inter partes review shall be heard by at least 3 members of the Patent Trial and Appeal Board, who shall be designated by the Director. Only the Patent Trial and Appeal Board may grant rehearings.

(d) Treatment of prior appointments.—The Secretary of Commerce may, in the Secretary's discretion, deem the appointment of an administrative patent judge who, before the date of the enactment of this subsection, held office pursuant to an appointment by the Director to take effect on the date on which the Director initially appointed the administrative patent judge. It shall be a defense to a challenge to the appointment of an administrative patent judge on the basis of the judge's having been originally appointed by the Director that the administrative patent judge so appointed was acting as a de facto officer.

HISTORY:

(Added Nov. 29, 1999, P.L. 106-113, Div B, § 1000(a)(9), 113 Stat. 1536; Nov. 2, 2002, P.L. 107-273, Div C, Title V, Subtitle B, § 13203(a)(2), 116 Stat. 1902; Aug. 12, 2008, P.L. 110-313, § 1(a)(1), 122 Stat. 3014.)

(America Invents Act § 7(a)(1).)

§ 7. Library

The Director shall maintain a library of scientific and other works and periodicals, both foreign and domestic, in the Patent and Trademark Office to aid the officers in the discharge of their duties.

HISTORY:

(July 19, 1952, ch 950, § 1, 66 Stat. 793; Jan. 2, 1975, P.L. 93-596, § 1, 88 Stat. 1949; Nov. 29, 1999, P.L. 106-113, Div B, § 1000(a)(9), 113 Stat. 1536; Nov. 2, 2002, P.L. 107-273, Div C, Title III, Subtitle B, § 13206(b)(1)(B), 116 Stat. 1906.)

§ 8. Classification of patents

The Director may revise and maintain the classification by subject matter of United States letters patent, and such other patents and printed publications as may be necessary or practicable, for the purpose of determining with readiness and accuracy the novelty of inventions for which applications for patent are filed.

35 USC § 8

HISTORY:

(July 19, 1952, ch 950, § 1, 66 Stat. 794; Nov. 29, 1999, P.L. 106-113, Div B, § 1000(a)(9), 113 Stat. 1536; Nov. 2, 2002, P.L. 107-273, Div C, Title III, Subtitle B, § 13206(b)(1)(B), 116 Stat. 1906.)

§ 9. Certified copies of records

The Director may furnish certified copies of specifications and drawings of patents issued by the Patent and Trademark Office, and of other records available either to the public or to the person applying therefor.

HISTORY:

(July 19, 1952, ch 950, § 1, 66 Stat. 794; Jan. 2, 1975, P.L. 93-596, § 1, 88 Stat. 1949; Nov. 29, 1999, P.L. 106-113, Div B, § 1000(a)(9), 113 Stat. 1536; Nov. 2, 2002, P.L. 107-273, Div C, Title III, Subtitle B, § 13206(b)(1)(B), 116 Stat. 1906.)

§ 10. Publications

(a) The Director may publish in printed, typewritten, or electronic form, the following:

1. Patents and published applications for patents, including specifications and drawings, together with copies of the same. The Patent and Trademark Office may print the headings of the drawings for patents for the purpose of photolithography.

2. Certificates of trade-mark registrations, including statements and drawings, together with copies of the same.

3. The Official Gazette of the United States Patent and Trademark Office.

4. Annual indexes of patents and patentees, and of trade-marks and registrants.

5. Annual volumes of decisions in patent and trade-mark cases.

6. Pamphlet copies of the patent laws and rules of practice, laws and rules relating to trade-marks, and circulars or other publications relating to the business of the Office.

(b) The Director may exchange any of the publications specified in items 3, 4, 5, and 6 of subsection (a) of this section for publications desirable for the use of the Patent and Trademark Office.

HISTORY:

(July 19, 1952, ch 950, § 1, 66 Stat. 794; Jan. 2, 1975, P.L. 93-596, § 1, 88 Stat. 1949; Nov. 29, 1999, P.L. 106-113, Div B, § 1000(a)(9), 113 Stat. 1536; Nov. 2, 2002, P.L. 107-273, Div C, Title III, Subtitle B, §§ 13205(2)(A), 13206(b)(1)(B), (3)(A), 116 Stat. 1903, 1906.)

§ 11. Exchange of copies of patents and applications with foreign countries

The Director may exchange copies of specifications and drawings of United States patents and published applications for patents for those of foreign countries. The Director shall not enter into an agreement to provide such copies of specifications and drawings of United States patents and applications to a foreign country, other than a NAFTA country or a WTO member country, without the express authorization of the Secretary of Commerce. For purposes of this section, the terms "NAFTA country" and "WTO member country" have the meanings given those terms in section 104(b) [35 USC § 104(b)].

HISTORY:

(July 19, 1952, ch 950, § 1, 66 Stat. 794; Nov. 29, 1999, P.L. 106-113, Div B, § 1000(a)(9), 113 Stat. 1536; Nov. 2, 2002, P.L. 107-273, Div C, Title III, Subtitle B, §§ 13205(2)(B), 13206(b)(1)(B), 116 Stat. 1903, 1906.)

§ 12. Copies of patents and applications for public libraries

The Director may supply copies of specifications and drawings of patents and published applications for patents in printed or electronic form to public libraries in the United States which shall maintain such copies for the use of the public, at the rate for each year's issue established for this purpose in section 41(d) ~~of this title~~ [35 USC § 41(d)].

HISTORY:

(July 19, 1952, ch 950, § 1, 66 Stat. 794; Aug. 27, 1982, P.L. 97-247, § 15, 96 Stat. 321; Nov. 29, 1999, P.L. 106-113, Div B, § 1000(a)(9), 113 Stat. 1536; Nov. 2, 2002, P.L. 107-273, Div C, Title III, Subtitle B, §§ 13205(2)(C), 13206(b)(1)(B), (3)(B), 116 Stat. 1903, 1906.)

(America Invents Act § 20(j)(1))

§ 13. Annual report to Congress

The Director shall report to the Congress, not later than 180 days after the end of each fiscal year, the moneys received and expended by the Office, the purposes for which the moneys were spent, the quality and quantity of the work of the Office, the nature of training provided to examiners, the evaluation of the Commissioner of Patents and the Commissioner of Trademarks by the Secretary of Commerce, the compensation of the Commissioners, and other information relating to the Office.

HISTORY:

(July 19, 1952, ch 950, § 1, 66 Stat. 794; Nov. 29, 1999, P.L. 106-113, Div B, § 1000(a)(9), 113 Stat. 1536.)

[§ 14. Redesignated]

CHAPTER 2. PROCEEDINGS IN THE PATENT AND TRADEMARK OFFICE

§ 21. Filing date and day for taking action

(a) The Director may by rule prescribe that any paper or fee required to be filed in the Patent and Trademark Office will be considered filed in the Office on the date on which it was deposited with the United States Postal Service or would have been deposited with the United States Postal Service but for postal service interruptions or emergencies designated by the Director.

(b) When the day, or the last day, for taking any action or paying any fee in the United States Patent and Trademark Office falls on Saturday, Sunday, or a federal holiday within the District of Columbia, the action may be taken, or the fee paid, on the next succeeding secular or business day.

HISTORY:

(July 19, 1952, ch 950, § 1, 66 Stat. 794; Jan. 2, 1975, P.L. 93-596, § 1, 88 Stat. 1949; Aug. 27, 1982, P.L. 97-247, § 12, 96 Stat. 321; Nov. 29, 1999, P.L. 106-113, Div B, § 1000(a)(9), 113 Stat. 1536; Nov. 2, 2002, P.L. 107-273, Div C, Title III, Subtitle B, § 13206(b)(1)(B), 116 Stat. 1906.)

§ 22. Printing of papers filed

The Director may require papers filed in the Patent and Trademark Office to be printed, typewritten, or on an electronic medium.

HISTORY:

(July 19, 1952, ch 950, § 1, 66 Stat. 795; Jan. 2, 1975, P.L. 93-596, § 1, 88 Stat. 1949; Nov. 29, 1999, P.L. 106-113, Div B, § 1000(a)(9), 113 Stat. 1536; Nov. 2, 2002, P.L. 107-273, Div C, Title III, Subtitle B, § 13206(b)(1)(B), 116 Stat. 1906.)

§ 23. Testimony in Patent and Trademark Office cases

The Director may establish rules for taking affidavits and depositions required in cases in the Patent and Trademark Office. Any officer authorized by law to take depositions to be used in the courts of the United States, or of the State where he resides, may take such affidavits and depositions.

35 USC § 23

HISTORY:

(July 19, 1952, ch 950, § 1, 66 Stat. 795; Jan. 2, 1975, P.L. 93-596, § 1, 88 Stat. 1949; Nov. 29, 1999, P.L. 106-113, Div B, § 1000(a)(9), 113 Stat. 1536; Nov. 2, 2002, P.L. 107-273, Div C, Title III, Subtitle B, § 13206(b)(1)(B), 116 Stat. 1906.)

§ 24. Subpoenas, witnesses

The clerk of any United States court for the district wherein testimony is to be taken for use in any contested case in the Patent and Trademark Office, shall, upon the application of any party thereto, issue a subpoena for any witness residing or being within such district, commanding him to appear and testify before an officer in such district authorized to take depositions and affidavits, at the time and place stated in the subpoena. The provisions of the Federal Rules of Civil Procedure relating to the attendance of witnesses and to the production of documents and things shall apply to contested cases in the Patent and Trademark Office.

Every witness subpoenaed and in attendance shall be allowed the fees and traveling expenses allowed to witnesses attending the United States district courts.

A judge of a court whose clerk issued a subpoena may enforce obedience to the process or punish disobedience as in other like cases, on proof that a witness, served with such subpoena, neglected or refused to appear or to testify. No witness shall be deemed guilty of contempt for disobeying such subpoena unless his fees and traveling expenses in going to, and returning from, and one day's attendance at the place of examination, are paid or tendered him at the time of the service of the subpoena; nor for refusing to disclose any secret matter except upon appropriate order of the court which issued the subpoena.

HISTORY:

(July 19, 1952, ch 950, § 1, 66 Stat. 795; Jan. 2, 1975, P.L. 93-596, § 1, 88 Stat. 1949.)

§ 25. Declaration in lieu of oath

(a) The Director may by rule prescribe that any document to be filed in the Patent and Trademark Office and which is required by any law, rule, or other regulation to be under oath may be subscribed to by a written declaration in such form as the Director may prescribe, such declaration to be in lieu of the oath otherwise required.

(b) Whenever such written declaration is used, the document must warn the declarant that willful false statements and the like are punishable by fine or imprisonment, or both (18 U.S.C. 1001).

HISTORY:

(Added March 26, 1964, P.L. 88-292, § 1, 78 Stat. 171; Jan. 2, 1975, P.L. 93-596, § 1, 88 Stat. 1949; Nov. 29, 1999, P.L. 106-113, Div B, § 1000(a)(9), 113 Stat. 1536; Nov. 2, 2002, P.L. 107-273, Div C, Title III, Subtitle B, § 13206(b)(1)(B), 116 Stat. 1906.)

§ 26. Effect of defective execution

Any document to be filed in the Patent and Trademark Office and which is required by any law, rule, or other regulation to be executed in a specified manner may be provisionally accepted by the Director despite a defective execution, provided a properly executed document is submitted within such time as may be prescribed.

HISTORY:

(Added March 26, 1964, P.L. 88-292, § 1, 78 Stat. 171; Jan. 2, 1975, P.L. 93-596, § 1, 88 Stat. 1949; Nov. 29, 1999, P.L. 106-113, Div B, § 1000(a)(9), 113 Stat. 1536; Nov. 2, 2002, P.L. 107-273, Div C, Title III, Subtitle B, § 13206(b)(1)(B), 116 Stat. 1906.)

[§ 31. Repealed]

§ 32. Suspension or exclusion from practice

The Director may, after notice and opportunity for a hearing suspend or exclude, either generally or in any particular case, from further practice before the Patent and Trademark Office, any person, agent, or attorney shown to be incompetent or disreputable, or guilty of gross misconduct, or who does not comply with the regulations established under section 2(b)(2)(D) of this title [35 USC § 2(b)(2)(D)], or who shall, by word, circular, letter, or advertising, with intent to defraud in any manner, deceive, mislead, or threaten any applicant or prospective applicant, or other person having immediate or prospective business before the Office. The reasons for any such suspension or exclusion shall be duly recorded. The Director shall have the discretion to designate any attorney who is an officer or employee of the United States Patent and Trademark Office to conduct the hearing required by this section. A proceeding under this section shall be commenced not later than the earlier of either the date that is 10 years after the date on which the misconduct forming the basis for the proceeding occurred, or 1 year after the date on which the misconduct forming the basis for the proceeding is made known to an officer or employee of the Office as prescribed in the regulations established under section 2(b)(2)(D). The United States District Court for the District of Columbia United States District Court for the Eastern District of Virginia, under such conditions and upon such proceedings as it by its rules determines, may review the action of the Director upon the petition of the person so refused recognition or so suspended or excluded.

HISTORY:

(July 19, 1952, ch 950, § 1, 66 Stat. 795; Jan. 2, 1975, P.L. 93-596, § 1, 88 Stat. 1949; Nov. 29, 1999, P.L. 106-113, Div B, § 1000(a)(9), 113 Stat. 1536; Nov. 2, 2002, P.L. 107-273, Div C, Title III, Subtitle B, § 13206(b)(1)(B), 116 Stat. 1906.)

(America Invents Act §§ 3(k)(1); 9(a); 20(j)(1).)

§ 33. Unauthorized representation as practitioner

Whoever, not being recognized to practice before the Patent and Trademark Office, holds himself out or permits himself to be held out as so recognized, or as being qualified to prepare or prosecute applications for patent, shall be fined not more than $ 1,000 for each offense.

HISTORY:

(July 19, 1952, ch 950, § 1, 66 Stat. 796; Jan. 2, 1975, P.L. 93-596, § 1, 88 Stat. 1949.)

§ 41. Patent fees; patent and trademark search systems

(a) The Director shall charge the following fees:

(1)(A) On filing each application for an original patent, except in design or plant cases, $ 690.

(B) In addition, on filing or on presentation at any other time, $ 78 for each claim in independent form which is in excess of 3, $ 18 for each claim (whether independent or dependent) which is in excess of 20, and $ 260 for each application containing a multiple dependent claim.

(C) On filing each provisional application for an original patent, $ 150.

(2) For issuing each original or reissue patent, except in design or plant cases, $ 1,210.

(3) In design and plant cases—

(A) on filing each design application, $ 310;

(B) on filing each plant application, $ 480;

(C) on issuing each design patent, $ 430; and

(D) on issuing each plant patent, $ 580.

(4)(A) On filing each application for the reissue of a patent, $ 690.

(B) In addition, on filing or on presentation at any other time, $ 78 for each claim in independent form which is in excess of the number of independent claims of the original patent, and $ 18 for each claim (whether independent or dependent) which is in excess of 20 and also in excess of the number of claims of the original patent.

(5) On filing each disclaimer, $ 110.

(6)(A) On filing an appeal from the examiner to the Board of Patent Appeals and Interferences, $ 300.

(B) In addition, on filing a brief in support of the appeal, $ 300, and on requesting an oral hearing in the appeal before the Board of Patent Appeals and Interferences, $ 260.

(7) On filing each petition for the revival of an unintentionally abandoned application for a patent, for the unintentionally delayed payment of the fee for issuing each patent, or for an unintentionally delayed response by the patent owner in any reexamination proceeding, $ 1,210, unless the petition is filed under section 133 or 151 of this title [35 USC § 133 or 151], in which case the fee shall be $ 110.

(8) For petitions for 1-month extensions of time to take actions required by the Director in an application—

(A) on filing a first petition, $ 110;

(B) on filing a second petition, $ 270; and

(C) on filing a third petition or subsequent petition, $ 490.

(9) Basic national fee for an international application where the Patent and Trademark Office was the International Preliminary Examining Authority and the International Searching Authority, $ 670.

(10) Basic national fee for an international application where the Patent and Trademark Office was the International Searching Authority but not the International Preliminary Examining Authority, $ 690.

(11) Basic national fee for an international application where the Patent and Trademark Office was neither the International Searching Authority nor the International Preliminary Examining Authority, $ 970.

(12) Basic national fee for an international application where the international preliminary examination fee has been paid to the Patent and Trademark Office, and the international preliminary examination report states that the provisions of Article 33(2), (3), and (4) of the Patent Cooperation Treaty have been satisfied for all claims in the application entering the national stage, $ 96.

(13) For filing or later presentation of each independent claim in the national stage of an international application in excess of 3, $ 78.

(14) For filing or later presentation of each claim (whether independent or dependent) in a national stage of an international application in excess of 20, $ 18.

(15) For each national stage of an international application containing a multiple dependent claim, $ 260.

For the purpose of computing fees, a multiple dependent claim referred to in section 112 of this title [35 USC § 112] or any claim depending therefrom shall be considered as separate dependent claims in accordance with the number of claims to which reference is made.

~~Errors in payment of the additional fees may be rectified in accordance with regulations of the Director.~~

~~(b) The Director shall charge the following fees for maintaining in force all patents based on applications filed on or after December 12, 1980:~~

~~(1) 3 years and 6 months after grant, $ 830.~~

~~(2) 7 years and 6 months after grant, $ 1,900.~~

~~(3) 11 years and 6 months after grant, $ 2,910.~~

~~Unless payment of the applicable maintenance fee is received in the Patent and Trademark Office on or before the date the fee is due or within a grace period of 6 months thereafter, the patent will expire as of the end of such grace period. The Director may require the payment of a surcharge as a condition of accepting within such 6-month grace period the payment of an applicable maintenance fee. No fee may be established for maintaining a design or plant patent in force.~~

(a) General fees.—The Director shall charge the following fees:

(1) Filing and basic national fees.—

(A) On filing each application for an original patent, except for design, plant, or provisional applications, $330.

(B) On filing each application for an original design patent, $220.

(C) On filing each application for an original plant patent, $220.

(D) On filing each provisional application for an original patent, $220.

(E) On filing each application for the reissue of a patent, $330.

(F) The basic national fee for each international application filed under the treaty defined in section 351(a) entering the national stage under section 371, $330.

(G) In addition, excluding any sequence listing or computer program listing filed in an electronic medium as prescribed by the Director, for any application the specification and drawings of which exceed 100 sheets of paper (or equivalent as prescribed by the Director if filed in an electronic medium), $270 for each additional 50 sheets of paper (or equivalent as prescribed by the Director if filed in an electronic medium) or fraction thereof.

(2) Excess claims fees.—

(A) In general.—In addition to the fee specified in paragraph (1)—

(i) on filing or on presentation at any other time, $220 for each claim in independent form in excess of 3;

(ii) on filing or on presentation at any other time, $52 for each claim (whether dependent or independent) in excess of 20; and

(iii) for each application containing a multiple dependent claim, $390.

(B) Multiple dependent claims.—For the purpose of computing fees under subparagraph (A), a multiple dependent claim referred to in section 112 or any claim depending therefrom shall be considered as separate dependent claims in accordance with the number of claims to which reference is made.

(C) Refunds; errors in payment.—The Director may by regulation provide for a refund of any part of the fee specified in subparagraph (A) for any claim that is canceled before an examination on the merits, as prescribed by the Director, has been made of the application under section 131. Errors in payment of the additional fees under this paragraph may be rectified in accordance with regulations prescribed by the Director.

(3) Examination fees.—

(A) In general.—

35 USC § 41

(i) For examination of each application for an original patent, except for design, plant, provisional, or international applications, $220.

(ii) For examination of each application for an original design patent, $140.

(iii) For examination of each application for an original plant patent, $170.

(iv) For examination of the national stage of each international application, $220.

(v) For examination of each application for the reissue of a patent, $650.

(B) Applicability of other fee provisions.—The provisions of paragraphs (3) and (4) of section 111(a) relating to the payment of the fee for filing the application shall apply to the payment of the fee specified in subparagraph (A) with respect to an application filed under section 111(a). The provisions of section 371(d) relating to the payment of the national fee shall apply to the payment of the fee specified in subparagraph (A) with respect to an international application.

(4) Issue fees.—

(A) For issuing each original patent, except for design or plant patents, $1,510.

(B) For issuing each original design patent, $860.

(C) For issuing each original plant patent, $1,190.

(D) For issuing each reissue patent, $1,510.

(5) Disclaimer fee.—On filing each disclaimer, $140.

(6) Appeal fees.—

(A) On filing an appeal from the examiner to the Patent Trial and Appeal Board, $540.

(B) In addition, on filing a brief in support of the appeal, $540, and on requesting an oral hearing in the appeal before the Patent Trial and Appeal Board, $1,080.

(7) Revival fees.—On filing each petition for the revival of an unintentionally abandoned application for a patent, for the unintentionally delayed payment of the fee for issuing each patent, or for an unintentionally delayed response by the patent owner in any reexamination proceeding, $1,620, unless the petition is filed under section 133 or 151, in which case the fee shall be $540.

(8) Extension fees.—For petitions for 1-month extensions of time to take actions required by the Director in an application—

(A) on filing a first petition, $130;

(B) on filing a second petition, $360; and

(C) on filing a third or subsequent petition, $620.

(b) Maintenance fees.—

(1) In general.—The Director shall charge the following fees for maintaining in force all patents based on applications filed on or after December 12, 1980:

(A) Three years and 6 months after grant, $980.

(B) Seven years and 6 months after grant, $2,480.

(C) Eleven years and 6 months after grant, $4,110.

(2) Grace period; surcharge.—Unless payment of the applicable maintenance fee under paragraph (1) is received in the Office on or before the date the fee is due or within a grace period of 6 months thereafter, the patent shall expire as of the end of such grace period. The Director may require the payment of a surcharge as a condition of accepting within such 6-month grace period the payment of an applicable maintenance fee.

(3) No maintenance fee for design or plant patent.—No fee may be established for maintaining a design or plant patent in force.

(c)(1) The Director

(c) Delays in payment of maintenance fees.—

(1) Acceptance.—The Director may accept the payment of any maintenance fee required by subsection (b) of this section which is made within twenty-four months after the six-month grace period if the delay is shown to the satisfaction of the Director to have been unintentional, or at any time after the six-month grace period if the delay is shown to the satisfaction of the Director to have been unavoidable. The Director may require the payment of a surcharge as a condition of accepting payment of any maintenance fee after the six-month grace period. If the Director accepts payment of a maintenance fee after the six-month grace period, the patent shall be considered as not having expired at the end of the grace period.

~~(2) A patent~~ **(2) Effect on rights of others.**—A patent, the term of which has been maintained as a result of the acceptance of a payment of a maintenance fee under this subsection, shall not abridge or affect the right of any person or that person's successors in business who made, purchased, offered to sell, or used anything protected by the patent within the United States, or imported anything protected by the patent into the United States after the 6-month grace period but prior to the acceptance of a maintenance fee under this subsection, to continue the use of, to offer for sale, or to sell to others to be used, offered for sale, or sold, the specific thing so made, purchased, offered for sale, used, or imported. The court before which such matter is in question may provide for the continued manufacture, use, offer for sale, or sale of the thing made, purchased, offered for sale, or used within the United States, or imported into the United States, as specified, or for the manufacture, use, offer for sale, or sale in the United States of which substantial preparation was made after the 6-month grace period but before the acceptance of a maintenance fee under this subsection, and the court may also provide for the continued practice of any process that is practiced, or for the practice of which substantial preparation was made, after the 6-month grace period but before the acceptance of a maintenance fee under this subsection, to the extent and under such terms as the court deems equitable for the protection of investments made or business commenced after the 6-month grace period but before the acceptance of a maintenance fee under this subsection.

~~(d) The Director shall establish fees for all other processing, services, or materials relating to patents not specified in this section to recover the estimated average cost to the Office of such processing, services, or materials, except that the Director shall charge the following fees for the following services:~~

~~(1) For recording a document affecting title, $ 40 per property.~~

~~(2) For each photocopy, $ .25 per page.~~

~~(3) For each black and white copy of a patent, $ 3.~~

~~The yearly fee for providing a library specified in section 13 of this title [35 USC § 13] with uncertified printed copies of the specifications and drawings for all patents in that year shall be $ 50.~~

(d) Patent Search and Other Fees.—

(1) Patent search fees.—

(A) In general.—The Director shall charge the fees specified under subparagraph (B) for the search of each application for a patent, except for provisional applications. The Director shall adjust the fees charged under this paragraph to ensure that the fees recover an amount not to exceed the estimated average cost to the Office of searching applications for patent by Office personnel.

(B) Specific fees.—The fees referred to in subparagraph (A) are—

(i) $540 for each application for an original patent, except for design, plant, provisional, or international applications;

(ii) $100 for each application for an original design patent;

(iii) $330 for each application for an original plant patent;

(iv) $540 for the national stage of each international application; and

(v) $540 for each application for the reissue of a patent.

(C) **Applicability of other provisions.**—The provisions of paragraphs (3) and (4) of section 111(a) relating to the payment of the fee for filing the application shall apply to the payment of the fee specified in this paragraph with respect to an application filed under section 111(a). The provisions of section 371(d) relating to the payment of the national fee shall apply to the payment of the fee specified in this paragraph with respect to an international application.

(D) **Refunds.**—The Director may by regulation provide for a refund of any part of the fee specified in this paragraph for any applicant who files a written declaration of express abandonment as prescribed by the Director before an examination has been made of the application under section 131.

(2) **Other fees.—**

(A) **In general.**—The Director shall establish fees for all other processing, services, or materials relating to patents not specified in this section to recover the estimated average cost to the Office of such processing, services, or materials, except that the Director shall charge the following fees for the following services:

(i) For recording a document affecting title, $40 per property.

(ii) For each photocopy, $.25 per page.

(iii) For each black and white copy of a patent, $3.

(B) **Copies for libraries.**—The yearly fee for providing a library specified in section 12 with uncertified printed copies of the specifications and drawings for all patents in that year shall be $50.

(e) ~~The Director~~ **Waiver of fees; copies regarding notice.**—The Director may waive the payment of any fee for any service or material related to patents in connection with an occasional or incidental request made by a department or agency of the Government, or any officer thereof. The Director may provide any applicant issued a notice under section 132 ~~of this title~~ [35 USC § 132] with a copy of the specifications and drawings for all patents referred to in that notice without charge.

(f) ~~The fees~~ **Adjustment of fees.**—The fees established in subsections (a) and (b) of this section may be adjusted by the Director on October 1, 1992, and every year thereafter, to reflect any fluctuations occurring during the previous 12 months in the Consumer Price Index, as determined by the Secretary of Labor. Changes of less than 1 per centum may be ignored.

~~(g) No fee established by the Director under this section shall take effect until at least 30 days after notice of the fee has been published in the Federal Register and in the Official Gazette of the Patent and Trademark Office.~~

~~(h)(1) Fees charged under subsection (a) or (b) shall be reduced by 50 percent with respect to their application to any small business concern as defined under section 3 of the Small Business Act, and to any independent inventor or nonprofit organization as defined in regulations issued by the Director.~~

~~(2) With respect to its application to any entity described in paragraph (1), any surcharge or fee charged under subsection (c) or (d) shall not be higher than the surcharge or fee required of any other entity under the same or substantially similar circumstances.~~

(h) Fees for small entities.—

(1) Reductions in fees.—Subject to paragraph (3), fees charged under subsections (a), (b), and (d)(1) shall be reduced by 50 percent with respect to their application to any small business concern as defined under section 3 of the Small Business Act, and to any independent inventor or nonprofit organization as defined in regulations issued by the Director.

(2) Surcharges and other fees.—With respect to its application to any entity described in paragraph (1), any surcharge or fee charged under subsection (c) or (d) shall not be higher than the surcharge or fee required of any other entity under the same or substantially similar circumstances.

(3) Reduction for electronic filing.—The fee charged under subsection (a)(1)(A) shall be reduced by 75 percent with respect to its application to any entity to which paragraph (1) applies, if the application is filed by electronic means as prescribed by the Director.

~~(i)(1) The Director~~ (i) **Electronic patent and trademark data.—**

(1) Maintenance of collections.—The Director shall maintain, for use by the public, paper, microform, or electronic collections of United States patents, foreign patent documents, and United States trademark registrations arranged to permit search for and retrieval of information. The Director may not impose fees directly for the use of such collections, or for the use of the public patent or trademark search rooms or libraries.

~~(2) The Director~~ (2) **Availability of automated search systems.**—The Director shall provide for the full deployment of the automated search systems of the Patent and Trademark Office so that such systems are available for use by the public, and shall assure full access by the public to, and dissemination of, patent and trademark information, using a variety of automated methods, including electronic bulletin boards and remote access by users to mass storage and retrieval systems.

~~(3) The Director~~ (3) **Access fees.**—The Director may establish reasonable fees for access by the public to the automated search systems of the Patent and Trademark Office. If such fees are established, a limited amount of free access shall be made available to users of the systems for purposes of education and training. The Director may waive the payment by an individual of fees authorized by this subsection upon a showing of need or hardship, and if such a waiver is in the public interest.

~~(4) The Director~~ (4) **Annual report to congress.**—The Director shall submit to the Congress an annual report on the automated search systems of the Patent and Trademark Office and the access by the public to such systems. The Director shall also publish such report in the Federal Register. The Director shall provide an opportunity for the submission of comments by interested persons on each such report.

HISTORY:

(July 19, 1952, ch 950, § 1, 66 Stat. 796; July 24, 1965, P.L. 89-83, §§ 1, 2, 79 Stat. 259; Jan. 2, 1975, P.L. 93-596, § 1, 88 Stat. 1949; Nov. 14, 1975, P.L. 94-131, § 3, 89 Stat. 690; Dec. 12, 1980, P.L. 96-517, § 2, 94 Stat. 3017; Aug. 27, 1982, P.L. 97-247, § 3(a)-(e), 96 Stat. 317; Sept. 8, 1982, P.L. 97-256, Title I, § 101(1)-(4), 96 Stat. 816; Nov. 8, 1984, P.L. 98-622, Title II, § 204(a), 98 Stat. 3388; Nov. 6, 1986, P.L. 99-607, § 1(b)(2), 100 Stat. 3470; Dec. 10, 1991, P.L. 102-204, § 5(a)-(c)(1), (d)(1), (2)(A), 105 Stat. 1637—1639; Oct. 23, 1992, P.L. 102-444, § 1, 106 Stat. 2245; Dec. 8, 1994, P.L. 103-465, Title V, Subtitle C, §§ 532(b)(2), 533(b)(1), 108 Stat. 4986, 4988; Nov. 10, 1998, P.L. 105-358, § 3, 112 Stat. 3272; Nov. 29, 1999, P.L. 106-113, Div B, § 1000(a) (9), 113 Stat. 1536; Nov. 2, 2002, P.L. 107-273, Div C, Title III, Subtitle B, § 13206(b)(1)(B), 116 Stat. 1906.)

(America Invents Act §§ 11(a), (b)(1)-(2), (c), (d), (e)(1)-(3), (4)(A)-(D); 20(j)(1))

§ 42. Patent and Trademark Office funding

(a) All fees for services performed by or materials furnished by the Patent and Trademark Office will be payable to the Director.

(b) All fees paid to the Director and all appropriations for defraying the costs of the activities of the Patent and Trademark Office will be credited to the Patent and Trademark Office Appropriation Account in the Treasury of the United States.

~~(c)~~ **(c)(1)** To the extent and in the amounts provided in advance in appropriations Acts, fees authorized in this title or any other Act to be charged or established by the Director shall be collected by and ~~shall be available~~ shall, subject to paragraph (3), be available to the Director to carry out the activities of the Patent and Trademark Office. ~~All fees available to the Director under section 31 of the Trademark Act of 1946 [15 USC § 1113] shall be used only for the processing of trademark registrations and for other activities, services, and materials relating to trademarks and to cover a proportionate share of the administrative costs of the Patent and Trademark Office.~~

(2) There is established in the Treasury a Patent and Trademark Fee Reserve Fund. If fee collections by the Patent and Trademark Office for a fiscal year exceed the amount appropriated to the Office for that fiscal year, fees collected in excess of the appropriated amount shall be deposited in the Patent and Trademark Fee Reserve Fund. To the extent and in the amounts provided in appropriations Acts, amounts in the Fund shall be made available until expended only for obligation and expenditure by the Office in accordance with paragraph (3).

(3)(A) Any fees that are collected under sections 41, 42, and 376, and any surcharges on such fees, may only be used for expenses of the Office relating to the processing of patent applications and for other activities, services, and materials relating to patents and to cover a share of the administrative costs of the Office relating to patents.

(B) Any fees that are collected under section 31 of the Trademark Act of 1946, and any surcharges on such fees, may only be used for expenses of the Office relating to the processing of trademark registrations and for other activities, services, and materials relating to trademarks and to cover a share of the administrative costs of the Office relating to trademarks.

(d) The Director may refund any fee paid by mistake or any amount paid in excess of that required.

(e) The Secretary of Commerce shall, on the day each year on which the President submits the annual budget to the Congress, provide to the Committees on the Judiciary of the Senate and the House of Representatives—

(1) a list of patent and trademark fee collections by the Patent and Trademark Office during the preceding fiscal year;

(2) a list of activities of the Patent and Trademark Office during the preceding fiscal year which were supported by patent fee expenditures, trademark fee expenditures, and appropriations;

(3) budget plans for significant programs, projects, and activities of the Office, including out-year funding estimates;

(4) any proposed disposition of surplus fees by the Office; and

(5) such other information as the committees consider necessary.

HISTORY:

(July 19, 1952, ch 950, § 1, 66 Stat. 796; Nov. 14, 1975, P.L. 94-131, § 4, 89 Stat. 690; Dec. 12, 1980, P.L. 96-517, § 3, 94 Stat. 3018; Aug. 27, 1982, P.L. 97-247, § 3(g), 96 Stat. 319; Sept. 13, 1982, P.L. 97-258, § 3(i), 96 Stat. 1065; Dec. 10, 1991, P.L. 102-204, §§ 4, 5(e), 105 Stat. 1637, 1640; Nov. 10, 1998, P.L. 105-358, § 4, 112 Stat. 3274; Nov. 29, 1999, P.L. 106-113, Div B, § 1000(a)(9), 113 Stat. 1536; Nov. 2, 2002, P.L. 107-273, Div C, Title III, Subtitle B, § 13206(b)(1)(B), 116 Stat. 1906.)

(America Invents Act § 22(a)(1)-(4).)

PART II. PATENTABILITY OF INVENTIONS AND GRANT OF PATENTS

CHAPTER 10. PATENTABILITY OF INVENTIONS

§ 100. Definitions

When used in this title [35 USC §§ 1 et seq.] unless the context otherwise indicates—

(a) The term "invention" means invention or discovery.

(b) The term "process" means process, art or method, and includes a new use of a known process, machine, manufacture, composition of matter, or material.

(c) The terms "United States" and "this country" mean the United States of America, its territories and possessions.

(d) The word "patentee" includes not only the patentee to whom the patent was issued but also the successors in title to the patentee.

(e) The term "third-party requester" means a person requesting ex parte reexamination under section 302 [35 USC § 302] ~~or inter partes reexamination under section 311 [35 USC § 311]~~ who is not the patent owner.

(f) The term "inventor" means the individual or, if a joint invention, the individuals collectively who invented or discovered the subject matter of the invention.

(g) The terms "joint inventor" and "coinventor" mean any 1 of the individuals who invented or discovered the subject matter of a joint invention.

(h) The term "joint research agreement" means a written contract, grant, or cooperative agreement entered into by 2 or more persons or entities for the performance of experimental, developmental, or research work in the field of the claimed invention.

(i)(1) The term "effective filing date" for a claimed invention in a patent or application for patent means—

(A) if subparagraph (B) does not apply, the actual filing date of the patent or the application for the patent containing a claim to the invention; or

(B) the filing date of the earliest application for which the patent or application is entitled, as to such invention, to a right of priority under section 119, 365(a), or 365(b) or to the benefit of an earlier filing date under section 120, 121, or 365(c).

(2) The effective filing date for a claimed invention in an application for reissue or reissued patent shall be determined by deeming the claim to the invention to have been contained in the patent for which reissue was sought.

(j) The term "claimed invention" means the subject matter defined by a claim in a patent or an application for a patent.

HISTORY:

(July 19, 1952, ch 950, § 1, 66 Stat. 797; Nov. 29, 1999, P.L. 106-113, Div B, § 1000(a)(9), 113 Stat. 1536.)

(America Invents Act § 3(a)(1)-(2).)

§ 101. Inventions patentable

Whoever invents or discovers any new and useful process, machine, manufacture, or composition of matter, or any new and useful improvement thereof, may obtain a patent therefor, subject to the conditions and requirements of this title [35 USC §§ 1 et seq.].

HISTORY:

(July 19, 1952, ch 950, § 1, 66 Stat. 797.)

~~§ 102. Conditions for patentability; novelty and loss of right to patent~~

~~A person shall be entitled to a patent unless—~~

35 USC § 102

(a) the invention was known or used by others in this country, or patented or described in a printed publication in this or a foreign country, before the invention thereof by the applicant for patent, or

(b) the invention was patented or described in a printed publication in this or a foreign country or in public use or on sale in this country, more than one year prior to the date of the application for patent in the United States, or

(c) he has abandoned the invention, or

(d) the invention was first patented or caused to be patented, or was the subject of an inventor's certificate, by the applicant or his legal representatives or assigns in a foreign country prior to the date of the application for patent in this country on an application for patent or inventor's certificate filed more than twelve months before the filing of the application in the United States, or

(e) the invention was described in (1) an application for patent, published under section 122(b) [35 USC § 122(b)], by another filed in the United States before the invention by the applicant for patent or (2) a patent granted on an application for patent by another filed in the United States before the invention by the applicant for patent, except that an international application filed under the treaty defined in section 351(a) [35 USC § 351(a)] shall have the effects for the purposes of this subsection of an application filed in the United States only if the international application designated the United States and was published under Article 21(2) of such treaty in the English language; or

(f) he did not himself invent the subject matter sought to be patented, or

(g)(1) during the course of an interference conducted under section 135 [35 USC § 135] or section 291 [35 USC § 291], another inventor involved therein establishes, to the extent permitted in section 104 [35 USC § 104], that before such person's invention thereof the invention was made by such other inventor and not abandoned, suppressed, or concealed, or (2) before such person's invention thereof, the invention was made in this country by another inventor who had not abandoned, suppressed, or concealed it. In determining priority of invention under this subsection, there shall be considered not only the respective dates of conception and reduction to practice of the invention, but also the reasonable diligence of one who was first to conceive and last to reduce to practice, from a time prior to conception by the other.

§ 102. Conditions for patentability; novelty

(a) Novelty; Prior Art.—A person shall be entitled to a patent unless—

(1) the claimed invention was patented, described in a printed publication, or in public use, on sale, or otherwise available to the public before the effective filing date of the claimed invention; or

(2) the claimed invention was described in a patent issued under section 151, or in an application for patent published or deemed published under section 122(b), in which the patent or application, as the case may be, names another inventor and was effectively filed before the effective filing date of the claimed invention.

(b) Exceptions.—

(1) Disclosures made 1 year or less before the effective filing date of the claimed invention.—A disclosure made 1 year or less before the effective filing date of a claimed invention shall not be prior art to the claimed invention under subsection (a)(1) if—

(A) the disclosure was made by the inventor or joint inventor or by another who obtained the subject matter disclosed directly or indirectly from the inventor or a joint inventor; or

(B) the subject matter disclosed had, before such disclosure, been publicly disclosed by the inventor or a joint inventor or another who obtained the subject matter disclosed directly or indirectly from the inventor or a joint inventor.

(2) Disclosures appearing in applications and patents.—A disclosure shall not be prior art to a claimed invention under subsection (a)(2) if—

(A) the subject matter disclosed was obtained directly or indirectly from the inventor or a joint inventor;

(B) the subject matter disclosed had, before such subject matter was effectively filed under subsection (a)(2), been publicly disclosed by the inventor or a joint inventor or another who obtained the subject matter disclosed directly or indirectly from the inventor or a joint inventor; or

(C) the subject matter disclosed and the claimed invention, not later than the effective filing date of the claimed invention, were owned by the same person or subject to an obligation of assignment to the same person.

(c) Common Ownership Under Joint Research Agreements.—Subject matter disclosed and a claimed invention shall be deemed to have been owned by the same person or subject to an obligation of assignment to the same person in applying the provisions of subsection (b)(2)(C) if—

(1) the subject matter disclosed was developed and the claimed invention was made by, or on behalf of, 1 or more parties to a joint research agreement that was in effect on or before the effective filing date of the claimed invention;

(2) the claimed invention was made as a result of activities undertaken within the scope of the joint research agreement; and

(3) the application for patent for the claimed invention discloses or is amended to disclose the names of the parties to the joint research agreement.

(d) Patents and Published Applications Effective as Prior Art.—For purposes of determining whether a patent or application for patent is prior art to a claimed invention under subsection (a)(2), such patent or application shall be considered to have been effectively filed, with respect to any subject matter described in the patent or application—

(1) if paragraph (2) does not apply, as of the actual filing date of the patent or the application for patent; or

(2) if the patent or application for patent is entitled to claim a right of priority under section 119, 365(a), or 365(b), or to claim the benefit of an earlier filing date under section 120, 121, or 365(c), based upon 1 or more prior filed applications for patent, as of the filing date of the earliest such application that describes the subject matter.

HISTORY:

(July 19, 1952, ch 950, § 1, 66 Stat. 797; July 28, 1972, P.L. 92-358, § 2, 86 Stat. 502; Nov. 14, 1975, P.L. 94-131, § 5, 89 Stat. 691; Nov. 29, 1999, P.L. 106-113, Div B, § 1000(a)(9), 113 Stat. 1536; Nov. 2, 2002, P.L. 107-273, Div C, Title III, Subtitle B, § 13205(1), 116 Stat. 1902.)

(America Invents Act § 3(b)(1).)

§ 103. Conditions for patentability; non-obvious subject matter

(a) A patent may not be obtained though the invention is not identically disclosed or described as set forth in section 102 of this title [35 USC § 102], if the differences between the subject matter sought to be patented and the prior art are such that the subject matter as a whole would have been obvious at the time the invention was made to a person having ordinary skill in the art to which said subject matter pertains. Patentability shall not be negatived by the manner in which the invention was made.

35 USC § 103

(b)(1) Notwithstanding subsection (a), and upon timely election by the applicant for patent to proceed under this subsection, a biotechnological process using or resulting in a composition of matter that is novel under section 102 [35 USC § 102] and nonobvious under subsection (a) of this section shall be considered nonobvious if—

(A) claims to the process and the composition of matter are contained in either the same application for patent or in separate applications having the same effective filing date; and

(B) the composition of matter, and the process at the time it was invented, were owned by the same person or subject to an obligation of assignment to the same person.

(2) A patent issued on a process under paragraph (1)—

(A) shall also contain the claims to the composition of matter used in or made by that process, or

(B) shall, if such composition of matter is claimed in another patent, be set to expire on the same date as such other patent, notwithstanding section 154 [35 USC § 154].

(3) For purposes of paragraph (1), the term "biotechnological process" means—

(A) a process of genetically altering or otherwise inducing a single- or multi-celled organism to—

(i) express an exogenous nucleotide sequence,

(ii) inhibit, eliminate, augment, or alter expression of an endogenous nucleotide sequence, or

(iii) express a specific physiological characteristic not naturally associated with said organism;

(B) cell fusion procedures yielding a cell line that expresses a specific protein, such as a monoclonal antibody; and

(C) a method of using a product produced by a process defined by subparagraph (A) or (B), or a combination of subparagraphs (A) and (B).

(c)(1) Subject matter developed by another person, which qualifies as prior art only under one or more of subsections (e), (f), and (g) of section 102 of this title [35 USC § 102], shall not preclude patentability under this section where the subject matter and the claimed invention were, at the time the claimed invention was made, owned by the same person or subject to an obligation of assignment to the same person.

(2) For purposes of this subsection, subject matter developed by another person and a claimed invention shall be deemed to have been owned by the same person or subject to an obligation of assignment to the same person if—

(A) the claimed invention was made by or on behalf of parties to a joint research agreement that was in effect on or before the date the claimed invention was made;

(B) the claimed invention was made as a result of activities undertaken within the scope of the joint research agreement; and

(C) the application for patent for the claimed invention discloses or is amended to disclose the names of the parties to the joint research agreement.

(3) For purposes of paragraph (2), the term "joint research agreement" means a written contract, grant, or cooperative agreement entered into by two or more persons or entities for the performance of experimental, developmental, or research work in the field of the claimed invention.

§ 103. Conditions for patentability; non-obvious subject matter

A patent for a claimed invention may not be obtained, notwithstanding that the claimed invention is not identically disclosed as set forth in section 102, if the differences between the claimed invention and the prior art are such that the claimed invention as a whole would have been obvious before the effective filing date of the claimed invention to a person having ordinary skill in the art to which the claimed invention pertains. Patentability shall not be negated by the manner in which the invention was made.

HISTORY:

(July 19, 1952, ch 950, § 1, 66 Stat. 798; Nov. 8, 1984, P.L. 98-622, Title I, § 103, 98 Stat. 3384; Nov. 1, 1995, P.L. 104-41, § 1, 109 Stat. 351; Nov. 29, 1999, P.L. 106-113, Div B, § 1000(a)(9), 113 Stat. 1536; Dec. 10, 2004, P.L. 108-453, § 2, 118 Stat. 3596.)

(America Invents Act § 3(c).)

§ 104. Invention made abroad

(a) In general.

(1) Proceedings. In proceedings in the Patent and Trademark Office, in the courts, and before any other competent authority, an applicant for a patent, or a patentee, may not establish a date of invention by reference to knowledge or use thereof, or other activity with respect thereto, in a foreign country other than a NAFTA country or a WTO member country, except as provided in sections 119 and 365 of this title [35 USC §§ 119 and 365].

(2) Rights. If an invention was made by a person, civil or military—

(A) while domiciled in the United States, and serving in any other country in connection with operations by or on behalf of the United States,

(B) while domiciled in a NAFTA country and serving in another country in connection with operations by or on behalf of that NAFTA country, or

(C) while domiciled in a WTO member country and serving in another country in connection with operations by or on behalf of that WTO member country,

that person shall be entitled to the same rights of priority in the United States with respect to such invention as if such invention had been made in the United States, that NAFTA country, or that WTO member country, as the case may be.

(3) Use of information. To the extent that any information in a NAFTA country or a WTO member country concerning knowledge, use, or other activity relevant to proving or disproving a date of invention has not been made available for use in a proceeding in the Patent and Trademark Office, a court, or any other competent authority to the same extent as such information could be made available in the United States, the Director, court, or such other authority shall draw appropriate inferences, or take other action permitted by statute, rule, or regulation, in favor of the party that requested the information in the proceeding.

(b) Definitions. As used in this section—

(1) the term "NAFTA country" has the meaning given that term in section 2(4) of the North American Free Trade Agreement Implementation Act [19 USC § 3301(4)]; and

(2) the term "WTO member country" has the meaning given that term in section 2(10) of the Uruguay Round Agreements Act [19 USC § 3501(10)].

HISTORY:

(July 19 1952, ch 950, § 1, 66 Stat. 798; Jan. 2, 1975, P.L. 93-596, § 1, 88 Stat. 1949; Nov. 14, 1975, P.L. 94-131, § 6, 89 Stat. 691; Nov. 8, 1984, P.L. 98-622, Title IV, § 403(a), 98 Stat. 3392; Dec. 8, 1993, P.L. 103-182, Title III, Subtitle C, § 331, 107 Stat. 2113; Dec. 8, 1994, P.L. 103-465, Title V, Subtitle C, § 531(a), 108 Stat. 4982; Nov. 29, 1999, P.L. 106-113, Div B, § 1000(a)(9), 113 Stat. 1536; Nov. 2, 2002, P.L. 107-273, Div C, Title III, Subtitle B, § 13206(b)(1)(B), 116 Stat. 1906.)

(America Invents Act § 3(d).)

35 USC § 105

§ 105. Inventions in outer space

(a) Any invention made, used or sold in outer space on a space object or component thereof under the jurisdiction or control of the United States shall be considered to be made, used or sold within the United States for the purposes of this title, except with respect to any space object or component thereof that is specifically identified and otherwise provided for by an international agreement to which the United States is a party, or with respect to any space object or component thereof that is carried on the registry of a foreign state in accordance with the Convention on Registration of Objects Launched into Outer Space.

(b) Any invention made, used or sold in outer space on a space object or component thereof that is carried on the registry of a foreign state in accordance with the Convention on Registration of Objects Launched into Outer Space, shall be considered to be made, used or sold within the United States for the purposes of this title if specifically so agreed in an international agreement between the United States and the state of registry.

HISTORY:

(Added Nov. 15, 1990, P.L. 101-580, § 1(a), 104 Stat. 2863.)

CHAPTER 11. APPLICATION FOR PATENT

§ 111. Application

(a) In general.

(1) Written application. An application for patent shall be made, or authorized to be made, by the inventor, except as otherwise provided in this title, in writing to the Director.

(2) Contents. Such application shall include—

(A) a specification as prescribed by section 112 of this title [35 USC § 112];

(B) a drawing as prescribed by section 113 of this title [35 USC § 113]; and

(C) an oath by the applicant or declaration as prescribed by section 115 of this title [35 USC § 115].

(3) Fee and oath or declaration. The application must be accompanied by the fee required by law. The fee and oath or declaration may be submitted after the specification and any required drawing are submitted, within such period and under such conditions, including the payment of a surcharge, as may be prescribed by the Director.

(4) Failure to submit. Upon failure to submit the fee and oath or declaration within such prescribed period, the application shall be regarded as abandoned, unless it is shown to the satisfaction of the Director that the delay in submitting the fee and oath or declaration was unavoidable or unintentional. The filing date of an application shall be the date on which the specification and any required drawing are received in the Patent and Trademark Office.

(b) Provisional application.

(1) Authorization. A provisional application for patent shall be made or authorized to be made by the inventor, except as otherwise provided in this title, in writing to the Director. Such application shall include—

(A) a specification as prescribed by the first paragraph of section 112 of this title [35 USC § 112] section 112(a); and

(B) a drawing as prescribed by section 113 of this title [35 USC § 113].

(2) Claim. A claim, as required by the second through fifth paragraphs of section 112 [35 USC § 112], subsections (b) through (e) of section 112, shall not be required in a provisional application.

44

(3) Fee.

(A) The application must be accompanied by the fee required by law.

(B) The fee may be submitted after the specification and any required drawing are submitted, within such period and under such conditions, including the payment of a surcharge, as may be prescribed by the Director.

(C) Upon failure to submit the fee within such prescribed period, the application shall be regarded as abandoned, unless it is shown to the satisfaction of the Director that the delay in submitting the fee was unavoidable or unintentional.

(4) Filing date. The filing date of a provisional application shall be the date on which the specification and any required drawing are received in the Patent and Trademark Office.

(5) Abandonment. Notwithstanding the absence of a claim, upon timely request and as prescribed by the Director, a provisional application may be treated as an application filed under subsection (a). Subject to section 119(e)(3) ~~of this title~~ [35 USC § 119(e)(3)], if no such request is made, the provisional application shall be regarded as abandoned 12 months after the filing date of such application and shall not be subject to revival after such 12-month period.

(6) Other basis for provisional application. Subject to all the conditions in this subsection and section 119(e) ~~of this title~~ [35 USC § 119(e)], and as prescribed by the Director, an application for patent filed under subsection (a) may be treated as a provisional application for patent.

(7) No right of priority or benefit of earliest filing date. A provisional application shall not be entitled to the right of priority of any other application under section 119 or 365(a) ~~of this title~~ [35 USC § 119 or 365(a)] or to the benefit of an earlier filing date in the United States under section 120, 121, or 365(c) ~~of this title~~ [35 USC § 120, 121, or 365(c)].

(8) Applicable provisions. The provisions of this title relating to applications for patent shall apply to provisional applications for patent, except as otherwise provided, and except that provisional applications for patent shall not be subject to ~~sections 115, 131, 135, and 157~~ sections 131 and 135 ~~of this title~~.

HISTORY:

(July 19, 1952, ch 950, § 1, 66 Stat. 798; Aug. 27, 1982, P.L. 97-247, § 5, 96 Stat. 319; Dec. 8, 1994, P.L. 103-465, Title V, Subtitle C, § 532(b)(3), 108 Stat. 4986; Nov. 29, 1999, P.L. 106-113, Div B, § 1000(a)(9), 113 Stat. 1536; Nov. 2, 2002, P.L. 107-273, Div C, Title III, Subtitle B, § 13206(b)(1)(B), 116 Stat. 1906.)

(America Invents Act §§ 3(e)(2); 4(a)(3)(A)-(C), (d)(1)-(2); 20(j)(1).)

§ 112. Specification

~~The specification~~ **(a) In General.**—The specification shall contain a written description of the invention, and of the manner and process of making and using it, in such full, clear, concise, and exact terms as to enable any person skilled in the art to which it pertains, or with which it is most nearly connected, to make and use the same, and shall set forth the best mode contemplated by the inventor ~~of carrying out his invention~~ or joint inventor of carrying out the invention.

~~The specification~~ **(b) Conclusion.**—The specification shall conclude with one or more claims particularly pointing out and distinctly claiming the subject matter which the ~~applicant regards as his invention~~ inventor or a joint inventor regards as the invention.

~~A claim~~ **(c) Form.**—A claim may be written in independent or, if the nature of the case admits, in dependent or multiple dependent form.

~~Subject to the following paragraph,~~ **(d) Reference in Dependent Forms.**—Subject to subsection (e), a claim in dependent form shall contain a reference to a claim previously set

35 USC § 112

forth and then specify a further limitation of the subject matter claimed. A claim in dependent form shall be construed to incorporate by reference all the limitations of the claim to which it refers.

A claim (e) Reference in Multiple Dependent Form.—A claim in multiple dependent form shall contain a reference, in the alternative only, to more than one claim previously set forth and then specify a further limitation of the subject matter claimed. A multiple dependent claim shall not serve as a basis for any other multiple dependent claim. A multiple dependent claim shall be construed to incorporate by reference all the limitations of the particular claim in relation to which it is being considered.

An element (f) Element in Claim for a Combination.—An element in a claim for a combination may be expressed as a means or step for performing a specified function without the recital of structure, material, or acts in support thereof, and such claim shall be construed to cover the corresponding structure, material, or acts described in the specification and equivalents thereof.

HISTORY:

(July 19, 1952, ch 950, § 1, 66 Stat. 798; July 24, 1965, P.L. 89-83, § 9, 79 Stat. 261; Nov. 14, 1975, P.L. 94-131, § 7, 89 Stat. 691.)

(America Invents Act §§ 4(c)(1)(A)-(B), 2(A)-(B), (3)-(6).)

§ 113. Drawings

The applicant shall furnish a drawing where necessary for the understanding of the subject matter sought to be patented. When the nature of such subject matter admits of illustration by a drawing and the applicant has not furnished such a drawing, the Director may require its submission within a time period of not less than two months from the sending of a notice thereof. Drawings submitted after the filing date of the application may not be used (i) to overcome any insufficiency of the specification due to lack of an enabling disclosure or otherwise inadequate disclosure therein, or (ii) to supplement the original disclosure thereof for the purpose of interpretation of the scope of any claim.

HISTORY:

(July 19, 1952, ch 950, § 1, 66 Stat. 799; Nov. 14, 1975, P.L. 94-131, § 8, 89 Stat. 691; Nov. 29, 1999, P.L. 106-113, Div B, § 1000(a)(9), 113 Stat. 1536; Nov. 2, 2002, P.L. 107-273, Div C, Title III, Subtitle B, § 13206(b)(1)(B), 116 Stat. 1906.)

§ 114. Models, specimens

The Director may require the applicant to furnish a model of convenient size to exhibit advantageously the several parts of his invention.

When the invention relates to a composition of matter, the Director may require the applicant to furnish specimens or ingredients for the purpose of inspection or experiment.

HISTORY:

(July 19, 1952, ch 950, § 1, 66 Stat. 799; Nov. 29, 1999, P.L. 106-113, Div B, § 1000(a)(9), 113 Stat. 1536; Nov. 2, 2002, P.L. 107-273, Div C, Title III, Subtitle B, § 13206(b)(1)(B), 116 Stat. 1906.)

§ 115. Oath of applicant

The applicant shall make oath that he believes himself to be the original and first inventor of the process, machine, manufacture, or composition of matter, or improvement thereof, for which he solicits a patent; and shall state of what country he is a citizen. Such oath may be made before any person within the United States authorized by law to administer oaths, or, when made in a foreign country, before any diplomatic or consular officer of the United States authorized to administer oaths, or before any officer having an official seal and authorized to administer oaths in the foreign country in which the applicant may be, whose authority shall be proved by certificate of a diplomatic or consular officer of the United States, or apostille of an official designated by a foreign country which, by treaty or convention, accords like effect to apostilles of designated officials in the United States, and such oath is valid if it complies with the laws of the state or country where made. When the application is made as provided in this title by a person other than the inventor, the oath may be so varied in form that it can be made by him. For purposes of this section, a consular officer shall include any United States citizen serving overseas, authorized to perform notarial functions pursuant to section 1750 of the Revised Statutes, as amended (22 U.S.C. 4221).

§ 115. Inventor's oath or declaration

(a) **Naming the Inventor; Inventor's Oath or Declaration.**—An application for patent that is filed under section 111(a) or commences the national stage under section 371 shall include, or be amended to include, the name of the inventor for any invention claimed in the application. Except as otherwise provided in this section, each individual who is the inventor or a joint inventor of a claimed invention in an application for patent shall execute an oath or declaration in connection with the application.

(b) **Required Statements.**—An oath or declaration under subsection (a) shall contain statements that—

(1) the application was made or was authorized to be made by the affiant or declarant; and

(2) such individual believes himself or herself to be the original inventor or an original joint inventor of a claimed invention in the application.

(c) **Additional Requirements.**—The Director may specify additional information relating to the inventor and the invention that is required to be included in an oath or declaration under subsection (a).

(d) **Substitute Statement.**—

(1) **In general.**—In lieu of executing an oath or declaration under subsection (a), the applicant for patent may provide a substitute statement under the circumstances described in paragraph (2) and such additional circumstances that the Director may specify by regulation.

(2) **Permitted circumstances.**—A substitute statement under paragraph (1) is permitted with respect to any individual who—

(A) is unable to file the oath or declaration under subsection (a) because the individual—

(i) is deceased;

(ii) is under legal incapacity; or

(iii) cannot be found or reached after diligent effort; or

(B) is under an obligation to assign the invention but has refused to make the oath or declaration required under subsection (a).

(3) **Contents.**—A substitute statement under this subsection shall—

(A) identify the individual with respect to whom the statement applies;

(B) set forth the circumstances representing the permitted basis for the filing of the substitute statement in lieu of the oath or declaration under subsection (a); and

(C) contain any additional information, including any showing, required by the Director.

(e) **Making Required Statements in Assignment of Record.**—An individual who is under an obligation of assignment of an application for patent may include the required statements under subsections (b) and (c) in the assignment executed by the individual, in lieu of filing such statements separately.

(f) Time for Filing.—A notice of allowance under section 151 may be provided to an applicant for patent only if the applicant for patent has filed each required oath or declaration under subsection (a) or has filed a substitute statement under subsection (d) or recorded an assignment meeting the requirements of subsection (e).

(g) Earlier-Filed Application Containing Required Statements or Substitute Statement.—

(1) Exception.—The requirements under this section shall not apply to an individual with respect to an application for patent in which the individual is named as the inventor or a joint inventor and who claims the benefit under section 120, 121, or 365(c) of the filing of an earlier-filed application, if—

(A) an oath or declaration meeting the requirements of subsection (a) was executed by the individual and was filed in connection with the earlier-filed application;

(B) a substitute statement meeting the requirements of subsection (d) was filed in connection with the earlier filed application with respect to the individual; or

(C) an assignment meeting the requirements of subsection (e) was executed with respect to the earlier-filed application by the individual and was recorded in connection with the earlier-filed application.

(2) Copies of oaths, declarations, statements, or assignments.—Notwithstanding paragraph (1), the Director may require that a copy of the executed oath or declaration, the substitute statement, or the assignment filed in connection with the earlier-filed application be included in the later-filed application.

(h) Supplemental and Corrected Statements; Filing Additional Statements.—

(1) In general.—Any person making a statement required under this section may withdraw, replace, or otherwise correct the statement at any time. If a change is made in the naming of the inventor requiring the filing of 1 or more additional statements under this section, the Director shall establish regulations under which such additional statements may be filed.

(2) Supplemental statements not required.—If an individual has executed an oath or declaration meeting the requirements of subsection (a) or an assignment meeting the requirements of subsection (e) with respect to an application for patent, the Director may not thereafter require that individual to make any additional oath, declaration, or other statement equivalent to those required by this section in connection with the application for patent or any patent issuing thereon.

(3) Savings clause.—A patent shall not be invalid or unenforceable based upon the failure to comply with a requirement under this section if the failure is remedied as provided under paragraph (1).

(i) Acknowledgment of Penalties.—Any declaration or statement filed pursuant to this section shall contain an acknowledgment that any willful false statement made in such declaration or statement is punishable under section 1001 of title 18 by fine or imprisonment of not more than 5 years, or both.

HISTORY:

(July 19, 1952, ch 950, § 1, 66 Stat. 799; Aug. 27, 1982, P.L. 97-247, § 14(a), 96 Stat. 321; Oct. 21, 1998, P.L. 105-277, Div G, Title XXII, Ch 2, § 2222(d), 112 Stat. 2681-818.)

(America Invents Act § 4(a)(1).)

§ 116. Inventors

~~When~~ **(a) Joint Inventions.**—When an invention is made by two or more persons jointly, they shall apply for patent jointly and each make the required oath, except as otherwise provided in this title. Inventors may apply for a patent jointly even though (1) they did not physically work together or at the same time, (2) each did not make the same type or amount of contribution, or (3) each did not make a contribution to the subject matter of every claim of the patent.

~~If a joint inventor~~ **(b) Omitted Inventor.**—If a joint inventor refuses to join in an application for patent or cannot be found or reached after diligent effort, the application may be made by the other inventor on behalf of himself and the omitted inventor. The Director, on proof of the pertinent facts and after such notice to the omitted inventor as he prescribes, may grant a patent to the inventor making the application, subject to the same rights which the omitted inventor would have had if he had been joined. The omitted inventor may subsequently join in the application.

~~Whenever~~ **(c) Correction of Errors in Application.**—Whenever through error a person is named in an application for patent as the inventor, or through error an inventor is not named in an application, ~~and such error arose without any deceptive intention on his part,~~ the Director may permit the application to be amended accordingly, under such terms as he prescribes.

HISTORY:

(July 19, 1952, ch 950, § 1, 66 Stat. 799; Aug. 27, 1982, P.L. 97-247, § 6(a), 96 Stat. 320; Nov. 8, 1984, P.L. 98-622, Title I, § 104(a), 98 Stat. 3384; Nov. 29, 1999, P.L. 106-113, Div B, § 1000(a)(9), 113 Stat. 1536; Nov. 2, 2002, P.L. 107-273, Div C, Title III, Subtitle B, § 13206(b)(1)(B), 116 Stat. 1906.)

(America Invents Act §§ 20(a)(1), (2), (3)(A)-(B).)

§ 117. Death or incapacity of inventor

Legal representatives of deceased inventors and of those under legal incapacity may make application for patent upon compliance with the requirements and on the same terms and conditions applicable to the inventor.

§ 118. Filing by other than inventor

~~Whenever an inventor refuses to execute an application for patent, or cannot be found or reached after diligent effort, a person to whom the inventor has assigned or agreed in writing to assign the invention or who otherwise shows sufficient proprietary interest in the matter justifying such action, may make application for patent on behalf of and as agent for the inventor on proof of the pertinent facts and a showing that such action is necessary to preserve the rights of the parties or to prevent irreparable damage; and the Director may grant a patent to such inventor upon such notice to him as the Director deems sufficient, and on compliance with such regulations as he prescribes.~~

A person to whom the inventor has assigned or is under an obligation to assign the invention may make an application for patent. A person who otherwise shows sufficient proprietary interest in the matter may make an application for patent on behalf of and as agent for the inventor on proof of the pertinent facts and a showing that such action is appropriate to preserve the rights of the parties. If the Director grants a patent on an application filed under this section by a person other than the inventor, the patent shall be granted to the real party in interest and upon such notice to the inventor as the Director considers to be sufficient.

HISTORY:

(America Invents Act § 4(b)(1).)

§ 119. Benefit of earlier filing date; right of priority

(a) An application for patent for an invention filed in this country by any person who has, or whose legal representatives or assigns have, previously regularly filed an application for a patent for the same invention in a foreign country which affords similar privileges in the case of applications filed in the United States or to citizens of the United States, or in a WTO member country, shall have the same effect as the same application would have if filed in this country on the date on which the application for patent for the same invention was first filed in such foreign country, if the application in this country is filed within twelve months from the earliest date on which such foreign application was filed~~; but no patent shall be granted on any application for patent for an invention which had been patented or described in a printed publication in any country more than one year before the date of the actual filing of the application in this country, or which had been in public use or on sale in this country more than one year prior to such filing~~.

(b)(1) No application for patent shall be entitled to this right of priority unless a claim is filed in the Patent and Trademark Office, identifying the foreign application by specifying the application number on that foreign application, the intellectual property authority or country in or for which the application was filed, and the date of filing the application, at such time during the pendency of the application as required by the Director.

(2) The Director may consider the failure of the applicant to file a timely claim for priority as a waiver of any such claim. The Director may establish procedures, including the payment of a surcharge, to accept an unintentionally delayed claim under this section.

(3) The Director may require a certified copy of the original foreign application, specification, and drawings upon which it is based, a translation if not in the English language, and such other information as the Director considers necessary. Any such certification shall be made by the foreign intellectual property authority in which the foreign application was filed and show the date of the application and of the filing of the specification and other papers.

(c) In like manner and subject to the same conditions and requirements, the right provided in this section may be based upon a subsequent regularly filed application in the same foreign country instead of the first filed foreign application, provided that any foreign application filed prior to such subsequent application has been withdrawn, abandoned, or otherwise disposed of, without having been laid open to public inspection and without leaving any rights outstanding, and has not served, nor thereafter shall serve, as a basis for claiming a right of priority.

(d) Applications for inventors' certificates filed in a foreign country in which applicants have a right to apply, at their discretion, either for a patent or for an inventor's certificate shall be treated in this country in the same manner and have the same effect for purpose of the right of priority under this section as applications for patents, subject to the same conditions and requirements of this section as apply to applications for patents, provided such applicants are entitled to the benefits of the Stockholm Revision of the Paris Convention at the time of such filing.

(e)(1) An application for patent filed under section 111(a) or section 363 ~~of this title~~ [35 USC § 111(a) or 363] for an invention disclosed in the manner provided by ~~the first paragraph of section 112 of this title [35 USC § 112]~~ section 112(a) (other than the requirement to disclose the best mode) in a provisional application filed under section 111(b) ~~of this title~~ [35 USC § 111(b)], by an inventor or inventors named in the provisional application, shall have the same effect, as to such invention, as though filed on the date of the provisional application filed under section 111(b) ~~of this title~~ [35 USC § 111(b)], if the application for patent filed under section 111(a) or section 363 ~~of this title~~ [35 USC § 111(a) or 363] is filed not later than 12 months after the date on which the provisional application was filed and if it contains or is amended to contain a specific reference to the provisional application. No application shall be entitled to the benefit of an earlier filed provisional application under this subsection unless an amendment containing the specific reference to the earlier filed provisional application is submitted at such time during the pendency of the application as required by the Director. The Director may consider the failure to submit such an amendment within that time period as a waiver of any benefit under this subsection. The Director may establish procedures, including the payment of a surcharge, to accept an unintentionally delayed submission of an amendment under this subsection during the pendency of the application.

(2) A provisional application filed under section 111(b) ~~of this title~~ [35 USC § 111(b)] may not be relied upon in any proceeding in the Patent and Trademark Office unless the fee set forth in subparagraph (A) or (C) of section 41(a)(1) ~~of this title~~ [35 USC § 41(a)(1)] has been paid.

(3) If the day that is 12 months after the filing date of a provisional application falls on a Saturday, Sunday, or Federal holiday within the District of Columbia, the period of pendency of the provisional application shall be extended to the next succeeding secular or business day.

(f) Applications for plant breeder's rights filed in a WTO member country (or in a foreign UPOV Contracting Party) shall have the same effect for the purpose of the right of priority under subsections (a) through (c) of this section as applications for patents, subject to the same conditions and requirements of this section as apply to applications for patents.

(g) As used in this section—

(1) the term "WTO member country" has the same meaning as the term is defined in section 104(b)(2) ~~of this title~~ [35 USC § 104(b)(2)]; and

(2) the term "UPOV Contracting Party" means a member of the International Convention for the Protection of New Varieties of Plants.

HISTORY:

(July 19, 1952, ch 950, § 1, 66 Stat. 800; Oct. 3, 1961, P.L. 87-333, § 1, 75 Stat. 748; July 28, 1972, P.L. 92-358, § 1, 86 Stat. 501; Jan. 2, 1975, P.L. 93-596, § 1, 88 Stat. 1949; Dec. 8, 1994, P.L. 103-465, Title V, Subtitle C, § 532(b)(1), 108 Stat. 4985; Nov. 29, 1999, P.L. 106-113, Div B, § 1000(a)(9), 113 Stat. 1536; Nov. 2, 2002, P.L. 107-273, Div C, Title III, Subtitle B, § 13206(b)(2), 116 Stat. 1906.)

(America Invents Act §§ 3(g)(6); 15(b); 20(j)(1).)

§ 120. Benefit of earlier filing date in the United States

An application for patent for an invention disclosed in the manner provided by ~~the first paragraph of section 112 of this title [35 USC § 112]~~ section 112(a) (other than the requirement to disclose the best mode) in an application previously filed in the United States, or as provided by section 363 ~~of this title~~ [35 USC § 363], ~~which is filed by an inventor or inventors named~~ which names an inventor or joint inventor in the previously filed application shall have the same effect, as to such invention, as though filed on the date of the prior application, if filed before the patenting or abandonment of or termination of proceedings on the first application or on an application similarly entitled to the benefit of the filing date of the first application and if it contains or is amended to contain a specific reference to the earlier filed application. No application shall be entitled to the benefit of an earlier filed application under this section unless an amendment containing the specific reference to the earlier filed application is submitted at such time during the pendency of the application as required by

35 USC § 120

the Director. The Director may consider the failure to submit such an amendment within that time period as a waiver of any benefit under this section. The Director may establish procedures, including the payment of a surcharge, to accept an unintentionally delayed submission of an amendment under this section.

HISTORY:

(July 19, 1952, ch 950, § 1, 66 Stat. 800; Nov. 14, 1975, P.L. 94-131, § 9, 89 Stat. 691; Nov. 8, 1984, P.L. 98-622, Title I, § 104(b), 98 Stat. 3385; Nov. 29, 1999, P.L. 106-113, Div B, § 1000(a)(9), 113 Stat. 1536.)

(America Invents Act §§ 3(f); 15(b); 20(j)(1).)

§ 121. Divisional applications

If two or more independent and distinct inventions are claimed in one application, the Director may require the application to be restricted to one of the inventions. If the other invention is made the subject of a divisional application which complies with the requirements of section 120 ~~of this title~~ [35 USC § 120] it shall be entitled to the benefit of the filing date of the original application. A patent issuing on an application with respect to which a requirement for restriction under this section has been made, or on an application filed as a result of such a requirement, shall not be used as a reference either in the Patent and Trademark Office or in the courts against a divisional application or against the original application or any patent issued on either of them, if the divisional application is filed before the issuance of the patent on the other application. ~~If a divisional application is directed solely to subject matter described and claimed in the original application as filed, the Director may dispense with signing and execution by the inventor.~~ The validity of a patent shall not be questioned for failure of the Director to require the application to be restricted to one invention.

HISTORY:

(July 19, 1952, ch 950, § 1, 66 Stat. 800; Jan. 2, 1975, P.L. 93-596, § 1, 88 Stat. 1949; Nov. 29, 1999, P.L. 106-113, Div B, § 1000(a)(9), 113 Stat. 1536; Nov. 2, 2002, P.L. 107-273, Div C, Title III, Subtitle B, § 13206(b)(1)(B), 116 Stat. 1906.)

(America Invents Act §§ 4(a)(2); 20(j)(1))

§ 122. Confidential status of applications; publication of patent applications

(a) Confidentiality. Except as provided in subsection (b), applications for patents shall be kept in confidence by the Patent and Trademark Office and no information concerning the same given without authority of the applicant or owner unless necessary to carry out the provisions of an Act of Congress or in such special circumstances as may be determined by the Director.

(b) Publication.

(1) In general.

(A) Subject to paragraph (2), each application for a patent shall be published, in accordance with procedures determined by the Director, promptly after the expiration of a period of 18 months from the earliest filing date for which a benefit is sought under this title. At the request of the applicant, an application may be published earlier than the end of such 18-month period.

(B) No information concerning published patent applications shall be made available to the public except as the Director determines.

(C) Notwithstanding any other provision of law, a determination by the Director to release or not to release information concerning a published patent application shall be final and nonreviewable.

(2) Exceptions.

(A) An application shall not be published if that application is—

(i) no longer pending;

(ii) subject to a secrecy order under section 181 ~~of this title~~ [35 USC § 181];

(iii) a provisional application filed under section 111(b) ~~of this title~~ [35 USC § 111(b)]; or

(iv) an application for a design patent filed under chapter 16 ~~of this title~~ [35 USC §§ 171 et seq.].

(B)(i) If an applicant makes a request upon filing, certifying that the invention disclosed in the application has not and will not be the subject of an application filed in another country, or under a multilateral international agreement, that requires publication of applications 18 months after filing, the application shall not be published as provided in paragraph (1).

(ii) An applicant may rescind a request made under clause (i) at any time.

(iii) An applicant who has made a request under clause (i) but who subsequently files, in a foreign country or under a multilateral international agreement specified in clause (i), an application directed to the invention disclosed in the application filed in the Patent and Trademark Office, shall notify the Director of such filing not later than 45 days after the date of the filing of such foreign or international application. A failure of the applicant to provide such notice within the prescribed period shall result in the application being regarded as abandoned, unless it is shown to the satisfaction of the Director that the delay in submitting the notice was unintentional.

(iv) If an applicant rescinds a request made under clause (i) or notifies the Director that an application was filed in a foreign country or under a multilateral international agreement specified in clause (i), the application shall be published in accordance with the provisions of paragraph (1) on or as soon as is practical after the date that is specified in clause (i).

(v) If an applicant has filed applications in one or more foreign countries, directly or through a multilateral international agreement, and such foreign filed applications corresponding to an application filed in the Patent and Trademark Office or the description of the invention in such foreign filed applications is less extensive than the application or description of the invention in the application filed in the Patent and Trademark Office, the applicant may submit a redacted copy of the application filed in the Patent and Trademark Office eliminating any part or description of the invention in such application that is not also contained in any of the corresponding applications filed in a foreign country. The Director may only publish the redacted copy of the application unless the redacted copy of the application is not received within 16 months after the earliest effective filing date for which a benefit is sought under this title. The provisions of section 154(d) [35 USC § 154(d)] shall not apply to a claim if the description of the invention published in the redacted application filed under this clause with respect to the claim does not enable a person skilled in the art to make and use the subject matter of the claim.

(c) Protest and pre-issuance opposition. The Director shall establish appropriate procedures to ensure that no protest or other form of pre-issuance opposition to the grant of a patent on an application may be initiated after publication of the application without the express written consent of the applicant.

(d) National security. No application for patent shall be published under subsection (b) (1) if the publication or disclosure of such invention would be detrimental to the national security. The Director shall establish appropriate procedures to ensure that such applications are promptly identified and the secrecy of such inventions is maintained in accordance with chapter 17 ~~of this title~~ [35 USC §§ 181 et seq.].

(e) Preissuance Submissions by Third Parties.—

(1) In general.—Any third party may submit for consideration and inclusion in the record of a patent application, any patent, published patent application, or other printed publication of potential relevance to the examination of the application, if such submission is made in writing before the earlier of—

(A) the date a notice of allowance under section 151 is given or mailed in the application for patent; or

(B) the later of—

(i) 6 months after the date on which the application for patent is first published under section 122 by the Office, or

(ii) the date of the first rejection under section 132 of any claim by the examiner during the examination of the application for patent.

(2) Other requirements.—Any submission under paragraph (1) shall—

(A) set forth a concise description of the asserted relevance of each submitted document;

(B) be accompanied by such fee as the Director may prescribe; and

(C) include a statement by the person making such submission affirming that the submission was made in compliance with this section.

HISTORY:

(July 19, 1952, ch 950, § 1, 66 Stat. 801; Jan. 2, 1975, P.L. 93-596, § 1, 88 Stat. 1949; Nov. 29, 1999, P.L. 106-113, Div B, § 1000(a)(9), 113 Stat. 1536.)

(America Invents Act §§ 8(a); 20(j)(1).)

§ 123. Micro entity defined

(a) In general.—For purposes of this title, the term "micro entity" means an applicant who makes a certification that the applicant—

(1) qualifies as a small entity, as defined in regulations issued by the Director;

(2) has not been named as an inventor on more than 4 previously filed patent applications, other than applications filed in another country, provisional applications under section 111(b), or international applications filed under the treaty defined in section 351(a) for which the basic national fee under section 41(a) was not paid;

(3) did not, in the calendar year preceding the calendar year in which the applicable fee is being paid, have a gross income, as defined in section 61(a) of the Internal Revenue Code of 1986, exceeding 3 times the median household income for that preceding calendar year, as most recently reported by the Bureau of the Census; and

(4) has not assigned, granted, or conveyed, and is not under an obligation by contract or law to assign, grant, or convey, a license or other ownership interest in the application concerned to an entity that, in the calendar year preceding the calendar year in which the applicable fee is being paid, had a gross income, as defined in section 61(a) of the Internal Revenue Code of 1986, exceeding 3 times the median household income for that preceding calendar year, as most recently reported by the Bureau of the Census.

(b) Applications Resulting From Prior Employment.—An applicant is not considered to be named on a previously filed application for purposes of subsection (a)(2) if the applicant has assigned, or is under an obligation by contract or law to assign, all ownership rights in the application as the result of the applicant's previous employment.

(c) Foreign Currency Exchange Rate.—If an applicant's or entity's gross income in the preceding calendar year is not in United States dollars, the average currency exchange rate, as reported by the Internal Revenue Service, during that calendar year shall be used to determine whether the applicant's or entity's gross income exceeds the threshold specified in paragraphs (3) or (4) of subsection (a).

(d) Institutions of higher education.—For purposes of this section, a micro entity shall include an applicant who certifies that—

(1) the applicant's employer, from which the applicant obtains the majority of the applicant's income, is an institution of higher education as defined in section 101(a) of the Higher Education Act of 1965 (20 U.S.C. 1001(a)); or

(2) the applicant has assigned, granted, conveyed, or is under an obligation by contract or law, to assign, grant, or convey, a license or other ownership interest in the particular applications to such an institution of higher education.

(e) Director's authority.—In addition to the limits imposed by this section, the Director may, in the Director's discretion, impose income limits, annual filing limits, or other limits on who may qualify as a micro entity pursuant to this section if the Director determines that such additional limits are reasonably necessary to avoid an undue impact on other patent applicants or owners or are otherwise reasonably necessary and appropriate. At least 3 months before any limits proposed to be imposed pursuant to this subsection take effect, the Director shall inform the Committee on the Judiciary of the House of Representatives and the Committee on the Judiciary of the Senate of any such proposed limits.

HISTORY:

(America Invents Act § 10(g)(1))

CHAPTER 12. EXAMINATION OF APPLICATION

§ 131. Examination of application

The Director shall cause an examination to be made of the application and the alleged new invention; and if on such examination it appears that the applicant is entitled to a patent under the law, the Director shall issue a patent therefor.

HISTORY:

(July 19, 1952, ch 950, § 1, 66 Stat. 801; Nov. 29, 1999, P.L. 106-113, Div B, § 1000(a)(9), 113 Stat. 1536; Nov. 2, 2002, P.L. 107-273, Div C, Title III, Subtitle B, § 13206(b)(1)(B), 116 Stat. 1906.)

§ 132. Notice of rejection; reexamination

(a) Whenever, on examination, any claim for a patent is rejected, or any objection or requirement made, the Director shall notify the applicant thereof, stating the reasons for such rejection, or objection or requirement, together with such information and references as may be useful in judging of the propriety of continuing the prosecution of his application; and if after receiving such notice, the applicant persists in his claim for a patent, with or without amendment, the application shall be reexamined. No amendment shall introduce new matter into the disclosure of the invention.

(b) The Director shall prescribe regulations to provide for the continued examination of applications for patent at the request of the applicant. The Director may establish appropriate fees for such continued examination and shall provide a 50 percent reduction in such fees for small entities that qualify for reduced fees under section 41(h)(1) of this title [35 USC § 41(h)(1)].

35 USC § 132

HISTORY:

(July 19, 1952, ch 950, § 1, 66 Stat. 801; Nov. 29, 1999, P.L. 106-113, Div B, § 1000(a)(9), 113 Stat. 1536; Nov. 2, 2002, P.L. 107-273, Div C, Title III, Subtitle B, § 13206(b)(1)(B), 116 Stat. 1906.)

(America Invents Act § 20(j)(1).)

§ 133. Time for prosecuting application

Upon failure of the applicant to prosecute the application within six months after any action therein, of which notice has been given or mailed to the applicant, or within such shorter time, not less than thirty days, as fixed by the Director in such action, the application shall be regarded as abandoned by the parties thereto, unless it be shown to the satisfaction of the Director that such delay was unavoidable.

HISTORY:

(July 19, 1952, ch 950, § 1, 66 Stat. 801; Nov. 29, 1999, P.L. 106-113, Div B, § 1000(a)(9), 113 Stat. 1536; Nov. 2, 2002, P.L. 107-273, Div C, Title III, Subtitle B, § 13206(b)(1)(B), 116 Stat. 1906.)

~~§ 134. Appeal to the Board of Patent Appeals and Interferences~~

§ 134. Appeal to the Patent Trial and Appeal Board

(a) Patent applicant. An applicant for a patent, any of whose claims has been twice rejected, may appeal from the decision of the primary examiner to the ~~Board of Patent Appeals and Interferences~~ Patent Trial and Appeal Board, having once paid the fee for such appeal.

(b) Patent owner. A patent owner in ~~any reexamination proceeding~~ a reexamination may appeal from the final rejection of any claim by the primary examiner to the ~~Board of Patent Appeals and Interferences~~ Patent Trial and Appeal Board, having once paid the fee for such appeal.

~~(c) Third-party. A third-party requester in an inter partes proceeding may appeal to the Board of Patent Appeals and Interferences Patent Trial and Appeal Board from the final decision of the primary examiner favorable to the patentability of any original or proposed amended or new claim of a patent, having once paid the fee for such appeal.~~

HISTORY:

(July 19, 1952, ch 950, § 1, 66 Stat. 801; Nov. 8, 1984, P.L. 98-622, Title II, § 204(b)(1), 98 Stat. 3388; Nov. 29, 1999, P.L. 106-113, Div B, § 1000(a)(9), 113 Stat. 1536; Nov. 2, 2002, P.L. 107-273, Div C, Title III, Subtitle A, § 13106(b), Subtitle B, § 13202(b)(1), 116 Stat. 1901.)

(America Invents Act §§ 3(j)(1), (3); 7(b)(1), (2).)

~~§ 135. Interferences~~

~~(a) Whenever an application is made for a patent which, in the opinion of the Director, would interfere with any pending application, or with any unexpired patent, an interference may be declared and the Director shall give notice of such declaration to the applicants, or applicant and patentee, as the case may be. The Board of Patent Appeals and Interferences shall determine questions of priority of the inventions and may determine questions of patentability. Any final decision, if adverse to the claim of an applicant, shall constitute the final refusal by the Patent and Trademark Office of the claims involved, and the Director may issue a patent to the applicant who is adjudged the prior inventor. A final judgment adverse to a patentee from which no appeal or other review has been or can be taken or had shall constitute cancellation of the claims involved in the patent, and notice of such cancellation shall be endorsed on copies of the patent distributed after such cancellation by the Patent and Trademark Office.~~

~~(b)(1) A claim which is the same as, or for the same or substantially the same subject mat-~~

~~ter as, a claim of an issued patent may not be made in any application unless such a claim is made prior to one year from the date on which the patent was granted.~~

~~(2) A claim which is the same as, or for the same or substantially the same subject matter as, a claim of an application published under section 122(b) of this title [35 USC § 122(b)] may be made in an application filed after the application is published only if the claim is made before 1 year after the date on which the application is published.~~

~~(c) Any agreement or understanding between parties to an interference, including any collateral agreements referred to therein, made in connection with or in contemplation of the termination of the interference, shall be in writing and a true copy thereof filed in the Patent and Trademark Office before the termination of the interference as between the said parties to the agreement or understanding. If any party filing the same so requests, the copy shall be kept separate from the file of the interference, and made available only to Government agencies on written request, or to any person on a showing of good cause. Failure to file the copy of such agreement or understanding shall render permanently unenforceable such agreement or understanding and any patent of such parties involved in the interference or any patent subsequently issued on any application of such parties so involved. The Director may, however, on a showing of good cause for failure to file within the time prescribed, permit the filing of the agreement or understanding during the six-month period subsequent to the termination of the interference as between the parties to the agreement or understanding.~~

~~The Director shall give notice to the parties or their attorneys of record, a reasonable time prior to said termination, of the filing requirement of this section. If the Director gives such notice at a later time, irrespective of the right to file such agreement or understanding within the six-month period on a showing of good cause, the parties may file such agreement or understanding within sixty days of the receipt of such notice.~~

~~Any discretionary action of the Director under this subsection shall be reviewable under section 10 of the Administrative Procedure Act.~~

~~(d) Parties to a patent interference, within such time as may be specified by the Director by regulation, may determine such contest or any aspect thereof by arbitration. Such arbitration shall be governed by the provisions of title 9 [9 USC §§ 1 et seq.] to the extent such title is not inconsistent with this section. The parties shall give notice of any arbitration award to the Director, and such award shall, as between the parties to the arbitration, be dispositive of the issues to which it relates. The arbitration award shall be unenforceable until such notice is given. Nothing in this subsection shall preclude the Director from determining patentability of the invention involved in the interference.~~

§ 135. Derivation proceedings

(a) **Institution of Proceeding.**—An applicant for patent may file a petition to institute a derivation proceeding in the Office. The petition shall set forth with particularity the basis for finding that an inventor named in an earlier application derived the claimed invention from an inventor named in the petitioner's application and, without authorization, the earlier application claiming such invention was filed. Any such petition may be filed only within the 1-year period beginning on the date of the first publication of a claim to an invention that is the same or substantially the same as the earlier application's claim to the invention, shall be made under oath, and shall be supported by substantial evidence. Whenever the Director determines that a petition filed under this subsection demonstrates that the standards for instituting a derivation proceeding are met, the Director may institute a derivation proceeding. The determination by the Director whether to institute a derivation proceeding shall be final and nonappealable.

(b) **Determination by Patent Trial and Appeal Board.**—In a derivation proceeding instituted under subsection (a), the Patent Trial and Appeal Board shall determine whether an inventor named in the earlier application derived the claimed invention from an inventor named in the petitioner's application and, without authorization, the earlier application claiming such invention was filed. In appropriate circumstances, the Patent Trial and Appeal Board may correct the naming of the inventor in any application or patent at issue. The Director shall prescribe regulations setting forth standards for the conduct of derivation proceedings, including requiring parties to provide sufficient evidence to prove and rebut a claim of derivation.

(c) **Deferral of Decision.**—The Patent Trial and Appeal Board may defer action on a petition for a derivation proceeding until the expiration of the 3-month period beginning on the date on which the Director issues a patent that includes the claimed invention that is the subject of the petition. The Patent Trial and Appeal Board also may defer action on a petition for a derivation proceeding, or stay the proceeding after it has been instituted, until the termination of a proceeding under chapter 30, 31, or 32 involving the patent of the earlier applicant.

(d) **Effect of Final Decision.**—The final decision of the Patent Trial and Appeal Board, if adverse to claims in an application for patent, shall constitute the final refusal by the Office on those claims. The final decision of the Patent Trial and Appeal Board, if adverse to claims in a patent, shall, if no appeal or other review of the decision has been or can be taken or had, constitute cancellation of those claims, and notice of such cancellation shall be endorsed on copies of the patent distributed after such cancellation.

(e) **Settlement.**—Parties to a proceeding instituted under subsection (a) may terminate the proceeding by filing a written statement reflecting the agreement of the parties as to the correct inventors of the claimed invention in dispute. Unless the Patent Trial and Appeal Board finds the agreement to be inconsistent with the evidence of record, if any, it shall take action consistent with the agreement. Any written settlement or understanding of the parties shall be filed with the Director. At the request of a party to the proceeding, the agreement or understanding shall be treated as business confidential information, shall be kept separate from the file of the involved patents or applications, and shall be made available only to Government agencies on written request, or to any person on a showing of good cause.

(f) **Arbitration.**—Parties to a proceeding instituted under subsection (a) may, within such time as may be specified by the Director by regulation, determine such contest or any aspect thereof by arbitration. Such arbitration shall be governed by the provisions of title 9, to the extent such title is not inconsistent with this section. The parties shall give notice of any arbitration award to the Director, and such award shall, as between the parties to the arbitration, be dispositive of the issues to which it relates. The arbitration award shall be unenforceable until such notice is given. Nothing in this subsection shall preclude the Director from determining the patentability of the claimed inventions involved in the proceeding.

HISTORY:

(July 19, 1952, ch 950, § 1, 66 Stat. 801; Oct. 15, 1962, P.L. 87-831, 76 Stat. 958; Jan. 2, 1975, P.L. 93-596, § 1, 88 Stat. 1949; Nov. 8, 1984, P.L. 98-622, Title I, § 105, Title II, § 202, 98 Stat. 3385, 3386; Nov. 29, 1999, P.L. 106-113, Div B, § 1000(a)(9), 113 Stat. 1536; Nov. 2, 2002, P.L. 107-273, Div C, Title III, Subtitle B, § 13206(b)(1)(B), 116 Stat. 1906.)

(America Invents Act § 3(i).)

CHAPTER 13. REVIEW OF PATENT AND TRADEMARK OFFICE

§ 141. Appeal to Court of Appeals for the Federal Circuit

An applicant dissatisfied with the decision in an appeal to the Board of Patent Appeals

~~and Interferences under section 134 of this title [35 USC § 134] may appeal the decision to the United States Court of Appeals for the Federal Circuit. By filing such an appeal the applicant waives his or her right to proceed under section 145 of this title [35 USC § 145]. A patent owner, or a third-party requester in an inter partes reexamination proceeding, who is in any reexamination proceeding dissatisfied with the final decision in an appeal to the Board of Patent Appeals and Interferences under section 134 [35 USC § 134] may appeal the decision only to the United States Court of Appeals for the Federal Circuit. A party to an interference dissatisfied with the decision of the Board of Patent Appeals and Interferences on the interference may appeal the decision to the United States Court of Appeals for the Federal Circuit, but such appeal shall be dismissed if any adverse party to such interference, within twenty days after the appellant has filed notice of appeal in accordance with section 142 of this title [35 USC § 142], files notice with the Director that the party elects to have all further proceedings conducted as provided in section 146 of this title [35 USC § 146]. If the appellant does not, within thirty days after the filing of such notice by the adverse party, file a civil action under section 146 [35 USC § 146], the decision appealed from shall govern the further proceedings in the case.~~

§ 141. Appeal to Court of Appeals for the Federal Circuit

   (a) **Examinations.**—An applicant who is dissatisfied with the final decision in an appeal to the Patent Trial and Appeal Board under section 134(a) may appeal the Board's decision to the United States Court of Appeals for the Federal Circuit. By filing such an appeal, the applicant waives his or her right to proceed under section 145.

   (b) **Reexaminations.**—A patent owner who is dissatisfied with the final decision in an appeal of a reexamination to the Patent Trial and Appeal Board under section 134(b) may appeal the Board's decision only to the United States Court of Appeals for the Federal Circuit.

   (c) **Post-Grant and Inter Partes Reviews.**—A party to an inter partes review or a post-grant review who is dissatisfied with the final written decision of the Patent Trial and Appeal Board under section 318(a) or 328(a) (as the case may be) may appeal the Board's decision only to the United States Court of Appeals for the Federal Circuit.

   (d) **Derivation Proceedings.**—A party to a derivation proceeding who is dissatisfied with the final decision of the Patent Trial and Appeal Board in the proceeding may appeal the decision to the United States Court of Appeals for the Federal Circuit, but such appeal shall be dismissed if any adverse party to such derivation proceeding, within 20 days after the appellant has filed notice of appeal in accordance with section 142, files notice with the Director that the party elects to have all further proceedings conducted as provided in section 146. If the appellant does not, within 30 days after the filing of such notice by the adverse party, file a civil action under section 146, the Board's decision shall govern the further proceedings in the case.

HISTORY:

   (July 19, 1952, ch 950, § 1, 66 Stat. 802; April 2, 1982, P.L. 97-164, Title I, Part B, § 163(a)(7), (b)(2), 96 Stat. 49, 50; Nov. 8, 1984, P.L. 98-622, Title II, § 203(a), 98 Stat. 3387; Nov. 29, 1999, P.L. 106-113, Div B, § 1000(a)(9), 113 Stat. 1536; Nov. 2, 2002, P.L. 107-273, Div C, Title III, Subtitle A, § 13106(c), Subtitle B, § 13206(b)(1)(B), 116 Stat. 1901, 1906.)

   (America Invents Act § 7(c)(1).)

§ 142. Notice of appeal

   When an appeal is taken to the United States Court of Appeals for the Federal Circuit, the appellant shall file in the Patent and Trademark Office a written notice of appeal directed to the Director, within such time after the date of the decision from which the appeal is taken as the Director prescribes, but in no case less than 60 days after that date.

35 USC § 142

HISTORY:

(July 19, 1952, ch 950, § 1, 66 Stat. 802; Jan. 2, 1975, P.L. 93-596, § 1, 88 Stat. 1949; April 2, 1982, P.L. 97-164, Title I, Part B, § 163(a)(7), 96 Stat. 49; Nov. 8, 1984, P.L. 98-620, Title IV, Subtitle C, § 414(a), 98 Stat. 3363; Nov. 29, 1999, P.L. 106-113, Div B, § 1000(a)(9), 113 Stat. 1536; Nov. 2, 2002, P.L. 107-273, Div C, Title III, Subtitle B, § 13206(b)(1)(B), 116 Stat. 1906.)

§ 143. Proceedings on appeal

With respect to an appeal described in section 142 ~~of this title~~ [35 USC § 142], the Director shall transmit to the United States Court of Appeals for the Federal Circuit a certified list of the documents comprising the record in the Patent and Trademark Office. The court may request that the Director forward the original or certified copies of such documents during pendency of the appeal. ~~In an ex parte case or any reexamination case, the Director shall submit to the court in writing the grounds for the decision of the Patent and Trademark Office, addressing all the issues involved in the appeal.~~ In an ex parte case, the Director shall submit to the court in writing the grounds for the decision of the Patent and Trademark Office, addressing all of the issues raised in the appeal. The Director shall have the right to intervene in an appeal from a decision entered by the Patent Trial and Appeal Board in a derivation proceeding under section 135 or in an inter partes or post-grant review under chapter 31 or 32. ~~The court shall, before hearing an appeal, give notice of the time and place of the hearing to the Director and the parties in the appeal.~~

HISTORY:

(July 19, 1952, ch 950, § 1, 66 Stat. 802; Jan. 2, 1975, P.L. 93-596, § 1, 88 Stat. 1949; April 2, 1982, P.L. 97-164, Title I, Part B, § 163(a)(7), 96 Stat. 49; Nov. 8, 1984, P.L. 98-620, Title IV, Subtitle C, § 414(a), 98 Stat. 3363; Nov. 29, 1999, P.L. 106-113, Div B, § 1000(a)(9), 113 Stat. 1536; Nov. 2, 2002, P.L. 107-273, Div C, Title V, Subtitle B, §§ 13202(b)(2), 13206(b)(1)(B), 116 Stat. 1901, 1906.)

(America Invents Act §§ 7(c)(3)(A), (B); 20(j)(1).)

§ 144. Decision on appeal

The United States Court of Appeals for the Federal Circuit shall review the decision from which an appeal is taken on the record before the Patent and Trademark Office. Upon its determination the court shall issue to the Director its mandate and opinion, which shall be entered of record in the Patent and Trademark Office and shall govern the further proceedings in the case.

HISTORY:

(July 19, 1952, ch 950, § 1, 66 Stat. 802; Jan. 2, 1975, P.L. 93-596, § 1, 88 Stat. 1949; April 2, 1982, P.L. 97-164, Title I, Part B, § 163(a)(7) in part, 96 Stat. 49; Nov. 8, 1984, P.L. 98-620, Title IV, Subtitle C, § 414(a), 98 Stat. 3363; Nov. 29, 1999, P.L. 106-113, Div B, § 1000(a)(9), 113 Stat. 1536; Nov. 2, 2002, P.L. 107-273, Div C, Title III, Subtitle B, § 13206(b)(1)(B), 116 Stat. 1906.)

§ 145. Civil action to obtain patent

An applicant dissatisfied with the decision of the ~~Board of Patent Appeals and Interferences~~ Patent Trial and Appeal Board in an appeal under section 134(a) ~~of this title~~ [35 USC § 134(a)] may, unless appeal has been taken to the United States Court of Appeals for the Federal Circuit, have remedy by civil action against the Director in the ~~United States District Court for the District of Columbia~~ United States District Court for the Eastern District of Virginia if commenced within such time after such decision, not less than sixty days, as the Director appoints. The court may adjudge that such applicant is entitled to receive a patent for his invention, as specified in any of his claims involved in the decision of the ~~Board of Patent Appeals and Interferences~~ Patent Trial and Appeal Board, as the facts in the case may appear and such adjudication shall authorize the Director to issue such patent on compliance with the requirements of law. All the expenses of the proceedings shall be paid by the applicant.

HISTORY:

(July 19, 1952, ch 950, § 1, 66 Stat. 803; April 2, 1982, P.L. 97-164, Title I, Part B, § 163(a)(7) in part, 96 Stat. 49; Nov. 8, 1984, P.L. 98-622, Title II § 203(b), 98 Stat. 3387; Nov. 29, 1999, P.L. 106-113, Div B, § 1000(a)(9), 113 Stat. 1536; Nov. 2, 2002, P.L. 107-273, Div C, Title III, Subtitle B, § 13206(b)(1)(B), 116 Stat. 1906.)

(America Invents Act §§ 3(j)(1); 9(a); 20(j)(1).)

§ 146. ~~Civil action in case of interference~~

§ 146. Civil action in case of derivation proceeding

Any party to ~~an interference~~ a derivation proceeding dissatisfied with the decision of the ~~Board of Patent Appeals and Interferences~~ Patent Trial and Appeal Board on ~~the interference~~ the derivation proceeding, may have remedy by civil action, if commenced within such time after such decision, not less than sixty days, as the Director appoints or as provided in section 141 ~~of this title~~ [35 USC § 141], unless he has appealed to the United States Court of Appeals for the Federal Circuit, and such appeal is pending or has been decided. In such suits the record in the Patent and Trademark Office shall be admitted on motion of either party upon the terms and conditions as to costs, expenses, and the further cross-examination of the witnesses as the court imposes, without prejudice to the right of the parties to take further testimony. The testimony and exhibits of the record in the Patent and Trademark Office when admitted shall have the same effect as if originally taken and produced in the suit.

Such suit may be instituted against the party in interest as shown by the records of the Patent and Trademark Office at the time of the decision complained of, but any party in interest may become a party to the action. If there be adverse parties residing in a plurality of districts not embraced within the same state, or an adverse party residing in a foreign country, the ~~United States District Court for the District of Columbia~~ United States District Court for the Eastern District of Virginia shall have jurisdiction and may issue summons against the adverse parties directed to the marshal of any district in which any adverse party resides. Summons against adverse parties residing in foreign countries may be served by publication or otherwise as the court directs. The Director shall not be a necessary party but he shall be notified of the filing of the suit by the clerk of the court in which it is filed and shall have the right to intervene. Judgment of the court in favor of the right of an applicant to a patent shall authorize the Director to issue such patent on the filing in the Patent and Trademark Office of a certified copy of the judgment and on compliance with the requirements of law.

HISTORY:

(July 19, 1952, ch 950, § 1, 66 Stat. 803; Jan. 2, 1975, P.L. 93-596, § 1, 88 Stat. 1949; April 2, 1982, P.L. 97-164, Title I, Part B, § 163(a)(7) in part, 96 Stat. 49; Nov. 8, 1984, P.L. 98-622, Title II, § 203(c), 98 Stat. 3387; Nov. 29, 1999, P.L. 106-113, Div B, § 1000(a)(9), 113 Stat. 1536; Nov. 2, 2002, P.L. 107-273, Div C, Title III, Subtitle B, § 13206(b)(1)(B), 116 Stat. 1906.)

(America Invents Act §§ 3(j)(1), (2(A)(i) and (ii), (4), 9(a); 20(j)(1))

CHAPTER 14. ISSUE OF PATENT

§ 151. Issue of patent

If it appears that applicant is entitled to a patent under the law, a written notice of allowance of the application shall be given or mailed to the applicant. The notice shall specify a sum, constituting the issue fee or a portion thereof, which shall be paid within three months thereafter.

35 USC § 151

Upon payment of this sum the patent shall issue, but if payment is not timely made, the application shall be regarded as abandoned.

Any remaining balance of the issue fee shall be paid within three months from the sending of a notice thereof and, if not paid, the patent shall lapse at the termination of this three-month period. In calculating the amount of a remaining balance, charges for a page or less may be disregarded.

If any payment required by this section is not timely made, but is submitted with the fee for delayed payment and the delay in payment is shown to have been unavoidable, it may be accepted by the Director as though no abandonment or lapse had ever occurred.

HISTORY:

(July 19, 1952, ch 950, § 1, 66 Stat. 803; July 24, 1965, P.L. 89-83, § 4, 79 Stat. 260; Jan. 2, 1975, P.L. 93-601, § 3, 88 Stat. 1956; Nov. 29, 1999, P.L. 106-113, Div B, § 1000(a)(9), 113 Stat. 1536; Nov. 2, 2002, P.L. 107-273, Div C, Title III, Subtitle B, § 13206(b)(1)(B), 116 Stat. 1906.)

§ 152. Issue of patent to assignee

Patents may be granted to the assignee of the inventor of record in the Patent and Trademark Office, upon the application made and the specification sworn to by the inventor, except as otherwise provided in this title [35 USC §§ 1 et seq.].

HISTORY:

(July 19, 1952, ch 950, § 1, 66 Stat. 804; Jan. 2, 1975, P.L. 93-596, § 1, 88 Stat. 1949.)

§ 153. How issued

Patents shall be issued in the name of the United States of America, under the seal of the Patent and Trademark Office, and shall be signed by the Director or have his signature placed thereon and shall be recorded in the Patent and Trademark Office.

HISTORY:

(July 19, 1952, ch 950, § 1, 66 Stat. 804; Jan. 2, 1975, P.L. 93-596, § 1, 88 Stat. 1949; Nov. 29, 1999, P.L. 106-113, Div B, § 1000(a)(9), 113 Stat. 1536; Nov. 2, 2002, P.L. 107-273, Div C, Title III, Subtitle B, §§ 13203(c), 13206(b)(1)(B), 116 Stat. 1902, 1906.)

§ 154. Contents and term of patent; provisional rights

(a) In general.

(1) Contents. Every patent shall contain a short title of the invention and a grant to the patentee, his heirs or assigns, of the right to exclude others from making, using, offering for sale, or selling the invention throughout the United States or importing the invention into the United States, and, if the invention is a process, of the right to exclude others from using, offering for sale or selling throughout the United States, or importing into the United States, products made by that process, referring to the specification for the particulars thereof.

(2) Term. Subject to the payment of fees under this title, such grant shall be for a term beginning on the date on which the patent issues and ending 20 years from the date on which the application for the patent was filed in the United States or, if the application contains a specific reference to an earlier filed application or applications under section 120, 121, or 365(c) of this title, from the date on which the earliest such application was filed.

(3) Priority. Priority under section 119, 365(a), or 365(b) of this title shall not be taken into account in determining the term of a patent.

(4) Specification and drawing. A copy of the specification and drawing shall be annexed to the patent and be a part of such patent.

(b) Adjustment of patent term

(1) Patent term guarantees.

(A) Guarantee of prompt patent and trademark office responses. Subject to the limitations under paragraph (2), if the issue of an original patent is delayed due to the failure of the Patent and Trademark Office to—

(i) provide at least one of the notifications under section 132 ~~of this title~~ or a notice of allowance under section 151 ~~of this title~~ not later than 14 months after—

(I) the date on which an application was filed under section 111(a) ~~of this title~~; or

(II) the date on which an international application fulfilled the requirements of section 371 ~~of this title~~;

(ii) respond to a reply under section 132, or to an appeal taken under section 134, within 4 months after the date on which the reply was filed or the appeal was taken;

(iii) act on an application within 4 months after the date of a decision by the ~~Board of Patent Appeals and Interferences~~ Patent Trial and Appeal Board under section 134 or 135 or a decision by a Federal court under section 141, 145, or 146 in a case in which allowable claims remain in the application; or

(iv) issue a patent within 4 months after the date on which the issue fee was paid under section 151 and all outstanding requirements were satisfied,

the term of the patent shall be extended 1 day for each day after the end of the period specified in clause (i), (ii), (iii), or (iv), as the case may be, until the action described in such clause is taken.

(B) Guarantee of no more than 3-year application pendency. Subject to the limitations under paragraph (2), if the issue of an original patent is delayed due to the failure of the United States Patent and Trademark Office to issue a patent within 3 years after the actual filing date of the application in the United States, not including—

(i) any time consumed by continued examination of the application requested by the applicant under section 132(b);

(ii) any time consumed by a proceeding under section 135(a), any time consumed by the imposition of an order under section 181, or any time consumed by appellate review by the ~~Board of Patent Appeals and Interferences~~ Patent Trial and Appeal Board or by a Federal court; or

(iii) any delay in the processing of the application by the United States Patent and Trademark Office requested by the applicant except as permitted by paragraph (3)(C),

the term of the patent shall be extended 1 day for each day after the end of that 3-year period until the patent is issued.

~~(C) Guarantee or adjustments for delays due to interferences, secrecy orders, and appeals.~~ **(C) Guarantee of adjustments for delays due to derivation proceedings, secrecy orders, and appeals.**—Subject to the limitations under paragraph (2), if the issue of an original patent is delayed due to—

(i) a proceeding under section 135(a);

(ii) the imposition of an order under section 181; or

(iii) appellate review by the ~~Board of Patent Appeals and Interferences~~ Patent Trial and Appeal Board or by a Federal court in a case in which the patent was issued under a decision in the review reversing an adverse determination of patentability,

the term of the patent shall be extended 1 day for each day of the pendency of the proceeding, order, or review, as the case may be.

(2) Limitations.

(A) In general. To the extent that periods of delay attributable to grounds specified in paragraph (1) overlap, the period of any adjustment granted under this subsection shall not exceed the actual number of days the issuance of the patent was delayed.

(B) Disclaimed term. No patent the term of which has been disclaimed beyond a specified date may be adjusted under this section beyond the expiration date specified in the disclaimer.

(C) Reduction of period of adjustment.

(i) The period of adjustment of the term of a patent under paragraph (1) shall be reduced by a period equal to the period of time during which the applicant failed to engage in reasonable efforts to conclude prosecution of the application.

(ii) With respect to adjustments to patent term made under the authority of paragraph (1)(B), an applicant shall be deemed to have failed to engage in reasonable efforts to conclude processing or examination of an application for the cumulative total of any periods of time in excess of 3 months that are taken to respond to a notice from the Office making any rejection, objection, argument, or other request, measuring such 3-month period from the date the notice was given or mailed to the applicant.

(iii) The Director shall prescribe regulations establishing the circumstances that constitute a failure of an applicant to engage in reasonable efforts to conclude processing or examination of an application.

(3) Procedures for patent term adjustment determination.

(A) The Director shall prescribe regulations establishing procedures for the application for and determination of patent term adjustments under this subsection.

(B) Under the procedures established under subparagraph (A), the Director shall—

(i) make a determination of the period of any patent term adjustment under this subsection, and shall transmit a notice of that determination with the written notice of allowance of the application under section 151; and

(ii) provide the applicant one opportunity to request reconsideration of any patent term adjustment determination made by the Director.

(C) The Director shall reinstate all or part of the cumulative period of time of an adjustment under paragraph (2)(C) if the applicant, prior to the issuance of the patent, makes a showing that, in spite of all due care, the applicant was unable to respond within the 3-month period, but in no case shall more than three additional months for each such response beyond the original 3-month period be reinstated.

(D) The Director shall proceed to grant the patent after completion of the Director's determination of a patent term adjustment under the procedures established under this subsection, notwithstanding any appeal taken by the applicant of such determination.

(4) Appeal of patent term adjustment determination.

(A) An applicant dissatisfied with a determination made by the Director under paragraph (3) shall have remedy by a civil action against the Director filed in the ~~United States District Court for the District of Columbia~~ United States District Court for the Eastern District of Virginia within 180 days after the grant of the patent. Chapter 7 of title 5 [5 USC §§ 701 et seq.], shall apply to such action. Any final judgment resulting in a change to the period of adjustment of the patent term shall be served on the Director, and the Director shall thereafter alter the term of the patent to reflect such change.

(B) The determination of a patent term adjustment under this subsection shall not be subject to appeal or challenge by a third party prior to the grant of the patent.

(c) Continuation.

(1) Determination. The term of a patent that is in force on or that results from an application filed before the date that is 6 months after the date of the enactment of the Uruguay Round Agreements Act shall be the greater of the 20-year term as provided in subsection (a), or 17 years from grant, subject to any terminal disclaimers.

(2) Remedies. The remedies of sections 283, 284, and 285 ~~of this title~~ shall not apply to acts which—

(A) were commenced or for which substantial investment was made before the date that is 6 months after the date of the enactment of the Uruguay Round Agreements Act; and

(B) became infringing by reason of paragraph (1).

(3) Remuneration. The acts referred to in paragraph (2) may be continued only upon the payment of an equitable remuneration to the patentee that is determined in an action brought under chapter 28 and chapter 29 (other than those provisions excluded by paragraph (2)) ~~of this title~~.

(d) Provisional rights.

(1) In general. In addition to other rights provided by this section, a patent shall include the right to obtain a reasonable royalty from any person who, during the period beginning on the date of publication of the application for such patent under section 122(b), or in the case of an international application filed under the treaty defined in section 351(a) designating the United States under Article 21(2)(a) of such treaty, the date of publication of the application, and ending on the date the patent is issued—

(A)(i) makes, uses, offers for sale, or sells in the United States the invention as claimed in the published patent application or imports such an invention into the United States; or

(ii) if the invention as claimed in the published patent application is a process, uses, offers for sale, or sells in the United States or imports into the United States products made by that process as claimed in the published patent application; and

(B) had actual notice of the published patent application and, in a case in which the right arising under this paragraph is based upon an international application designating the United States that is published in a language other than English, had a translation of the international application into the English language.

(2) Right based on substantially identical inventions. The right under paragraph (1) to obtain a reasonable royalty shall not be available under this subsection unless the invention as claimed in the patent is substantially identical to the invention as claimed in the published patent application.

(3) Time limitation on obtaining a reasonable royalty. The right under paragraph (1) to obtain a reasonable royalty shall be available only in an action brought not later than 6 years after the patent is issued. The right under paragraph (1) to obtain a reasonable royalty shall not be affected by the duration of the period described in paragraph (1).

(4) Requirements for international applications.

(A) Effective date. The right under paragraph (1) to obtain a reasonable royalty based upon the publication under the treaty defined in section 351(a) of an international application designating the United States shall commence on the date of publication under the treaty of the international application, or, if the publication under the treaty of the international application is in a language other than English, on the date on which the Patent and Trademark Office receives a translation of the publication in the English language.

(B) Copies. The Director may require the applicant to provide a copy of the international application and a translation thereof.

35 USC § 154

HISTORY:

(July 19, 1952, ch 950, § 1, 66 Stat. 804; July 24, 1965, P.L. 89-83, § 5, 79 Stat. 261; Dec. 12, 1980, P.L. 96-517, § 4, 94 Stat. 3018; Aug. 23, 1988, P.L. 100-418, Title IX, Subtitle A, § 9002, 102 Stat. 1563; Dec. 8, 1994, P.L. 103-465, Title V, Subtitle C, § 532(a)(1), 108 Stat. 4983; Oct. 11, 1996, P.L. 104-295, § 20(e)(1), 110 Stat. 3529; Nov. 29, 1999, P.L. 106-113, Div B, § 1000(a)(9), 113 Stat. 1536; Nov. 2, 2002, P.L. 107-273, Div C, Title III, Subtitle B, §§ 13204, 13206(a)(8), 116 Stat. 1902, 1904.)

(America Invents Act §§ 3(j)(1), 2(B); 9(a); 20(j)(1).)

§ 155. Patent term extension

Notwithstanding the provisions of section 154, the term of a patent which encompasses within its scope a composition of matter or a process for using such composition shall be extended if such composition or process has been subjected to a regulatory review by the Federal Food and Drug Administration pursuant to the Federal Food, Drug, and Cosmetic Act [21 USC §§ 301 et seq.] leading to the publication of regulation permitting the interstate distribution and sale of such composition or process and for which there has thereafter been a stay of regulation of approval imposed pursuant to section 409 of the Federal Food, Drug, and Cosmetic Act [21 USC § 348] which stay was in effect on January 1, 1981, by a length of time to be measured from the date such stay of regulation of approval was imposed until such proceedings are finally resolved and commercial marketing permitted. The patentee, his heirs, successors or assigns shall notify the Director within ninety days of the date of enactment of this section [enacted Jan. 3, 1983] or the date the stay of regulation of approval has been removed, whichever is later, of the number of the patent to be extended and the date the stay was imposed and the date commercial marketing was permitted. On receipt of such notice, the Director shall promptly issue to the owner of record of the patent a certificate of extension, under seal, stating the fact and length of the extension and identifying the composition of matter or process for using such composition to which such extension is applicable. Such certificate shall be recorded in the official file of each patent extended and such certificate shall be considered as part of the original patent, and an appropriate notice shall be published in the Official Gazette of the Patent and Trademark Office.

HISTORY:

(Added Jan. 4, 1983, P.L. 97-414, § 11(a), 96 Stat. 2065; Nov. 29, 1999, P.L. 106-113, Div B, § 1000(a) (9), 113 Stat. 1536; Nov. 2, 2002, P.L. 107-273, Div C, Title III, Subtitle B, § 13206(b)(1)(B), 116 Stat. 1906.)

(America Invents Act § 20(k).)

§ 155A. Patent term restoration

(a) Notwithstanding section 154 of this title, the term of each of the following patents shall be extended in accordance with this section:

(1) Any patent which encompasses within its scope a composition of matter which is a new drug product, if during the regulatory review of the product by the Federal Food and Drug Administration—

(A) the Federal Food and Drug Administration notified the patentee, by letter dated February 20, 1976, that such product's new drug application was not approvable under section 505(b)(1) of the Federal Food, Drug and Cosmetic Act [21 USC § 355(b)(1)];

(B) in 1977 the patentee submitted to the Federal Food and Drug Administration the results of a health effects test to evaluate the carcinogenic potential of such product;

(C) the Federal Food and Drug Administration approved, by letter dated December 18, 1979, the new drug application for such product; and

(D) the Federal Food and Drug Administration approved, by letter dated May 26, 1981, a supplementary application covering the facility for the production of such product.

(2) Any patent which encompasses within its scope a process for using the composition of matter described in paragraph (1).

(b) The term of any patent described in subsection (a) shall be extended for a period equal to the period beginning February 20, 1976, and ending May 26, 1981, and such patent shall have the effect as if originally issued with such extended term.

(c) The patentee of any patent described in subsection (a) of this section shall, within ninety days after the date of enactment of this section [enacted Oct. 13, 1983], notify the Director of the number of any patent so extended. On receipt of such notice, the Director shall conform such extension by placing a notice thereof in the official file of such patent and publishing an appropriate notice of such extension in the Official Gazette of the Patent and Trademark Office.

HISTORY:

(Added Oct. 13, 1983, P.L. 98-127, § 4(a), 97 Stat. 832; Nov. 29, 1999, P.L. 106-113, Div B, § 1000(a)(9), 113 Stat. 1536; Nov. 2, 2002, P.L. 107-273, Div C, Title III, Subtitle B, § 13206(b)(1)(B), 116 Stat. 1906.)

(America Invents Act § 20(k).)

§ 156. Extension of patent term

(a) The term of a patent which claims a product, a method of using a product, or a method of manufacturing a product shall be extended in accordance with this section from the original expiration date of the patent, which shall include any patent term adjustment granted under section 154(b), if—

(1) the term of the patent has not expired before an application is submitted under subsection (d)(1) for its extension;

(2) the term of the patent has never been extended under subsection (e)(1) of this section;

(3) an application for extension is submitted by the owner of record of the patent or its agent and in accordance with the requirements of paragraphs (1) through (4) of subsection (d);

(4) the product has been subject to a regulatory review period before its commercial marketing or use;

(5)(A) except as provided in subparagraph (B) or (C), the permission for the commercial marketing or use of the product after such regulatory review period is the first permitted commercial marketing or use of the product under the provision of law under which such regulatory review period occurred;

(B) in the case of a patent which claims a method of manufacturing the product which primarily uses recombinant DNA technology in the manufacture of the product, the permission for the commercial marketing or use of the product after such regulatory review period is the first permitted commercial marketing or use of a product manufactured under the process claimed in the patent; or

(C) for purposes of subparagraph (A), in the case of a patent which—

(i) claims a new animal drug or a veterinary biological product which (I) is not covered by the claims in any other patent which has been extended, and (II) has received permission for the commercial marketing or use in non-food-producing animals and in food-producing animals, and

(ii) was not extended on the basis of the regulatory review period for use in non-food-producing animals,

the permission for the commercial marketing or use of the drug or product after the regulatory review period for use in food-producing animals is the first permitted commercial marketing or use of the drug or product for administration to a food-producing animal.

The product referred to in paragraphs (4) and (5) is hereinafter in this section referred to as the "approved product".

(b) Except as provided in subsection (d)(5)(F), the rights derived from any patent the term of which is extended under this section shall during the period during which the term of the patent is extended—

    (1) in the case of a patent which claims a product, be limited to any use approved for the product—

        (A) before the expiration of the term of the patent—

            (i) under the provision of law under which the applicable regulatory review occurred, or

            (ii) under the provision of law under which any regulatory review described in paragraph (1), (4), or (5) of subsection (g) occurred, and

        (B) on or after the expiration of the regulatory review period upon which the extension of the patent was based;

    (2) in the case of a patent which claims a method of using a product, be limited to any use claimed by the patent and approved for the product—

        (A) before the expiration of the term of the patent—

            (i) under any provision of law under which an applicable regulatory review occurred, and

            (ii) under the provision of law under which any regulatory review described in paragraph (1), (4), or (5) of subsection (g) occurred, and

        (B) on or after the expiration of the regulatory review period upon which the extension of the patent was based; and

    (3) in the case of a patent which claims a method of manufacturing a product, be limited to the method of manufacturing as used to make—

        (A) the approved product, or

        (B) the product if it has been subject to a regulatory review period described in paragraph (1), (4), or (5) of subsection (g).

As used in this subsection, the term "product" includes an approved product.

(c) The term of a patent eligible for extension under subsection (a) shall be extended by the time equal to the regulatory review period for the approved product which period occurs after the date the patent is issued, except that—

    (1) each period of the regulatory review period shall be reduced by any period determined under subsection (d)(2)(B) during which the applicant for the patent extension did not act with due diligence during such period of the regulatory review period;

    (2) after any reduction required by paragraph (1), the period of extension shall include only one-half of the time remaining in the periods described in paragraphs (1)(B)(i), (2)(B)(i), (3)(B)(i), (4)(B)(i), and (5)(B)(i) of subsection (g);

    (3) if the period remaining in the term of a patent after the date of the approval of the approved product under the provision of law under which such regulatory review occurred when added to the regulatory review period as revised under paragraphs (1) and (2) exceeds fourteen years, the period of extension shall be reduced so that the total of both such periods does not exceed fourteen years; and

    (4) in no event shall more than one patent be extended under subsection (e)(1) for the same regulatory review period for any product.

(d)(1) To obtain an extension of the term of a patent under this section, the owner of record of the patent or its agent shall submit an application to the Director. Except as provided in paragraph (5), such an application may only be submitted within the sixty-day period beginning on the date the product received permission under the provision of law under which the applicable regulatory review period occurred for commercial marketing or use. The application shall contain—

(A) the identity of the approved product and the Federal statute under which regulatory review occurred;

(B) the identity of the patent for which an extension is being sought and the identity of each claim of such patent which claims the approved product or a method of using or manufacturing the approved product;

(C) information to enable the Director to determine under subsections (a) and (b) the eligibility of a patent for extension and the rights that will be derived from the extension and information to enable the Director and the Secretary of Health and Human Services or the Secretary of Agriculture to determine the period of the extension under subsection (g);

(D) a brief description of the activities undertaken by the applicant during the applicable regulatory review period with respect to the approved product and the significant dates applicable to such activities; and

(E) such patent or other information as the Director may require.

For purposes of determining the date on which a product receives permission under the second sentence of this paragraph, if such permission is transmitted after 4:30 P.M., Eastern Time, on a business day, or is transmitted on a day that is not a business day, the product shall be deemed to receive such permission on the next business day. For purposes of the preceding sentence, the term "business day" means any Monday, Tuesday, Wednesday, Thursday, or Friday, excluding any legal holiday under section 6103 of title 5.

(2)(A) Within 60 days of the submittal of an application for extension of the term of a patent under paragraph (1), the Director shall notify—

(i) the Secretary of Agriculture if the patent claims a drug product or a method of using or manufacturing a drug product and the drug product is subject to the Virus-Serum-Toxin Act, and

(ii) the Secretary of Health and Human Services if the patent claims any other drug product, a medical device, or a food additive or color additive or a method of using or manufacturing such a product, device, or additive and if the product, device, and additive are subject to the Federal Food, Drug, and Cosmetic Act,

of the extension application and shall submit to the Secretary who is so notified a copy of the application. Not later than 30 days after the receipt of an application from the Director, the Secretary receiving the application shall review the dates contained in the application pursuant to paragraph (1)(C) and determine the applicable regulatory review period, shall notify the Director of the determination, and shall publish in the Federal Register a notice of such determination.

(B)(i) If a petition is submitted to the Secretary making the determination under subparagraph (A), not later than 180 days after the publication of the determination under subparagraph (A), upon which it may reasonably be determined that the applicant did not act with due diligence during the applicable regulatory review period, the Secretary making the determination shall, in accordance with regulations promulgated by such Secretary, determine if the applicant acted with due diligence during the applicable regulatory review period. The Secretary making the determination shall make such determination not later than 90 days after the receipt of such a petition. For a drug product, device, or additive subject to the Federal Food, Drug, and Cosmetic Act or the Public Health Service Act, the Secretary may not delegate the authority to make the determination prescribed by this clause to an office below the Office of the Director of Food and Drugs. For a product subject to the Virus-Serum-Toxin Act, the Secretary of Agriculture may not delegate the authority to make the determination prescribed by this clause to an office below the Office of the Assistant Secretary for Marketing and Inspection Services.

(ii) The Secretary making a determination under clause (i) shall notify the Director of the determination and shall publish in the Federal Register a notice of such determination together with the factual and legal basis for such determination. Any interested person may request, within the 60-day period beginning on the publication of a determination, the Secretary making the determination to hold an informal hearing on the determination. If such a request is made within such period, such Secretary shall hold such hearing not later than 30 days after the date of the request, or at the request of the person making the request, not later than 60 days after such date. The Secretary who is holding the hearing shall provide notice of the hearing to the owner of the patent involved and to any interested person and provide the owner and any interested person an opportunity to participate in the hearing. Within 30 days after the completion of the hearing, such Secretary shall affirm or revise the determination which was the subject of the hearing and shall notify the Director of any revision of the determination and shall publish any such revision in the Federal Register.

(3) For the purposes of paragraph (2)(B), the term "due diligence" means that degree of attention, continuous directed effort, and timeliness as may reasonably be expected from, and are ordinarily exercised by, a person during a regulatory review period.

(4) An application for the extension of the term of a patent is subject to the disclosure requirements prescribed by the Director.

(5)(A) If the owner of record of the patent or its agent reasonably expects that the applicable regulatory review period described in paragraph (1)(B)(ii), (2)(B)(ii), (3)(B)(ii), (4)(B)(ii), or (5)(B)(ii) of subsection (g) that began for a product that is the subject of such patent may extend beyond the expiration of the patent term in effect, the owner or its agent may submit an application to the Director for an interim extension during the period beginning 6 months, and ending 15 days, before such term is due to expire. The application shall contain—

(i) the identity of the product subject to regulatory review and the Federal statute under which such review is occurring;

(ii) the identity of the patent for which interim extension is being sought and the identity of each claim of such patent which claims the product under regulatory review or a method of using or manufacturing the product;

(iii) information to enable the Director to determine under subsection (a)(1), (2), and (3) the eligibility of a patent for extension;

(iv) a brief description of the activities undertaken by the applicant during the applicable regulatory review period to date with respect to the product under review and the significant dates applicable to such activities; and

(v) such patent or other information as the Director may require.

(B) If the Director determines that, except for permission to market or use the product commercially, the patent would be eligible for an extension of the patent term under this section, the Director shall publish in the Federal Register a notice of such determination, including the identity of the product under regulatory review, and shall issue to the applicant a certificate of interim extension for a period of not more than 1 year.

(C) The owner of record of a patent, or its agent, for which an interim extension has been granted under subparagraph (B), may apply for not more than 4 subsequent interim extensions under this paragraph, except that, in the case of a patent subject to subsection (g)(6)(C), the owner of record of the patent, or its agent, may apply for only 1 subsequent interim extension under this paragraph. Each such subsequent application shall be made during the period beginning 60 days before, and ending 30 days before, the expiration of the preceding interim extension.

(D) Each certificate of interim extension under this paragraph shall be recorded in the official file of the patent and shall be considered part of the original patent.

(E) Any interim extension granted under this paragraph shall terminate at the end of the 60-day period beginning on the date on which the product involved receives permission for commercial marketing or use, except that, if within that 60-day period the applicant notifies the Director of such permission and submits any additional information under paragraph (1) of this subsection not previously contained in the application for interim extension, the patent shall be further extended, in accordance with the provisions of this section—

(**i**) for not to exceed 5 years from the date of expiration of the original patent term; or

(**ii**) if the patent is subject to subsection (g)(6)(C), from the date on which the product involved receives approval for commercial marketing or use.

(F) The rights derived from any patent the term of which is extended under this paragraph shall, during the period of interim extension—

(**i**) in the case of a patent which claims a product, be limited to any use then under regulatory review;

(**ii**) in the case of a patent which claims a method of using a product, be limited to any use claimed by the patent then under regulatory review; and

(**iii**) in the case of a patent which claims a method of manufacturing a product, be limited to the method of manufacturing as used to make the product then under regulatory review.

(e)(1) A determination that a patent is eligible for extension may be made by the Director solely on the basis of the representations contained in the application for the extension. If the Director determines that a patent is eligible for extension under subsection (a) and that the requirements of paragraphs (1) through (4) of subsection (d) have been complied with, the Director shall issue to the applicant for the extension of the term of the patent a certificate of extension, under seal, for the period prescribed by subsection (c). Such certificate shall be recorded in the official file of the patent and shall be considered as part of the original patent.

(2) If the term of a patent for which an application has been submitted under subsection (d)(1) would expire before a certificate of extension is issued or denied under paragraph (1) respecting the application, the Director shall extend, until such determination is made, the term of the patent for periods of up to one year if he determines that the patent is eligible for extension.

(f) For purposes of this section:

(1) The term "product" means:

(A) A drug product.

(B) Any medical device, food additive, or color additive subject to regulation under the Federal Food, Drug, and Cosmetic Act.

(2) The term "drug product" means the active ingredient of—

(A) a new drug, antibiotic drug, or human biological product (as those terms are used in the Federal Food, Drug, and Cosmetic Act and the Public Health Service Act), or

(B) a new animal drug or veterinary biological product (as those terms are used in the Federal Food, Drug, and Cosmetic Act and the Virus-Serum-Toxin Act) which is not primarily manufactured using recombinant DNA, recombinant RNA, hybridoma technology, or other processes involving site specific genetic manipulation techniques,

including any salt or ester of the active ingredient, as a single entity or in combination with another active ingredient.

(3) The term "major health or environmental effects test" means a test which is reasonably related to the evaluation of the health or environmental effects of a product, which requires at least six months to conduct, and the data from which is submitted to receive permission for commercial marketing or use. Periods of analysis or evaluation of test results are not to be included in determining if the conduct of a test required at least six months.

(4)(A) Any reference to section 351 is a reference to section 351 of the Public Health Service Act [42 USC § 262].

(B) Any reference to section 503, 505, 512, or 515 is a reference to section 503, 505, 512, or 515 of the Federal Food, Drug, and Cosmetic Act [21 USC § 353, 355, 360b, or 360e].

(C) Any reference to the Virus-Serum-Toxin Act is a reference to the Act of March 4, 1913 (21 U.S.C. 151-158).

(5) The term "informal hearing" has the meaning prescribed for such term by section 201(y) of the Federal Food, Drug, and Cosmetic Act.

(6) The term "patent" means a patent issued by the United States Patent and Trademark Office.

(7) The term "date of enactment" as used in this section means September 24, 1984, for a human drug product, a medical device, food additive, or color additive.

(8) The term "date of enactment" as used in this section means the date of enactment of the Generic Animal Drug and Patent Term Restoration Act for an animal drug or a veterinary biological product.

(g) For purposes of this section, the term "regulatory review period" has the following meanings:

(1)(A) In the case of a product which is a new drug, antibiotic drug, or human biological product, the term means the period described in subparagraph (B) to which the limitation described in paragraph (6) applies.

(B) The regulatory review period for a new drug, antibiotic drug, or human biological product is the sum of—

(i) The period beginning on the date an exemption under subsection (i) of section 505 or subsection (d) of section 507 became effective for the approved product and ending on the date an application was initially submitted for such drug product under section 351, 505, or 507, and

(ii) the period beginning on the date the application was initially submitted for the approved product under section 351 [42 USC § 262], subsection (b) of section 505, or section 507 [21 USC § 357] and ending on the date such application was approved under such section.

(2)(A) In the case of a product which is a food additive or color additive, the term means the period described in subparagraph (B) to which the limitation described in paragraph (6) applies.

(B) The regulatory review period for a food or color additive is the sum of—

(i) the period beginning on the date a major health or environmental effects test on the additive was initiated and ending on the date a petition was initially submitted with respect to the product under the Federal Food, Drug, and Cosmetic Act requesting the issuance of a regulation for use of the product, and

(ii) the period beginning on the date a petition was initially submitted with respect to the product under the Federal Food, Drug, and Cosmetic Act requesting the issuance of a regulation for use of the product, and ending on the date such regulation became effective or, if objections were filed to such regulation, ending on the date such objections were resolved and commercial marketing was permitted or, if commercial marketing was permitted and later revoked pending further proceedings as a result of such objections, ending on the date such proceedings were finally resolved and commercial marketing was permitted.

(3)(A) In the case of a product which is a medical device, the term means the period described in subparagraph (B) to which the limitation described in paragraph (6) applies.

(B) The regulatory review period for a medical device is the sum of—

(i) the period beginning on the date a clinical investigation on humans involving the device was begun and ending on the date an application was initially submitted with respect to the device under section 515, and

(ii) the period beginning on the date an application was initially submitted with respect to the device under section 515 and ending on the date such application was approved under such Act or the period beginning on the date a notice of completion of a product development protocol was initially submitted under section 515(f)(5) and ending on the date the protocol was declared completed under section 515(f)(6).

(4)(A) In the case of a product which is a new animal drug, the term means the period described in subparagraph (B) to which the limitation described in paragraph (6) applies.

(B) The regulatory review period for a new animal drug product is the sum of—

(i) the period beginning on the earlier of the date a major health or environmental effects test on the drug was initiated or the date an exemption under subsection (j) of section 512 became effective for the approved new animal drug product and ending on the date an application was initially submitted for such animal drug product under section 512, and

(ii) the period beginning on the date the application was initially submitted for the approved animal drug product under subsection (b) of section 512 and ending on the date such application was approved under such section.

(5)(A) In the case of a product which is a veterinary biological product, the term means the period described in subparagraph (B) to which the limitation described in paragraph (6) applies.

(B) The regulatory period for a veterinary biological product is the sum of—

(i) the period beginning on the date the authority to prepare an experimental biological product under the Virus-Serum-Toxin Act became effective and ending on the date an application for a license was submitted under the Virus-Serum-Toxin Act, and

(ii) the period beginning on the date an application for a license was initially submitted for approval under the Virus-Serum-Toxin Act and ending on the date such license was issued.

(6) A period determined under any of the preceding paragraphs is subject to the following limitations:

(A) If the patent involved was issued after the date of the enactment of this section, the period of extension determined on the basis of the regulatory review period determined under any such paragraph may not exceed five years.

(B) If the patent involved was issued before the date of the enactment of this section [enacted Sept. 24, 1984] and—

(i) no request for an exemption described in paragraph (1)(B) or (4)(B) was submitted and no request for the authority described in paragraph (5)(B) was submitted,

(ii) no major health or environmental effects test described in paragraph (2)(B) or (4)(B) was initiated and no petition for a regulation or application for registration described in such paragraph was submitted, or

(iii) no clinical investigation described in paragraph (3) was begun or product development protocol described in such paragraph was submitted,

before such date for the approved product the period of extension determined on the basis of the regulatory review period determined under any such paragraph may not exceed five years.

(C) If the patent involved was issued before the date of the enactment of this section [enacted Sept. 24, 1984] and if an action described in subparagraph (B) was taken before the date of the enactment of this section [enacted Sept. 24, 1984] with respect to the approved product and the commercial marketing or use of the product has not been approved before such date, the period of extension determined on the basis of the regulatory review period determined under such paragraph may not exceed two years or in the case of an approved product which is a new animal drug or veterinary biological product (as those terms are used in the Federal Food, Drug, and Cosmetic Act or the Virus-Serum-Toxin Act), three years.

(h) The Director may establish such fees as the Director determines appropriate to cover the costs to the Office of receiving and acting upon applications under this section.

HISTORY:

(Added Sept. 24, 1984, P.L. 98-417, Title II, § 201(a), 98 Stat. 1598; Nov. 16, 1988, P.L. 100-670, Title II, § 201(a)-(h), 102 Stat. 3984; Dec. 3, 1993, P.L. 103-179, §§ 5, 6, 107 Stat. 2040; Dec. 8, 1994, P.L. 103-465, Title V, Subtitle C, § 532(c)(1), 108 Stat. 4987; Nov. 21, 1997, P.L. 105-115, Title I, Subtitle B, § 125(b)(2)(P), 111 Stat. 2326; Nov. 29, 1999, P.L. 106-113, Div B, § 1000(a)(9), 113 Stat. 1536; Nov. 2, 2002, P.L. 107-273, Div C, Title III, Subtitle B, §§ 13206(a)(9), 13206(b)(1)(B), 116 Stat. 1904, 1906.)

(America Invents Act § 37(a).)

§ 157. ~~Statutory invention registration~~

~~(a) Notwithstanding any other provision of this title, the Director is authorized to publish a statutory invention registration containing the specification and drawings of a regularly filed application for a patent without examination if the applicant—~~

~~(1) meets the requirements of section 112 of this title;~~

~~(2) has complied with the requirements for printing, as set forth in regulations of the Director;~~

~~(3) waives the right to receive a patent on the invention within such period as may be prescribed by the Director; and~~

~~(4) pays application, publication, and other processing fees established by the Director. If an interference is declared with respect to such an application, a statutory invention registration may not be published unless the issue of priority of invention is finally determined in favor of the applicant.~~

~~(b) The waiver under subsection (a)(3) of this section by an applicant shall take effect upon publication of the statutory invention registration.~~

~~(c) A statutory invention registration published pursuant to this section shall have all of the attributes specified for patents in this title except those specified in section 183 and sections~~

~~271 through 289 of this title. A statutory invention registration shall not have any of the attributes specified for patents in any other provision of law other than this title. A statutory invention registration published pursuant to this section shall give appropriate notice to the public, pursuant to regulations which the Director shall issue, of the preceding provisions of this subsection. The invention with respect to which a statutory invention certificate is published is not a patented invention for purposes of section 292 of this title.~~

~~(d) The Director shall report to the Congress annually on the use of statutory invention registrations. Such report shall include an assessment of the degree to which agencies of the Federal Government are making use of the statutory invention registration system, the degree to which it aids the management of federally developed technology, and an assessment of the cost savings to the Federal Government of the use of such procedures.~~

HISTORY:

(Added Nov. 8, 1984, P.L. 98-622, Title I, § 102(a), 98 Stat. 3383; Nov. 29, 1999, P.L. 106-113, Div B, § 1000(a)(9), 113 Stat. 1536; Nov. 2, 2002, P.L. 107-273, Div C, Title III, Subtitle B, § 13206(b)(1)(B), 116 Stat. 1906.)

(America Invents Act § 3(e)(1).)

CHAPTER 15. PLANT PATENTS

§ 161. Patent for plants

Whoever invents or discovers and asexually reproduces any distinct and new variety of plant, including cultivated sports, mutants, hybrids, and newly found seedlings, other than a tuber propagated plant or a plant found in an uncultivated state, may obtain a patent therefor, subject to the conditions and requirements of this title [35 USC §§ 1 et seq.].

The provisions of this title [35 USC §§ 1 et seq.] relating to patents for inventions shall apply to patents for plants, except as otherwise provided.

HISTORY:

(July 19, 1952, ch 950, § 1, 66 Stat. 804; Sept. 3, 1954, ch 1259, 68 Stat. 1190.)

§ 162. Description, claim

No plant patent shall be declared invalid for noncompliance with section 112 ~~of this title~~ [35 USC § 112] if the description is as complete as is reasonably possible.

The claim in the specification shall be in formal terms to the plant shown and described.

HISTORY:

(July 19, 1952, ch 950, § 1, 66 Stat. 804.)

(America Invents Act § 20(j)(1).)

§ 163. Grant

In the case of a plant patent, the grant shall include the right to exclude others from asexually reproducing the plant, and from using, offering for sale, or selling the plant so reproduced, or any of its parts, throughout the United States, or from importing the plant so reproduced, or any parts thereof, into the United States.

HISTORY:

(July 19, 1952, ch 950, § 1, 66 Stat. 804; Oct. 27, 1998, § 3(a), 112 Stat. 2781.)

§ 164. Assistance of Department of Agriculture

The President may by Executive order direct the Secretary of Agriculture, in accordance with the requests of the Director, for the purpose of carrying into effect the provisions of this title with respect to plants (1) to furnish available information of the Department of

35 USC § 164

Agriculture, (2) to conduct through the appropriate bureau or division of the Department research upon special problems, or (3) to detail to the Director officers and employees of the Department.

HISTORY:

(July 19, 1952, ch 950, § 1, 66 Stat. 804; Nov. 29, 1999, P.L. 106-113, Div B, § 1000(a)(9), 113 Stat. 1536; Nov. 2, 2002, P.L. 107-273, Div C, Title III, Subtitle B, § 13206(b)(1)(B), 116 Stat. 1906.)

CHAPTER 16. DESIGNS

§ 171. Patents for designs

Whoever invents any new, original and ornamental design for an article of manufacture may obtain a patent therefor, subject to the conditions and requirements of this title [35 USC §§ 1 et seq.].

The provisions of this title [35 USC §§ 1 et seq.] relating to patents for inventions shall apply to patents for designs, except as otherwise provided.

HISTORY:

(July 19, 1952, ch 950, § 1, 66 Stat. 805.)

§ 172. Right of priority

The right of priority provided for by subsections (a) through (d) of section 119 [35 USC § 119] and the time specified in section 102(d) [35 USC § 102(d)] shall be six months in the case of designs. The right of priority provided for by section 119(e) of this title [35 USC § 119(e)] shall not apply to designs.

HISTORY:

(July 19, 1952, ch 950, § 1, 66 Stat. 805; Dec. 8, 1994, P.L. 103-465, Title V, Subtitle C, § 532(c)(2), 108 Stat. 4987.)

(America Invents Act §§ 3(g)(1); 20(j)(1).)

§ 173. Term of design patent

Patents for designs shall be granted for the term of fourteen years from the date of grant.

HISTORY:

(July 19, 1952, ch 950, § 1, 66 Stat. 805; Aug. 27, 1982, P.L. 97-247, § 16, 96 Stat. 321; Dec. 8, 1994, P.L. 103-465, Title V, Subtitle C, § 532(c)(3), 108 Stat. 4987.)

CHAPTER 17. SECRECY OF CERTAIN INVENTIONS AND FILING APPLICATIONS IN FOREIGN COUNTRY

§ 181. Secrecy of certain inventions and withholding of patent

Whenever publication or disclosure by the publication of an application or by the grant of a patent on an invention in which the Government has a property interest might, in the opinion of the head of the interested Government agency, be detrimental to the national security, the Commissioner of Patents upon being so notified shall order that the invention be kept secret and shall withhold the publication of the application or the grant of a patent therefor under the conditions set forth hereinafter.

Whenever the publication or disclosure of an invention by the publication of an application or by the granting of a patent, in which the Government does not have a property interest, might, in the opinion of the Commissioner of Patents, be detrimental to the national security, he shall make the application for patent in which such invention is disclosed available for inspection to the Atomic Energy Commission, the Secretary of Defense, and the chief officer of any other department or agency of the Government designated by the President as a defense agency of the United States.

Each individual to whom the application is disclosed shall sign a dated acknowledgment thereof, which acknowledgment shall be entered in the file of the application. If, in the opinion of the Atomic Energy Commission, the Secretary of a Defense Department, or the chief officer of another department or agency so designated, the publication or disclosure of the invention by the publication of an application or by the granting of a patent therefor would be detrimental to the national security, the Atomic Energy Commission, the Secretary of a Defense Department, or such other chief officer shall notify the Commissioner of Patents and the Commissioner of Patents shall order that the invention be kept secret and shall withhold the publication of the application or the grant of a patent for such period as the national interest requires, and notify the applicant thereof. Upon proper showing by the head of the department or agency who caused the secrecy order to be issued that the examination of the application might jeopardize the national interest, the Commissioner of Patents shall thereupon maintain the application in a sealed condition and notify the applicant thereof. The owner of an application which has been placed under a secrecy order shall have a right to appeal from the order to the Secretary of Commerce under rules prescribed by him.

An invention shall not be ordered kept secret and the publication of an application or the grant of a patent withheld for a period of more than one year. The Commissioner of Patents shall renew the order at the end thereof, or at the end of any renewal period, for additional periods of one year upon notification by the head of the department or the chief officer of the agency who caused the order to be issued that an affirmative determination has been made that the national interest continues so to require. An order in effect, or issued, during a time when the United States is at war, shall remain in effect for the duration of hostilities and one year following cessation of hostilities. An order in effect, or issued, during a national emergency declared by the President shall remain in effect for the duration of the national emergency and six months thereafter. The Commissioner of Patents may rescind any order upon notification by the heads of the departments and the chief officers of the agencies who caused the order to be issued that the publication or disclosure of the invention is no longer deemed detrimental to the national security.

HISTORY:

(July 19, 1952, ch 950, § 1, 66 Stat. 805; Nov. 29, 1999, P.L. 106-113, Div B, § 1000(a)(9), 113 Stat. 1536.)

§ 182. Abandonment of invention for unauthorized disclosure

The invention disclosed in an application for patent subject to an order made pursuant to section 181 of this title [35 USC § 181] may be held abandoned upon its being established by the Commissioner of Patents that in violation of said order the invention has been published or disclosed or that an application for a patent therefor has been filed in a foreign country by the inventor, his successors, assigns, or legal representatives, or anyone in privity with him or them, without the consent of the Commissioner of Patents. The abandonment shall be held to have occurred as of the time of violation. The consent of the Commissioner of Patents shall not be given without the concurrence of the heads of the departments and the chief officers of the agencies who caused the order to be issued. A holding of abandonment shall constitute forfeiture by the applicant, his successors, assigns, or legal representatives, or anyone in privity with him or them, of all claims against the United States based upon such invention.

HISTORY:

(July 19, 1952, ch 950, § 1, 66 Stat. 806; Nov. 29, 1999, P.L. 106-113, Div B, § 1000(a)(9), 113 Stat. 1536.)

(America Invents Act § 20(j)(1).)

§ 183. Right to compensation

An applicant, his successors, assigns, or legal representatives, whose patent is withheld as herein provided, shall have the right, beginning at the date the applicant is notified that, except for such order, his application is otherwise in condition for allowance, or February 1, 1952, whichever is later, and ending six years after a patent is issued thereon, to apply to the head of any department or agency who caused the order to be issued for compensation for the damage caused by the order of secrecy and/or for the use of the invention by the Government, resulting from his disclosure. The right to compensation for use shall begin on the date of the first use of the invention by the Government. The head of the department or agency is authorized, upon the presentation of a claim, to enter into an agreement with the applicant, his successors, assigns, or legal representatives, in full settlement for the damage and/or use. This settlement agreement shall be conclusive for all purposes notwithstanding any other provision of law to the contrary. If full settlement of the claim cannot be effected, the head of the department or agency may award and pay to such applicant, his successors, assigns, or legal representatives, a sum not exceeding 75 per centum of the sum which the head of the department or agency considers just compensation for the damage and/or use. A claimant may bring suit against the United States in the United States Claims Court [United States Court of Federal Claims] or in the District Court of the United States for the district in which such claimant is a resident for an amount which when added to the award shall constitute just compensation for the damage and/or use of the invention by the Government. The owner of any patent issued upon an application that was subject to a secrecy order issued pursuant to section 181 of this title [35 USC § 181], who did not apply for compensation as above provided, shall have the right, after the date of issuance of such patent, to bring suit in the United States Claims Court [United States Court of Federal Claims] for just compensation for the damage caused by reason of the order of secrecy and/or use by the Government of the invention resulting from his disclosure. The right to compensation for use shall begin on the date of the first use of the invention by the Government. In a suit under the provisions of this section the United States may avail itself of all defenses it may plead in an action under section 1498 of title 28. This section shall not confer a right of action on anyone or his successors, assigns, or legal representatives who, while in the full-time employment or service of the United States, discovered, invented, or developed the invention on which the claim is based.

HISTORY:

(July 19, 1952, ch 950, § 1, 66 Stat. 806; April 2, 1982, P.L. 97-164, Title I, Part B, § 160(a)(12), 96 Stat. 48.)

(America Invents Act § 20(j)(1).)

§ 184. Filing of application in foreign country

~~Except when~~ **(a) Filing in Foreign Country.**—Except when authorized by a license obtained from the Commissioner of Patents a person shall not file or cause or authorize to be filed in any foreign country prior to six months after filing in the United States an application for patent or for the registration of a utility model, industrial design, or model in respect of an invention made in this country. A license shall not be granted with respect to an invention subject to an order issued by the Commissioner of Patents pursuant to section 181 of this title [35 USC § 181] without the concurrence of the head of the departments and the chief officers of the agencies who caused the order to be issued. The license may be granted retroactively where an application has been filed abroad through error ~~and without deceptive intent~~ and the application does not disclose an invention within the scope of section 181 of this title [35 USC § 181].

~~The term~~ **(b) Application.**—The term "application" when used in this chapter [35 USC §§ 181 et seq.] includes applications and any modifications, amendments, or supplements thereto, or divisions thereof.

~~The scope~~ **(c) Subsequent modifications, amendments, and supplements.**—The scope of a license shall permit subsequent modifications, amendments, and supplements containing additional subject matter if the application upon which the request for the license is based is not, or was not, required to be made available for inspection under section 181 ~~of this title~~ [35 USC § 181] and if such modifications, amendments, and supplements do not change the general nature of the invention in a manner which would require such application to be made available for inspection under such section 181 [35 USC § 181]. In any case in which a license is not, or was not, required in order to file an application in any foreign country, such subsequent modifications, amendments, and supplements may be made, without a license, to the application filed in the foreign country if the United States application was not required to be made available for inspection under section 181 [35 USC § 181] and if such modifications, amendments, and supplements do not, or did not, change the general nature of the invention in a manner which would require the United States application to have been made available for inspection under such section 181 [35 USC § 181].

HISTORY:

(July 19, 1952, ch 950, § 1, 66 Stat. 807; Aug. 23, 1988, P.L. 100-418, Title IX, Subtitle B, § 9101(b)(1), 102 Stat. 1567; Nov. 29, 1999, P.L. 106-113, Div B, § 1000(a)(9), 113 Stat. 1536.)

(America Invents Act §§ 20(b)(1)(A)-(B), (2), (3); 20(j)(1).)

§ 185. Patent barred for filing without license

Notwithstanding any other provisions of law any person, and his successors, assigns, or legal representatives, shall not receive a United States patent for an invention if that person, or his successors, assigns, or legal representatives shall, without procuring the license prescribed in section 184 ~~of this title~~ [35 USC § 184], have made, or consented to or assisted another's making, application in a foreign country for a patent or for the registration of a utility model, industrial design, or model in respect of the invention. A United States patent issued to such person, his successors, assigns, or legal representatives shall be invalid, unless the failure to procure such license was through error ~~and without deceptive intent,~~ and the patent does not disclose subject matter within the scope of section 181 ~~of this title~~ [35 USC § 181].

HISTORY:

(July 19, 1952, ch 950, § 1, 66 Stat. 807; Aug. 23, 1988, P.L. 100-418, Title IX, Subtitle B, § 9101(b)(2), 102 Stat. 1568; Nov. 2, 2002, P.L. 107-273, Div C, Title III, Subtitle B, § 13206(a)(11), 116 Stat. 1904.)

(America Invents Act §§ 20(c), (j)(1).)

§ 186. Penalty

Whoever, during the period or periods of time an invention has been ordered to be kept secret and the grant of a patent thereon withheld pursuant to section 181 ~~of this title~~ [35 USC § 181], shall, with knowledge of such order and without due authorization, willfully publish or disclose or authorize or cause to be published or disclosed the invention, or material information with respect thereto, or whoever willfully, in violation of the provisions of section 184 ~~of this title~~ [35 USC § 184], shall file or cause or authorize to be filed in any foreign country an application for patent or for the registration of a utility model, industrial design, or model in respect of any invention made in the United States, shall, upon conviction, be fined not more than $ 10,000 or imprisoned for not more than two years, or both.

35 USC § 186

HISTORY:
(July 19, 1952, ch 950, § 1, 66 Stat. 807; Aug. 23, 1988, P.L. 100-418, Title IX, Subtitle B, § 9101(b)(3), 102 Stat. 1568.)
(America Invents Act §§ 20(j)(1).)

§ 187. Nonapplicability to certain persons

The prohibitions and penalties of this chapter [35 USC §§ 181 et seq.] shall not apply to any officer or agent of the United States acting within the scope of his authority, nor to any person acting upon his written instructions or permission.

HISTORY:
(July 19, 1952, ch 950, § 1, 66 Stat. 808.)

§ 188. Rules and regulations, delegation of power

The Atomic Energy Commission, the Secretary of a defense department, the chief officer of any other department or agency of the Government designated by the President as a defense agency of the United States, and the Secretary of Commerce, may separately issue rules and regulations to enable the respective department or agency to carry out the provisions of this chapter [35 USC §§ 181 et seq.], and may delegate any power conferred by this chapter [35 USC §§ 181 et seq.].

HISTORY:
(July 19, 1952, ch 950, § 1, 66 Stat. 808.)

CHAPTER 18. PATENT RIGHTS IN INVENTIONS MADE WITH FEDERAL ASSISTANCE

§ 200. Policy and objective

It is the policy and objective of the Congress to use the patent system to promote the utilization of inventions arising from federally supported research or development; to encourage maximum participation of small business firms in federally supported research and development efforts; to promote collaboration between commercial concerns and nonprofit organizations, including universities; to ensure that inventions made by nonprofit organizations and small business firms are used in a manner to promote free competition and enterprise without unduly encumbering future research and discovery; to promote the commercialization and public availability of inventions made in the United States by United States industry and labor; to ensure that the Government obtains sufficient rights in federally supported inventions to meet the needs of the Government and protect the public against nonuse or unreasonable use of inventions; and to minimize the costs of administering policies in this area.

HISTORY:
(Added Dec. 12, 1980, P.L. 96-517, § 6(a), 94 Stat. 3019; Nov. 1, 2000, P.L. 106-404, § 5, 114 Stat. 1745.)

§ 201. Definitions

As used in this chapter [35 USC §§ 200 et seq.]—

(a) The term "Federal agency" means any executive agency as defined in section 105 of title 5, and the military departments as defined by section 102 of title 5.

(b) The term "funding agreement" means any contract, grant, or cooperative agreement entered into between any Federal agency, other than the Tennessee Valley Authority, and any contractor for the performance of experimental, developmental, or research work funded in whole or in part by the Federal Government. Such term includes any assignment, substitution of parties, or subcontract of any type entered into for the performance of experimental, developmental, or research work under a funding agreement as herein defined.

(c) The term "contractor" means any person, small business firm, or nonprofit organization that is a party to a funding agreement.

(d) The term "invention" means any invention or discovery which is or may be patentable or otherwise protectable under this title [35 USC §§ 1 et seq.] or any novel variety of plant which is or may be protectable under the Plant Variety Protection Act (7 U.S.C 2321 et seq.).

(e) The term "subject invention" means any invention of the contractor conceived or first actually reduced to practice in the performance of work under a funding agreement: Provided, That in the case of a variety of plant, the date of determination (as defined in section 41(d) of the Plant Variety Protection Act (7 U.S.C. 2401(d))) must also occur during the period of contract performance.

(f) The term "practical application" means to manufacture in the case of a composition or product, to practice in the case of a process or method, or to operate in the case of a machine or system; and, in each case, under such conditions as to establish that the invention is being utilized and that its benefits are to the extent permitted by law or Government regulations available to the public on reasonable terms.

(g) The term "made" when used in relation to any invention means the conception or first actual reduction to practice of such invention.

(h) The term "small business firm" means a small business concern as defined at section 2 of Public Law 85-536 (15 U.S.C. 632) and implementing regulations of the Administrator of the Small Business Administration.

(i) The term "nonprofit organization" means universities and other institutions of higher education or an organization of the type described in section 501(c)(3) of the Internal Revenue Code of 1954 [1986] (26 U.S.C. 501(c)) and exempt from taxation under section 501(a) of the Internal Revenue Code (26 U.S.C. 501(a)) or any nonprofit scientific or educational organization qualified under a State nonprofit organization statute.

HISTORY:

(Added Dec. 12, 1980, P.L. 96-517, § 6(a), 94 Stat. 3019; Nov. 8, 1984, P.L. 98-620, Title V, § 501(1), (2), 98 Stat. 3364; Nov. 2, 2002, P.L. 107-273, Div C, Title III, Subtitle B, § 13206(a)(12), 116 Stat. 1904.)

§ 202. Disposition of rights

(a) Each nonprofit organization or small business firm may, within a reasonable time after disclosure as required by paragraph (c)(1) of this section, elect to retain title to any subject invention: Provided, however, That a funding agreement may provide otherwise (i) when the contractor is not located in the United States or does not have a place of business located in the United States or is subject to the control of a foreign government, (ii) in exceptional circumstances when it is determined by the agency that restriction or elimination of the right to retain title to any subject invention will better promote the policy and objectives of this chapter[,] (iii) when it is determined by a Government authority which is authorized by statute or Executive order to conduct foreign intelligence or counter-intelligence activities that the restriction or elimination of the right to retain title to any subject invention is necessary to protect the security of such activities or, (iv) when the funding agreement includes the operation of a Government-owned, contractor-operated facility of the Department of Energy primarily dedicated to that Department's naval nuclear propulsion or weapons related programs and all funding agreement limitations under this subparagraph on the contractor's right to elect title to a subject invention are limited to inventions occurring under the above two programs of the Department of Energy. The rights of the nonprofit organization or small business firm shall be subject to the provisions of paragraph (c) of this section and the other provisions of this chapter [35 USC §§ 200 et seq.].

(b)(1) The rights of the Government under subsection (a) shall not be exercised by a Federal agency unless it first determines that at least one of the conditions identified in clauses (i) through (iv) of subsection (a) exists. Except in the case of subsection (a)(iii), the agency shall file with the Secretary of Commerce, within thirty days after the award of the applicable funding agreement, a copy of such determination. In the case of a determination under subsection (a)(ii), the statement shall include an analysis justifying the determination. In the case of determinations applicable to funding agreements with small business firms, copies shall also be sent to the Chief Counsel for Advocacy of the Small Business Administration. If the Secretary of Commerce believes that any individual determination or pattern of determinations is contrary to the policies and objectives of this chapter or otherwise not in conformance with this chapter, the Secretary shall so advise the head of the agency concerned and the Administrator of the Office of Federal Procurement Policy, and recommend corrective actions.

(2) Whenever the Administrator of the Office of Federal Procurement Policy has determined that one or more Federal agencies are utilizing the authority of clause (i) or (ii) of subsection (a) of this section in a manner that is contrary to the policies and objectives of this chapter, the Administrator is authorized to issue regulations describing classes of situations in which agencies may not exercise the authorities of those clauses.

(3) If the contractor believes that a determination is contrary to the policies and objectives of this chapter or constitutes an abuse of discretion by the agency, the determination shall be subject to ~~the section 203(b)~~ section 203(b) [35 USC § 203(b)].

(4) [Redesignated]

(c) Each funding agreement with a small business firm or nonprofit organization shall contain appropriate provisions to effectuate the following:

(1) That the contractor disclose each subject invention to the Federal agency within a reasonable time after it becomes known to contractor personnel responsible for the administration of patent matters, and that the Federal Government may receive title to any subject invention not disclosed to it within such time.

(2) That the contractor make a written election within two years after disclosure to the Federal agency (or such additional time as may be approved by the Federal agency) whether the contractor will retain title to a subject invention: Provided,That in any case where ~~publication, on sale, or public use, has initiated the one-year statutory period in which valid patent protection can still be obtained in the United States~~ the 1-year period referred to in section 102(b) would end before the end of that 2-year period, the period for election may be shortened by the Federal agency to a date that is not more than sixty days ~~prior to the end of the statutory~~ before the end of that 1-year period: And provided further, That the Federal Government may receive title to any subject invention in which the contractor does not elect to retain rights or fails to elect rights within such times.

(3) That a contractor electing rights in a subject invention agrees to file a patent application prior to ~~any statutory bar date that may occur under this title [35 USC §§ 1 et seq.] due to publication, on sale, or public use~~ the expiration of the 1-year period referred to in section 102(b), and shall thereafter file corresponding patent applications in other countries in which it wishes to retain title within reasonable times, and that the Federal Government may receive title to any subject inventions in the United States or other countries in which the contractor has not filed patent applications on the subject invention within such times.

(4) With respect to any invention in which the contractor elects rights, the Federal agency shall have a nonexclusive, nontransferrable, irrevocable, paid-up license to practice or have practiced for or on behalf of the United States any subject invention throughout the world: Provided, That the funding agreement may provide for such additional rights, including the right to assign or have assigned foreign patent rights in the subject invention, as are determined by the agency as necessary for meeting the obligations of the United States under any treaty, international agreement, arrangement of cooperation, memorandum of understanding, or similar arrangement, including military agreement relating to weapons development and production.

(5) The right of the Federal agency to require periodic reporting on the utilization or efforts at obtaining utilization that are being made by the contractor or his licensees or assignees: Provided, That any such information as well as any information on utilization or efforts at obtaining utilization obtained as part of a proceeding under section 203 of this chapter [35 USC § 203] shall be treated by the Federal agency as commercial and financial information obtained from a person and privileged and confidential and not subject to disclosure under section 552 of title 5.

(6) An obligation on the part of the contractor, in the event a United States patent application is filed by or on its behalf or by any assignee of the contractor, to include within the specification of such application and any patent issuing thereon, a statement specifying that the invention was made with Government support and that the Government has certain rights in the invention.

(7) In the case of a nonprofit organization, (A) a prohibition upon the assignment of rights to a subject invention in the United States without the approval of the Federal agency, except where such assignment is made to an organization which has as one of its primary functions the management of inventions (provided that such assignee shall be subject to the same provisions as the contractor); (B) a requirement that the contractor share royalties with the inventor; (C) except with respect to a funding agreement for the operation of a Government-owned-contractor-operated facility, a requirement that the balance of any royalties or income earned by the contractor with respect to subject inventions, after payment of expenses (including payments to inventors) incidental to the administration of subject inventions, be utilized for the support of scientific research or education; (D) a requirement that, ~~except where it proves infeasible after a reasonable inquiry, in the licensing of subject inventions shall be given to small business firms; and~~ except where it is determined to be infeasible following a reasonable inquiry, a preference in the licensing of subject inventions shall be given to small business firms; and (E) with respect to a funding agreement for the operation of a Government-owned-contractor-operated facility, requirements (i) that after payment of patenting costs, licensing costs, payments to inventors, and other expenses incidental to the administration of subject inventions, 100 percent of the balance of any royalties or income earned and retained by the contractor during any fiscal year up to an amount equal to 5 percent of the annual budget of the facility, shall be used by the contractor for scientific research, development, and education consistent with the research and development mission and objectives of the facility, including activities that increase the licensing potential of other inventions of the facility; provided that if said balance exceeds 5 percent of the annual budget of the facility, that ~~75 percent~~ 15 percent of such excess shall be paid to the Treasury of the United States and the remaining ~~25 percent~~ 85 percent shall be used for the same purposes ~~as described above in this clause (D);~~ described above in this clause; and (ii) that, to the extent it provides the most effective technology transfer, the licensing of subject inventions shall be administered by contractor employees on location at the facility.

(8) The requirements of sections 203 and 204 of this chapter [35 USC §§ 203, 204].

(d) If a contractor does not elect to retain title to a subject invention in cases subject to this section, the Federal agency may consider and after consultation with the contractor grant requests for retention of rights by the inventor subject to the provisions of this Act and regulations promulgated hereunder.

(e) In any case when a Federal employee is a coinventor of any invention made with a nonprofit organization, a small business firm, or a non-Federal inventor, the Federal agency employing such coinventor may, for the purpose of consolidating rights in the invention and if it finds that it would expedite the development of the invention—

(1) license or assign whatever rights it may acquire in the subject invention to the nonprofit organization, small business firm, or non-Federal inventor in accordance with the provisions of this chapter [35 USC §§ 200 et seq.]; or

(2) acquire any rights in the subject invention from the nonprofit organization, small business firm, or non-Federal inventor, but only to the extent the party from whom the rights are acquired voluntarily enters into the transaction and no other transaction under this chapter [35 USC §§ 200 et seq.] is conditioned on such acquisition.

(f)(1) No funding agreement with a small business firm or nonprofit organization shall contain a provision allowing a Federal agency to require the licensing to third parties of inventions owned by the contractor that are not subject inventions unless such provision has been approved by the head of the agency and a written justification has been signed by the head of the agency. Any such provision shall clearly state whether the licensing may be required in connection with the practice of a subject invention, a specifically identified work object, or both. The head of the agency may not delegate the authority to approve provisions or sign justifications required by this paragraph.

(2) A Federal agency shall not require the licensing of third parties under any such provision unless the head of the agency determines that the use of the invention by others is necessary for the practice of a subject invention or for the use of a work object of the funding agreement and that such action is necessary to achieve the practical application of the subject invention or work object. Any such determination shall be on the record after an opportunity for an agency hearing. Any action commenced for judicial review of such determination shall be brought within sixty days after notification of such determination.

HISTORY:

(Added Dec. 12, 1980, P.L. 96-517, § 6(a), 94 Stat. 3020; Nov. 8, 1984, P.L. 98-620, Title V, § 501(3)-(8), 98 Stat. 3364; Dec. 10, 1991, P.L. 102-204, § 10, 105 Stat. 1641; Nov. 29, 1999, P.L. 106-113, Div B, § 1000(a)(9), 113 Stat. 1536; Nov. 1, 2000, P.L. 106-404, § 6(1), 114 Stat. 1745; Nov. 2, 2002, P.L. 107-273, Div C, Title III, Subtitle B, § 13206(a)(13), 116 Stat. 1905; March 11, 2009, P.L. 111-8, Div G, Title I, § 1301(h), 123 Stat. 829.)

(America Invents Act §§ 3(g)(7)(A)(i), (ii), and (B); 13(a)(1)-(3), 20(i)(2)(A)-(B).)

§ 203. March-in rights

(a) With respect to any subject invention in which a small business firm or nonprofit organization has acquired title under this chapter [35 USC §§ 200 et seq.], the Federal agency under whose funding agreement the subject invention was made shall have the right, in accordance with such procedures as are provided in regulations promulgated hereunder to require the contractor, an assignee or exclusive licensee of a subject invention to grant a nonexclusive, partially exclusive, or exclusive license in any field of use to a responsible applicant or applicants, upon terms that are reasonable under the circumstances, and if the contractor, assignee, or exclusive licensee refuses such request, to grant such a license itself, if the Federal agency determines that such—

(1) action is necessary because the contractor or assignee has not taken, or is not expected to take within a reasonable time, effective steps to achieve practical application of the subject invention in such field of use;

(2) action is necessary to alleviate health or safety needs which are not reasonably satisfied by the contractor, assignee, or their licensees;

(3) action is necessary to meet requirements for public use specified by Federal regulations and such requirements are not reasonably satisfied by the contractor, assignee, or licensees; or

(4) action is necessary because the agreement required by section 204 [35 USC § 204] has not been obtained or waived or because a licensee of the exclusive right to use or sell any subject invention in the United States is in breach of its agreement obtained pursuant to section 204 [35 USC § 204].

(b) A determination pursuant to this section or section 202(b)(4) [35 USC § 202(b)(4)] shall not be subject to chapter 71 of title 41 [41 USC §§ 7101 et seq.]. An administrative appeals procedure shall be established by regulations promulgated in accordance with section 206 [35 USC § 206]. Additionally, any contractor, inventor, assignee, or exclusive licensee adversely affected by a determination under this section may, at any time within sixty days after the determination is issued, file a petition in the United States Claims Court [United States Court of Federal Claims], which shall have jurisdiction to determine the appeal on the record and to affirm, reverse, remand or modify, as appropriate, the determination of the Federal agency. In cases described in paragraphs (1) and (3) of subsection (a), the agency's determination shall be held in abeyance pending the exhaustion of appeals or petitions filed under the preceding sentence.

HISTORY:

(Added Dec. 12, 1980, P.L. 96-517, § 6(a), 94 Stat. 3022; Nov. 8, 1984, P.L. 98-620, Title V, § 501(9), 98 Stat. 3367; Nov. 2, 2002, P.L. 107-273, Div C, Title III, Subtitle B, § 13206(a)(14), 116 Stat. 1905; Jan. 4, 2011, P.L. 111-350, § 5(i)(2), 124 Stat. 3850.)

§ 204. Preference for United States industry

Notwithstanding any other provision of this chapter, [35 USC §§ 200 et seq.], no small business firm or nonprofit organization which receives title to any subject invention and no assignee of any such small business firm or nonprofit organization shall grant to any person the exclusive right to use or sell any subject invention in the United States unless such person agrees that any products embodying the subject invention or produced through the use of the subject invention will be manufactured substantially in the United States. However, in individual cases, the requirement for such an agreement may be waived by the Federal agency under whose funding agreement the invention was made upon a showing by the small business firm, nonprofit organization, or assignee that reasonable but unsuccessful efforts have been made to grant licenses on similar terms to potential licensees that would be likely to manufacture substantially in the United States or that under the circumstances domestic manufacture is not commercially feasible.

HISTORY:

(Added Dec. 12, 1980, P.L. 96-517, § 6(a), 94 Stat. 3023.)

§ 205. Confidentiality

Federal agencies are authorized to withhold from disclosure to the public information disclosing any invention in which the Federal Government owns or may own a right, title, or

35 USC § 205

interest (including a nonexclusive license) for a reasonable time in order for a patent application to be filed. Furthermore, Federal agencies shall not be required to release copies of any document which is part of an application for patent filed with the United States Patent and Trademark Office or with any foreign patent office.

HISTORY:

(Added Dec. 12, 1980, P.L. 96-517, § 6(a), 94 Stat. 3023.)

§ 206. Uniform clauses and regulations

The Secretary of Commerce may issue regulations which may be made applicable to Federal agencies implementing the provisions of sections 202 through 204 of this chapter [35 USC §§ 202-204] and shall establish standard funding agreement provisions required under this chapter [35 USC §§ 200 et seq.]. The regulations and the standard funding agreement shall be subject to public comment before their issuance.

HISTORY:

(Added Dec. 12, 1980, P.L. 96-517, § 6(a), 94 Stat. 3023; Nov. 8, 1984, P.L. 98-620, Title V, § 501(10), 98 Stat. 3367.)

§ 207. Domestic and foreign protection of federally owned inventions

(a) Each Federal agency is authorized to—

(1) apply for, obtain, and maintain patents or other forms of protection in the United States and in foreign countries on inventions in which the Federal Government owns a right, title, or interest;

(2) grant nonexclusive, exclusive, or partially exclusive licenses under federally owned inventions, royalty-free or for royalties or other consideration, and on such terms and conditions, including the grant to the licensee of the right of enforcement pursuant to the provisions of chapter 29 of this title [35 USC §§ 281 et seq.] as determined appropriate in the public interest;

(3) undertake all other suitable and necessary steps to protect and administer rights to federally owned inventions on behalf of the Federal Government either directly or through contract, including acquiring rights for and administering royalties to the Federal Government in any invention, but only to the extent the party from whom the rights are acquired voluntarily enters into the transaction, to facilitate the licensing of a federally owned invention; and

(4) transfer custody and administration, in whole or in part, to another Federal agency, of the right, title or interest in any federally owned invention.

(b) For the purpose of assuring the effective management of Government-owned inventions, the Secretary of Commerce is authorized to—

(1) assist Federal agency efforts to promote the licensing and utilization of Government-owned inventions;

(2) assist Federal agencies in seeking protection and maintaining inventions in foreign countries, including the payment of fees and costs connected therewith; and

(3) consult with and advise Federal agencies as to areas of science and technology research and development with potential for commercial utilization.

HISTORY:

(Added Dec. 12, 1980, P.L. 96-517, § 6(a), 94 Stat. 3023; Nov. 8, 1984, P.L. 98-620, Title V, § 501(11), 98 Stat. 3367; Nov. 1, 2000, P.L. 106-404, § 6(2), 114 Stat. 1745.)

(America Invents Act § 20(j)(1).)

§ 208. Regulations governing Federal licensing

The Secretary of Commerce is authorized to promulgate regulations specifying the terms and conditions upon which any federally owned invention, other than inventions owned by the Tennessee Valley Authority, may be licensed on a nonexclusive, partially exclusive, or exclusive basis.

HISTORY:

(Added Dec. 12, 1980, P.L. 96-517, § 6(a), 94 Stat. 3024; Nov. 8, 1984, P.L. 98-620, Title V, § 501(12), 98 Stat. 3367.)

§ 209. Licensing federally owned inventions

(a) Authority. A Federal agency may grant an exclusive or partially exclusive license on a federally owned invention under section 207(a)(2) [35 USC § 207(a)(2)] only if—

(1) granting the license is a reasonable and necessary incentive to—

(A) call forth the investment capital and expenditures needed to bring the invention to practical application; or

(B) otherwise promote the invention's utilization by the public;

(2) the Federal agency finds that the public will be served by the granting of the license, as indicated by the applicant's intentions, plans, and ability to bring the invention to practical application or otherwise promote the invention's utilization by the public, and that the proposed scope of exclusivity is not greater than reasonably necessary to provide the incentive for bringing the invention to practical application, as proposed by the applicant, or otherwise to promote the invention's utilization by the public;

(3) the applicant makes a commitment to achieve practical application of the invention within a reasonable time, which time may be extended by the agency upon the applicant's request and the applicant's demonstration that the refusal of such extension would be unreasonable;

(4) granting the license will not tend to substantially lessen competition or create or maintain a violation of the Federal antitrust laws; and

(5) in the case of an invention covered by a foreign patent application or patent, the interests of the Federal Government or United States industry in foreign commerce will be enhanced.

(b) Manufacture in United States. A Federal agency shall normally grant a license under section 207(a)(2) [35 USC § 207(a)(2)] to use or sell any federally owned invention in the United States only to a licensee who agrees that any products embodying the invention or produced through the use of the invention will be manufactured substantially in the United States.

(c) Small business. First preference for the granting of any exclusive or partially exclusive licenses under section 207(a)(2) [35 USC § 207(a)(2)] shall be given to small business firms having equal or greater likelihood as other applicants to bring the invention to practical application within a reasonable time.

(d) Terms and conditions. Any licenses granted under section 207(a)(2) [35 USC § 207(a)(2)] shall contain such terms and conditions as the granting agency considers appropriate, and shall include provisions—

(1) retaining a ~~nontransferrable~~ nontransferable, irrevocable, paid-up license for any Federal agency to practice the invention or have the invention practiced throughout the world by or on behalf of the Government of the United States;

(2) requiring periodic reporting on utilization of the invention, and utilization efforts,

by the licensee, but only to the extent necessary to enable the Federal agency to determine whether the terms of the license are being complied with, except that any such report shall be treated by the Federal agency as commercial and financial information obtained from a person and privileged and confidential and not subject to disclosure under section 552 of title 5; and

(3) empowering the Federal agency to terminate the license in whole or in part if the agency determines that—

(A) the licensee is not executing its commitment to achieve practical application of the invention, including commitments contained in any plan submitted in support of its request for a license, and the licensee cannot otherwise demonstrate to the satisfaction of the Federal agency that it has taken, or can be expected to take within a reasonable time, effective steps to achieve practical application of the invention;

(B) the licensee is in breach of an agreement described in subsection (b);

(C) termination is necessary to meet requirements for public use specified by Federal regulations issued after the date of the license, and such requirements are not reasonably satisfied by the licensee; or

(D) the licensee has been found by a court of competent jurisdiction to have violated the Federal antitrust laws in connection with its performance under the license agreement.

(e) **Public notice.** No exclusive or partially exclusive license may be granted under section 207(a)(2) [35 USC § 207(a)(2)] unless public notice of the intention to grant an exclusive or partially exclusive license on a federally owned invention has been provided in an appropriate manner at least 15 days before the license is granted, and the Federal agency has considered all comments received before the end of the comment period in response to that public notice. This subsection shall not apply to the licensing of inventions made under a cooperative research and development agreement entered into under section 12 of the Stevenson-Wydler Technology Innovation Act of 1980 (15 U.S.C. 3710a).

(f) **Plan.** No Federal agency shall grant any license under a patent or patent application on a federally owned invention unless the person requesting the license has supplied the agency with a plan for development or marketing of the invention, except that any such plan shall be treated by the Federal agency as commercial and financial information obtained from a person and privileged and confidential and not subject to disclosure under section 552 of title 5.

HISTORY:

(Added Dec. 12, 1980, P.L. 96-517, § 6(a), 94 Stat. 3024; Nov. 1, 2000, P.L. 106-404, § 4(a), 114 Stat. 1743; Nov. 2, 2002, P.L. 107-273, Div C, Title III, Subtitle B, § 13206(15), 116 Stat. 1905.)

(America Invents Act § 20(i)(3).)

§ 210. Precedence of chapter

(a) This chapter [35 USC §§ 200 et seq.] shall take precedence over any other Act which would require a disposition of rights in subject inventions of small business firms or nonprofit organizations contractors in a manner that is inconsistent with this chapter [35 USC §§ 200 et seq.], including but not necessarily limited to the following:

(1) section 10(a) of the Act of June 29, 1935, as added by title I of the Act of August 14, 1946 (7 U.S.C. 427i(a); 60 Stat. 1085);

(2) section 205(a) of the Act of August 14, 1946 (7 U.S.C. 1624(a); 60 Stat. 1090);

(3) section 501(c) of the Federal Mine Safety and Health Act of 1977 (30 U.S.C. 951(c); 83 Stat. 742);

(4) section 30168(e) of title 49;

(5) section 12 of the National Science Foundation Act of 1950 (42 U.S.C. 1871[(a)]; 82 Stat. 360);

(6) section 152 of the Atomic Energy Act of 1954 (42 U.S.C. 2182; 68 Stat. 943);

(7) section 20135 of title 51 [35 USC § 20135];

(8) section 6 of the Coal Research and Development Act of 1960 (30 U.S.C. 666; 74 Stat. 337);

(9) section 4 of the Helium Act Amendments of 1960 (50 U.S.C. 167b; 74 Stat. 920);

(10) section 32 of the Arms Control and Disarmament Act of 1961 (22 U.S.C. 2572; 75 Stat. 634);

(11) section 9 of the Federal Nonnuclear Energy Research and Development Act of 1974 (42 U.S.C. 5908; 88 Stat. 1878);

(12) section 5(d) of the Consumer Product Safety Act (15 U.S.C. 2054(d); 86 Stat. 1211);

(13) section 3 of the Act of April 5, 1944 (30 U.S.C. 323; 58 Stat. 191);

(14) section 8001(c)(3) of the Solid Waste Disposal Act (42 U.S.C. 6981(c); 90 Stat. 2829);

(15) section 219 of the Foreign Assistance Act of 1961 (22 U.S.C. 2179; 83 Stat. 806);

(16) section 427(b) of the Federal Mine Health and Safety Act of 1977 (30 U.S.C. 937(b); 86 Stat. 155);

(17) section 306(d) of the Surface Mining and Reclamation Act of 1977 (30 U.S.C. 1226(d); 91 Stat. 455);

(18) section 21(d) of the Federal Fire Prevention and Control Act of 1974 (15 U.S.C. 2218(d); 88 Stat. 1548);

(19) section 6(b) of the Solar Photovoltaic Energy Research Development and Demonstration Act of 1978 (42 U.S.C. 5585(b); 92 Stat. 2516);

(20) section 12 of the Native Latex Commercialization and Economic Development Act of 1978 (7 U.S.C. 178j; 92 Stat. 2533); and

(21) section 408 of the Water Resources and Development Act of 1978 (42 U.S.C. 7879; 92 Stat. 1360).

The Act creating this chapter shall be construed to take precedence over any future Act unless that Act specifically cites this Act and provides that it shall take precedence over this Act.

(b) Nothing in this chapter [35 USC §§ 200 et seq.] is intended to alter the effect of the laws cited in paragraph (a) of this section or any other laws with respect to the disposition of rights in inventions made in the performance of funding agreements with persons other than nonprofit organizations or small business firms.

(c) Nothing in this chapter [35 USC §§ 200 et seq.] is intended to limit the authority of agencies to agree to the disposition of rights in inventions made in the performance of work under funding agreements with persons other than nonprofit organizations or small business firms in accordance with the Statement of Government Patent Policy issued on February 18, 1983, agency regulations, or other applicable regulations or to otherwise limit the authority of agencies to allow such persons to retain ownership of inventions except that all funding agreements, including those with other than small business firms and nonprofit organizations, shall include the requirements established in section 202(c)(4) [35 USC § 202(c)(4)] and section 203 of this title [35 USC § 203]. Any disposition of rights in inventions made in accordance with the Statement or implementing regulations, including any disposition occurring before enactment of this section, are hereby authorized.

(d) Nothing in this chapter [35 USC §§ 200 et seq.] shall be construed to require the disclosure of intelligence sources or methods or to otherwise affect the authority granted to the Director of Central Intelligence by statute or Executive order for the protection of intelligence sources or methods.

(e) The provisions of the Stevenson-Wydler Technology Innovation Act of 1980 [15 USC §§ 3701 et seq.] shall take precedence over the provisions of this chapter [35 USC §§ 200 et seq.] to the extent that they permit or require a disposition of rights in subject inventions which is inconsistent with this chapter [35 USC §§ 200 et seq.].

HISTORY:

(Added Dec. 12, 1980, P.L. 96-517, § 6(a), 94 Stat. 3026; Nov. 8, 1984, P.L. 98-620, Title V, § 501(13), 98 Stat. 3367; Oct. 20, 1986, P.L. 99-502, § 9(c), 100 Stat. 1796; July 5, 1994, P.L. 103-272, § 5(j), 108 Stat. 1375; March 7, 1996, P.L. 104-113, § 7, 110 Stat. 779; Nov. 13, 1998, P.L. 105-393, Title II, § 220(c)(2), 112 Stat. 3625; Nov. 2, 2002, P.L. 107-273, Div C, Title III, Subtitle B, § 13206(a)(16), 116 Stat. 1905; Aug. 8, 2005, P.L. 109-58, Title X, § 1009(a)(2), 119 Stat. 934; Dec. 18, 2010, P.L. 111-314, § 4(c), 124 Stat. 3440.)

(America Invents Act § 20(j)(1).)

§ 211. Relationship to antitrust laws

Nothing in this chapter [35 USC §§ 200 et seq.] shall be deemed to convey to any person immunity from civil or criminal liability, or to create any defenses to actions, under any antitrust law.

HISTORY:

(Added Dec. 12, 1980, P.L. 96-517, § 6(a), 94 Stat. 3027.)

§ 212. Disposition of rights in educational awards

No scholarship, fellowship, training grant, or other funding agreement made by a Federal agency primarily to an awardee for educational purposes will contain any provision giving the Federal agency any rights to inventions made by the awardee.

HISTORY:

(Added Nov. 8, 1984, P.L. 98-620, Title V, § 501(14), 98 Stat. 3368.)

PART III. PATENTS AND PROTECTION OF PATENT RIGHTS

CHAPTER 25. AMENDMENT AND CORRECTION OF PATENTS

§ 251. Reissue of defective patents

~~Whenever~~ **(a) In general.**—Whenever any patent is, through error ~~without any deceptive intention~~, deemed wholly or partly inoperative or invalid, by reason of a defective specification or drawing, or by reason of the patentee claiming more or less than he had a right to claim in the patent, the Director shall, on the surrender of such patent and the payment of the fee required by law, reissue the patent for the invention disclosed in the original patent, and in accordance with a new and amended application, for the unexpired part of the term of the original patent. No new matter shall be introduced into the application for reissue.

~~The Director~~ **(b) Multiple reissued patents.**—The Director may issue several reissued patents for distinct and separate parts of the thing patented, upon demand of the applicant, and upon payment of the required fee for a reissue for each of such reissued patents.

~~The provisions~~ **(c) Applicability of this title.**—The provisions of this title relating to applications for patent shall be applicable to applications for reissue of a patent, except that application for reissue may be made and sworn to by the assignee of the entire interest if the application does not seek to enlarge the scope of the claims of the original patent or the application for the original patent was filed by the assignee of the entire interest.

~~No reissued patent~~ **(d) Reissue patent enlarging scope of claims.**—No reissued patent shall be granted enlarging the scope of the claims of the original patent unless applied for within two years from the grant of the original patent.

HISTORY:

(July 19, 1952, ch 950, § 1, 66 Stat. 808; Nov. 29, 1999, P.L. 106-113, Div B, § 1000(a)(9), 113 Stat. 1536; Nov. 2, 2002, P.L. 107-273, Div C, Title III, Subtitle B, § 13206(b)(1)(B), 116 Stat. 1906..)

(America Invents Act § 4(b)(2); 20(d)(1)(A)-(B), (2)-(4).)

§ 252. Effect of reissue

The surrender of the original patent shall take effect upon the issue of the reissued patent, and every reissued patent shall have the same effect and operation in law, on the trial of actions for causes thereafter arising, as if the same had been originally granted in such amended form, but in so far as the claims of the original and reissued patents are substantially identical, such surrender shall not affect any action then pending nor abate any cause of action then existing, and the reissued patent, to the extent that its claims are substantially identical with the original patent, shall constitute a continuation thereof and have effect continuously from the date of the original patent.

A reissued patent shall not abridge or affect the right of any person or that person's successors in business who, prior to the grant of a reissue, made, purchased, offered to sell, or used within the United States, or imported into the United States, anything patented by the reissued patent, to continue the use of, to offer to sell, or to sell to others to be used, offered for sale, or sold, the specific thing so made, purchased, offered for sale, used, or imported unless the making, using, offering for sale, or selling of such thing infringes a valid claim of the reissued patent which was in the original patent. The court before which such matter is in question may provide for the continued manufacture, use, offer for sale, or sale of the thing made, purchased, offered for sale, used, or imported as specified, or for the manufacture, use, offer for sale, or sale in the United States of which substantial preparation was made before the grant of the reissue, and the court may also provide for the continued practice of any process patented by the reissue that is practiced, or for the practice of which substantial preparation was made, before the grant of the reissue, to the extent and under such terms as the court deems equitable for the protection of investments made or business commenced before the grant of the reissue.

HISTORY:

(July 19, 1952, ch 950, § 1, 66 Stat. 808; Dec. 8, 1994, P.L. 103-465, Title V, Subtitle C, § 533(b)(2), 108 Stat. 4989; Nov. 29, 1999, P.L. 106-113, Div B, § 1000(a)(9), 113 Stat. 1536.)

§ 253. Disclaimer

~~Whenever, without any deceptive intention,~~ **(a) In general.**—Whenever a claim of a patent is invalid the remaining claims shall not thereby be rendered invalid. A patentee, whether of the whole or any sectional interest therein, may, on payment of the fee required by law, make disclaimer of any complete claim, stating therein the extent of his interest in such patent. Such disclaimer shall be in writing, and recorded in the Patent and Trademark Office; and it shall thereafter be considered as part of the original patent to the extent of the interest possessed by the disclaimant and by those claiming under him.

~~In like manner~~ **(b) Additional disclaimer or dedication.**—In the manner set forth in subsection (a), any patentee or applicant may disclaim or dedicate to the public the entire term, or any terminal part of the term, of the patent granted or to be granted.

HISTORY:

(July 19, 1952, ch 950, § 1, 66 Stat. 809; Jan. 2, 1975, P.L. 93-596, § 1, 88 Stat. 1949.)

(America Invents Act § 20(e)(1)-(2).)

§ 254. Certificate of correction of Patent and Trademark Office mistake

Whenever a mistake in a patent, incurred through the fault of the Patent and Trademark Office, is clearly disclosed by the records of the Office, the Director may issue a certificate of correction stating the fact and nature of such mistake, under seal, without charge, to be recorded in the records of patents. A printed copy thereof shall be attached to each printed copy of the patent, and such certificate shall be considered as part of the original patent. Every such patent, together with such certificate, shall have the same effect and operation in law on the trial of actions for causes thereafter arising as if the same had been originally issued in such corrected form. The Director may issue a corrected patent without charge in lieu of and with like effect as a certificate of correction.

HISTORY:

(July 19, 1952, ch 950, § 1, 66 Stat. 809; Jan. 2, 1975, P.L. 93-596, § 1, 88 Stat. 1949; Nov. 29, 1999, P.L. 106-113, Div B, § 1000(a)(9), 113 Stat. 1536; Nov. 2, 2002, P.L. 107-273, Div C, Title III, Subtitle B, § 13206(b)(1)(B), 116 Stat. 1906.)

§ 255. Certificate of correction of applicant's mistake

Whenever a mistake of a clerical or typographical nature, or of minor character, which was not the fault of the Patent and Trademark Office, appears in a patent and a showing has been made that such mistake occurred in good faith, the Director may, upon payment of the required fee, issue a certificate of correction, if the correction does not involve such changes in the patent as would constitute new matter or would require re-examination. Such patent, together with the certificate, shall have the same effect and operation in law on the trial of actions for causes thereafter arising as if the same had been originally issued in such corrected form.

HISTORY:

(July 19, 1952, ch 950, § 1, 66 Stat. 809; Jan. 2, 1975, P.L. 93-596, § 1, 88 Stat. 1949; Nov. 29, 1999, P.L. 106-113, Div B, § 1000(a)(9), 113 Stat. 1536; Nov. 2, 2002, P.L. 107-273, Div C, Title III, Subtitle B, § 13206(b)(1)(B), 116 Stat. 1906.)

§ 256. Correction of named inventor

~~Whenever~~ **(a) Correction.**—Whenever through error a person is named in an issued patent as the inventor, or through error an inventor is not named in an issued patent ~~and such error arose without any deceptive intention on his part~~, the Director may, on application of all the parties and assignees, with proof of the facts and such other requirements as may be imposed, issue a certificate correcting such error.

~~The error~~ **(b) Patent valid if error corrected.**—The error of omitting inventors or naming persons who are not inventors shall not invalidate the patent in which such error occurred if it can be corrected as provided in this section. The court before which such matter is called in question may order correction of the patent on notice and hearing of all parties concerned and the Director shall issue a certificate accordingly.

HISTORY:

(July 19, 1952, ch 950, § 1, 66 Stat. 810; Aug. 27, 1982, P.L. 97-247, § 6(b), 96 Stat. 320; Nov. 29, 1999, P.L. 106-113, Div B, § 1000(a)(9), 113 Stat. 1536; Nov. 2, 2002, P.L. 107-273, Div C, Title III, Subtitle B, § 13206(b)(1)(B), 116 Stat. 1906.)

(America Invents Act § 20(f)(1)(A)-(B), (2).)

§ 257. Supplemental examinations to consider, reconsider, or correct information

(a) Request for supplemental examination.—A patent owner may request supplemental examination of a patent in the Office to consider, reconsider, or correct information believed to be relevant to the patent, in accordance with such requirements as the Director may establish. Within 3 months after the date a request for supplemental examination meeting the requirements of this section is received, the Director shall conduct the supplemental examination and shall conclude such examination by issuing a certificate indicating whether the information presented in the request raises a substantial new question of patentability.

(b) Reexamination Ordered.—If the certificate issued under subsection (a) indicates that a substantial new question of patentability is raised by 1 or more items of information in the request, the Director shall order reexamination of the patent. The reexamination shall be conducted according to procedures established by chapter 30, except that the patent owner shall not have the right to file a statement pursuant to section 304. During the reexamination, the Director shall address each substantial new question of patentability identified during the supplemental examination, notwithstanding the limitations in chapter 30 relating to patents and printed publication or any other provision of such chapter.

(c) Effect.—

(1) In general.—A patent shall not be held unenforceable on the basis of conduct relating to information that had not been considered, was inadequately considered, or was incorrect in a prior examination of the patent if the information was considered, reconsidered, or corrected during a supplemental examination of the patent. The making of a request under subsection (a), or the absence thereof, shall not be relevant to enforceability of the patent under section 282.

(2) Exceptions.—

(A) Prior allegations.—Paragraph (1) shall not apply to an allegation pled with particularity in a civil action, or set forth with particularity in a notice received by the patent owner under section 505(j)(2)(B)(iv)(II) of the Federal Food, Drug, and Cosmetic Act (21 U.S.C. 355(j)(2)(B)(iv)(II)), before the date of a supplemental examination request under subsection (a) to consider, reconsider, or correct information forming the basis for the allegation.

(B) Patent enforcement actions.—In an action brought under section 337(a) of the Tariff Act of 1930 (19 U.S.C. 1337(a)), or section 281 of this title, paragraph (1) shall not apply to any defense raised in the action that is based upon information that was considered, reconsidered, or corrected pursuant to a supplemental examination request under subsection (a), unless the supplemental examination, and any reexamination ordered pursuant to the request, are concluded before the date on which the action is brought.

(d) Fees and Regulations.—

(1) Fees.—The Director shall, by regulation, establish fees for the submission of a request for supplemental examination of a patent, and to consider each item of information submitted in the request. If reexamination is ordered under subsection (b), fees established and applicable to ex parte reexamination proceedings under chapter 30 shall be paid, in addition to fees applicable to supplemental examination.

(2) Regulations.—The Director shall issue regulations governing the form, content, and other requirements of requests for supplemental examination, and establishing procedures for reviewing information submitted in such requests.

(e) Fraud.—If the Director becomes aware, during the course of a supplemental examination or reexamination proceeding ordered under this section, that a material fraud on the Office may have been committed in connection with the patent that is the subject of the supplemental examination, then in addition to any other actions the Director is authorized to take, including the cancellation of any claims found to be invalid under section 307 as a result of a reexamination ordered under this section, the Director shall also refer the matter

35 USC § 257

to the Attorney General for such further action as the Attorney General may deem appropriate. Any such referral shall be treated as confidential, shall not be included in the file of the patent, and shall not be disclosed to the public unless the United States charges a person with a criminal offense in connection with such referral.

(f) Rule of construction.—Nothing in this section shall be construed—

(1) to preclude the imposition of sanctions based upon criminal or antitrust laws (including section 1001(a) of title 18, the first section of the Clayton Act, and section 5 of the Federal Trade Commission Act to the extent that section relates to unfair methods of competition);

(2) to limit the authority of the Director to investigate issues of possible misconduct and impose sanctions for misconduct in connection with matters or proceedings before the Office; or

(3) to limit the authority of the Director to issue regulations under chapter 3 relating to sanctions for misconduct by representatives practicing before the Office.

HISTORY:

(America Invents Act § 12(a).)

CHAPTER 26. OWNERSHIP AND ASSIGNMENT

§ 261. Ownership; assignment

Subject to the provisions of this title [35 USC §§ 1 et seq.], patents shall have the attributes of personal property.

Applications for patent, patents, or any interest therein, shall be assignable in law by an instrument in writing. The applicant, patentee, or his assigns or legal representatives may in like manner grant and convey an exclusive right under his application for patent, or patents, to the whole or any specified part of the United States.

A certificate of acknowledgment under the hand and official seal of a person authorized to administer oaths within the United States, or, in a foreign country, of a diplomatic or consular officer of the United States or an officer authorized to administer oaths whose authority is proved by a certificate of a diplomatic or consular officer of the United States, or apostille of an official designated by a foreign country which, by treaty or convention, accords like effect to apostilles of designated officials in the United States, shall be prima facie evidence of the execution of an assignment, grant or conveyance of a patent or application for patent.

An assignment, grant or conveyance shall be void as against any subsequent purchaser or mortgagee for a valuable consideration, without notice, unless it is recorded in the Patent and Trademark Office within three months from its date or prior to the date of such subsequent purchase or mortgage.

HISTORY:

(July 19, 1952, ch 950, § 1, 66 Stat. 810; Jan. 2, 1975, P.L. 93-596, § 1, 88 Stat. 1949; Aug. 27, 1982, P.L. 97-247, § 14(b), 96 Stat. 321.)

§ 262. Joint owners

In the absence of any agreement to the contrary, each of the joint owners of a patent may make, use, offer to sell, or sell the patented invention within the United States, or import the patented invention into the United States, without the consent of and without accounting to the other owners.

HISTORY:

(July 19, 1952, ch 950, § 1, 66 Stat. 810; Dec. 8, 1994, P.L. 103-465, Title V, Subtitle C, § 533(b)(3), 108 Stat. 4989.)

[§ 266. Repealed]

§ 267. Time for taking action in Government applications

Notwithstanding the provisions of sections 133 and 151 ~~of this title~~ [35 USC §§ 133 and 151], the Director may extend the time for taking any action to three years, when an application has become the property of the United States and the head of the appropriate department or agency of the Government has certified to the Director that the invention disclosed therein is important to the armament or defense of the United States.

HISTORY:

(July 19, 1952, ch 950, § 1, 66 Stat. 811; Nov. 29, 1999, P.L. 106-113, Div B, § 1000(a)(9), 113 Stat. 1536; Nov. 2, 2002, P.L. 107-273, Div C, Title III, Subtitle B, § 13206(b)(1)(B), 116 Stat. 1906.)

(America Invents Act § 20(j)(1).)

§ 271. Infringement of patent

(a) Except as otherwise provided in this title [35 USC §§ 1 et seq.], whoever without authority makes, uses, offers to sell, or sells any patented invention, within the United States or imports into the United States any patented invention during the term of the patent therefor, infringes the patent.

(b) Whoever actively induces infringement of a patent shall be liable as an infringer.

(c) Whoever offers to sell or sells within the United States or imports into the United States a component of a patented machine, manufacture, combination or composition, or a material or apparatus for use in practicing a patented process, constituting a material part of the invention, knowing the same to be especially made or especially adapted for use in an infringement of such patent, and not a staple article or commodity of commerce suitable for substantial noninfringing use, shall be liable as a contributory infringer.

(d) No patent owner otherwise entitled to relief for infringement or contributory infringement of a patent shall be denied relief or deemed guilty of misuse or illegal extension of the patent right by reason of his having done one or more of the following: (1) derived revenue from acts which if performed by another without his consent would constitute contributory infringement of the patent; (2) licensed or authorized another to perform acts which if performed without his consent would constitute contributory infringement of the patent; (3) sought to enforce his patent rights against infringement or contributory infringement; (4) refused to license or use any rights to the patent; or (5) conditioned the license of any rights to the patent or the sale of the patented product on the acquisition of a license to rights in another patent or purchase of a separate product, unless, in view of the circumstances, the patent owner has market power in the relevant market for the patent or patented product on which the license or sale is conditioned.

(e)(1) It shall not be an act of infringement to make, use, offer to sell, or sell within the United States or import into the United States a patented invention (other than a new animal drug or veterinary biological product (as those terms are used in the Federal Food, Drug, and Cosmetic Act and the Act of March 4, 1913) which is primarily manufactured using recombinant DNA, recombinant RNA, hybridoma technology, or other processes involving site specific genetic manipulation techniques) solely for uses reasonably related to the development and submission of information under a Federal law which regulates the manufacture, use, or sale of drugs or veterinary biological products.

(2) It shall be an act of infringement to submit—

(A) an application under section 505(j) of the Federal Food, Drug, and Cosmetic Act [21 USC § 355(j)] or described in section 505(b)(2) of such Act [21 USC § 355(b)(2)] for a drug claimed in a patent or the use of which is claimed in a patent,

(B) an application under section 512 of such Act [21 USC § 360b] or under the Act of March 4, 1913 (21 U.S.C. 151-158) for a drug or veterinary biological product which is not primarily manufactured using recombinant DNA, recombinant RNA, hybridoma technology, or other processes involving site specific genetic manipulation techniques and which is claimed in a patent or the use of which is claimed in a patent, or

(C)(i) with respect to a patent that is identified in the list of patents described in section 351(l)(3) of the Public Health Service Act [42 USC § 262(l)(3)] (including as provided under section 351(l)(7) of such Act [42 USC § 262(l)(7)]), an application seeking approval of a biological product, or

(ii) if the applicant for the application fails to provide the application and information required under section 351(l)(2)(A) of such Act [42 USC § 262(l)(2)(A)], an application seeking approval of a biological product for a patent that could be identified pursuant to section 351(l)(3)(A)(i) of such Act [42 USC § 262(l)(3)(A)(i)],

if the purpose of such submission is to obtain approval under such Act to engage in the commercial manufacture, use, or sale of a drug, veterinary biological product, or biological product claimed in a patent or the use of which is claimed in a patent before the expiration of such patent.

(3) In any action for patent infringement brought under this section, no injunctive or other relief may be granted which would prohibit the making, using, offering to sell, or selling within the United States or importing into the United States of a patented invention under paragraph (1).

(4) For an act of infringement described in paragraph (2)—

(A) the court shall order the effective date of any approval of the drug or veterinary biological product involved in the infringement to be a date which is not earlier than the date of the expiration of the patent which has been infringed,

(B) injunctive relief may be granted against an infringer to prevent the commercial manufacture, use, offer to sell, or sale within the United States or importation into the United States of an approved drug, veterinary biological product, or biological product,

(C) damages or other monetary relief may be awarded against an infringer only if there has been commercial manufacture, use, offer to sell, or sale within the United States or importation into the United States of an approved drug, veterinary biological product, or biological product, and

(D) the court shall order a permanent injunction prohibiting any infringement of the patent by the biological product involved in the infringement until a date which is not earlier than the date of the expiration of the patent that has been infringed under paragraph (2) (C), provided the patent is the subject of a final court decision, as defined in section 351(k) (6) of the Public Health Service Act [42 USC § 262(k)(6)], in an action for infringement of the patent under section 351(l)(6) of such Act [42 USC § 262(l)(6)], and the biological product has not yet been approved because of section 351(k)(7) of such Act [42 USC § 262(k)(7)].

The remedies prescribed by subparagraphs (A), (B), (C), and (D) are the only remedies which may be granted by a court for an act of infringement described in paragraph (2), except that a court may award attorney fees under section 285 [35 USC § 285].

(5) Where a person has filed an application described in paragraph (2) that includes a certification under subsection (b)(2)(A)(iv) or (j)(2)(A)(vii)(IV) of section 505 of the Federal Food, Drug, and Cosmetic Act (21 U.S.C. 355), and neither the owner of the patent that is the subject of the certification nor the holder of the approved application under subsection (b) of such section for the drug that is claimed by the patent or a use of which is claimed by the patent brought an action for infringement of such patent before the expiration of 45 days after the date on which the notice given under subsection (b)(3) or (j)(2)(B) of such section was received, the courts of the United States shall, to the extent consistent with the Constitution, have subject matter jurisdiction in any action brought by such person under section 2201 of title 28 for a declaratory judgment that such patent is invalid or not infringed.

(6)(A) Subparagraph (B) applies, in lieu of paragraph (4), in the case of a patent—

(i) that is identified, as applicable, in the list of patents described in section 351(l)(4) of the Public Health Service Act [42 USC § 262(l)(4)] or the lists of patents described in section 351(l)(5)(B) of such Act [42 USC § 262(l)(5)(B)] with respect to a biological product; and

(ii) for which an action for infringement of the patent with respect to the biological product—

(I) was brought after the expiration of the 30-day period described in subparagraph (A) or (B), as applicable, of section 351(l)(6) of such Act [42 USC § 262(l)(6)]; or

(II) was brought before the expiration of the 30-day period described in subclause (I), but which was dismissed without prejudice or was not prosecuted to judgment in good faith.

(B) In an action for infringement of a patent described in subparagraph (A), the sole and exclusive remedy that may be granted by a court, upon a finding that the making, using, offering to sell, selling, or importation into the United States of the biological product that is the subject of the action infringed the patent, shall be a reasonable royalty.

(C) The owner of a patent that should have been included in the list described in section 351(l)(3)(A) of the Public Health Service Act [42 USC § 262(l)(3)(A)], including as provided under section 351(l)(7) of such Act [42 USC § 262(l)(7)] for a biological product, but was not timely included in such list, may not bring an action under this section for infringement of the patent with respect to the biological product.

(f)(1) Whoever without authority supplies or causes to be supplied in or from the United States all or a substantial portion of the components of a patented invention, where such components are uncombined in whole or in part, in such manner as to actively induce the combination of such components outside of the United States in a manner that would infringe the patent if such combination occurred within the United States, shall be liable as an infringer.

(2) Whoever without authority supplies or causes to be supplied in or from the United States any component of a patented invention that is especially made or especially adapted for use in the invention and not a staple article or commodity of commerce suitable for substantial noninfringing use, where such component is uncombined in whole or in part, knowing that such component is so made or adapted and intending that such component will be combined outside of the United States in a manner that would infringe the patent if such combination occurred within the United States, shall be liable as an infringer.

(g) Whoever without authority imports into the United States or offers to sell, sells, or uses within the United States a product which is made by a process patented in the United States shall be liable as an infringer, if the importation, offer to sell, sale, or use of the product occurs during the term of such process patent. In an action for infringement of a process patent, no remedy may be granted for infringement on account of the noncommercial use or retail sale of a product unless there is no adequate remedy under this title for infringement on account of the importation or other use, offer to sell, or sale of that product. A product which is made by a patented process will, for purposes of this title, not be considered to be so made after—

(1) it is materially changed by subsequent processes; or

(2) it becomes a trivial and nonessential component of another product.

(h) As used in this section, the term "whoever" includes any State, any instrumentality of a State, and any officer or employee of a State or instrumentality of a State acting in his official capacity. Any State, and any such instrumentality, officer, or employee, shall be subject to the provisions of this title in the same manner and to the same extent as any nongovernmental entity.

(i) As used in this section, an "offer for sale" or an "offer to sell" by a person other than the patentee, or any designee of the patentee, is that in which the sale will occur before the expiration of the term of the patent.

HISTORY:

(July 19, 1952, ch 950, § 1, 66 Stat. 811; Sept. 24, 1984, P.L. 98-417, Title II, § 202, 98 Stat. 1603; Nov. 8, 1984, P.L. 98-622, Title I, § 101(a), 98 Stat. 3383; Aug. 23, 1988, P.L. 100-418, Title IX, Subtitle A, § 9003, 102 Stat. 1564; Nov. 16, 1988, P.L. 100-670, Title II, § 201(i), 102 Stat. 3988; Nov. 19, 1988, P.L. 100-703, Title II, § 201, 102 Stat. 4676; Oct. 28, 1992, P.L. 102-560, § 2(a)(1), 106 Stat. 4230; Dec. 8, 1994, P.L. 103-465, Title V, Subtitle C, § 533(a), 108 Stat. 4988; Dec. 8, 2003, P.L. 108-173, Title XI, Subtitle A, § 1101(d), 117 Stat. 2457; March 23, 2010, P.L. 111-148, Title VII, Subtitle A, § 7002(c)(1), 124 Stat. 815.)

§ 272. Temporary presence in the United States

The use of any invention in any vessel, aircraft or vehicle of any country which affords similar privileges to vessels, aircraft or vehicles of the United States, entering the United States temporarily or accidentally, shall not constitute infringement of any patent, if the invention is used exclusively for the needs of the vessel, aircraft or vehicle and is not offered for sale or sold in or used for the manufacture of anything to be sold in or exported from the United States.

HISTORY:

(July 19, 1952, ch 950, § 1, 66 Stat. 812; Dec. 8, 1994, P.L. 103-465, Title V, Subtitle C, § 533(b)(4), 108 Stat. 4989.)

§ 273. Defense to infringement based on earlier inventor

(a) Definitions. For purposes of this section—

(1) the terms "commercially used" and "commercial use" mean use of a method in the United States, so long as such use is in connection with an internal commercial use or an actual arm's-length sale or other arm's-length commercial transfer of a useful end result, whether or not the subject matter at issue is accessible to or otherwise known to the public, except that the subject matter for which commercial marketing or use is subject to a premarketing regulatory review period during which the safety or efficacy of the subject matter is established, including any period specified in section 156(g) [35 USC § 156(g)], shall be deemed "commercially used" and in "commercial use" during such regulatory review period;

(2) in the case of activities performed by a nonprofit research laboratory, or nonprofit entity such as a university, research center, or hospital, a use for which the public is the

intended beneficiary shall be considered to be a use described in paragraph (1), except that the use—

(A) may be asserted as a defense under this section only for continued use by and in the laboratory or nonprofit entity; and

(B) may not be asserted as a defense with respect to any subsequent commercialization or use outside such laboratory or nonprofit entity;

(3) the term "method" means a method of doing or conducting business; and

(4) the "effective filing date" of a patent is the earlier of the actual filing date of the application for the patent or the filing date of any earlier United States, foreign, or international application to which the subject matter at issue is entitled under section 119, 120, or 365 of this title [35 USC § 119, 120, or 365].

(b) Defense to infringement.

(1) In general. It shall be a defense to an action for infringement under section 271 of this title [35 USC § 271] with respect to any subject matter that would otherwise infringe one or more claims for a method in the patent being asserted against a person, if such person had, acting in good faith, actually reduced the subject matter to practice at least 1 year before the effective filing date of such patent, and commercially used the subject matter before the effective filing date of such patent.

(2) Exhaustion of right. The sale or other disposition of a useful end product produced by a patented method, by a person entitled to assert a defense under this section with respect to that useful end result shall exhaust the patent owner's rights under the patent to the extent such rights would have been exhausted had such sale or other disposition been made by the patent owner.

(3) Limitations and qualifications of defense. The defense to infringement under this section is subject to the following:

(A) **Patent.** A person may not assert the defense under this section unless the invention for which the defense is asserted is for a method.

(B) **Derivation.** A person may not assert the defense under this section if the subject matter on which the defense is based was derived from the patentee or persons in privity with the patentee.

(C) **Not a general license.** The defense asserted by a person under this section is not a general license under all claims of the patent at issue, but extends only to the specific subject matter claimed in the patent with respect to which the person can assert a defense under this chapter, except that the defense shall also extend to variations in the quantity or volume of use of the claimed subject matter, and to improvements in the claimed subject matter that do not infringe additional specifically claimed subject matter of the patent.

(4) Burden of proof. A person asserting the defense under this section shall have the burden of establishing the defense by clear and convincing evidence.

(5) Abandonment of use. A person who has abandoned commercial use of subject matter may not rely on activities performed before the date of such abandonment in establishing a defense under this section with respect to actions taken after the date of such abandonment.

(6) Personal defense. The defense under this section may be asserted only by the person who performed the acts necessary to establish the defense and, except for any transfer to the patent owner, the right to assert the defense shall not be licensed or assigned or transferred to another person except as an ancillary and subordinate part of a good faith assignment or transfer for other reasons of the entire enterprise or line of business to which the defense relates.

(7) Limitation on sites. A defense under this section, when acquired as part of a good faith assignment or transfer of an entire enterprise or line of business to which the defense relates, may only be asserted for uses at sites where the subject matter that would otherwise infringe one or more of the claims is in use before the later of the effective filing date of the patent or the date of the assignment or transfer of such enterprise or line of business.

(8) Unsuccessful assertion of defense. If the defense under this section is pleaded by a person who is found to infringe the patent and who subsequently fails to demonstrate a reasonable basis for asserting the defense, the court shall find the case exceptional for the purpose of awarding attorney fees under section 285 of this title [35 USC § 285].

(9) Invalidity. A patent shall not be deemed to be invalid under section 102 or 103 of this title [35 USC § 102 or 103] solely because a defense is raised or established under this section.

§ 273. Defense to infringement based on prior commercial use

(a) In general.—A person shall be entitled to a defense under section 282(b) with respect to subject matter consisting of a process, or consisting of a machine, manufacture, or composition of matter used in a manufacturing or other commercial process, that would otherwise infringe a claimed invention being asserted against the person if—

(1) such person, acting in good faith, commercially used the subject matter in the United States, either in connection with an internal commercial use or an actual arm's length sale or other arm's length commercial transfer of a useful end result of such commercial use; and

(2) such commercial use occurred at least 1 year before the earlier of either—

(A) the effective filing date of the claimed invention; or

(B) the date on which the claimed invention was disclosed to the public in a manner that qualified for the exception from prior art under section 102(b).

(b) Burden of proof.—A person asserting a defense under this section shall have the burden of establishing the defense by clear and convincing evidence.

(c) Additional commercial uses.—

(1) Premarketing regulatory review.—Subject matter for which commercial marketing or use is subject to a premarketing regulatory review period during which the safety or efficacy of the subject matter is established, including any period specified in section 156(g), shall be deemed to be commercially used for purposes of subsection (a)(1) during such regulatory review period.

(2) Nonprofit laboratory use.—A use of subject matter by a nonprofit research laboratory or other nonprofit entity, such as a university or hospital, for which the public is the intended beneficiary, shall be deemed to be a commercial use for purposes of subsection (a)(1), except that a defense under this section may be asserted pursuant to this paragraph only for continued and noncommercial use by and in the laboratory or other nonprofit entity.

(d) Exhaustion of rights.—Notwithstanding subsection (e)(1), the sale or other disposition of a useful end result by a person entitled to assert a defense under this section in connection with a patent with respect to that useful end result shall exhaust the patent owner's rights under the patent to the extent that such rights would have been exhausted had such sale or other disposition been made by the patent owner.

(e) Limitations and Exceptions.—

(1) Personal defense.—

(A) In general.—A defense under this section may be asserted only by the person who performed or directed the performance of the commercial use described in subsection (a), or by an entity that controls, is controlled by, or is under common control with such person.

(B) Transfer of right.—Except for any transfer to the patent owner, the right to assert a defense under this section shall not be licensed or assigned or transferred to another person except as an ancillary and subordinate part of a good-faith assignment or transfer for other reasons of the entire enterprise or line of business to which the defense relates.

(C) Restriction on sites.—A defense under this section, when acquired by a person as part of an assignment or transfer described in subparagraph (B), may only be asserted for uses at sites where the subject matter that would otherwise infringe a claimed invention is in use before the later of the effective filing date of the claimed invention or the date of the assignment or transfer of such enterprise or line of business.

(2) Derivation.—A person may not assert a defense under this section if the subject matter on which the defense is based was derived from the patentee or persons in privity with the patentee.

(3) Not a general license.—The defense asserted by a person under this section is not a general license under all claims of the patent at issue, but extends only to the specific subject matter for which it has been established that a commercial use that qualifies under this section occurred, except that the defense shall also extend to variations in the quantity or volume of use of the claimed subject matter, and to improvements in the claimed subject matter that do not infringe additional specifically claimed subject matter of the patent.

(4) Abandonment of use.—A person who has abandoned commercial use (that qualifies under this section) of subject matter may not rely on activities performed before the date of such abandonment in establishing a defense under this section with respect to actions taken on or after the date of such abandonment.

(5) University exception.—

(A) In general.—A person commercially using subject matter to which subsection (a) applies may not assert a defense under this section if the claimed invention with respect to which the defense is asserted was, at the time the invention was made, owned or subject to an obligation of assignment to either an institution of higher education (as defined in section 101(a) of the Higher Education Act of 1965 (20 U.S.C. 1001(a)), or a technology transfer organization whose primary purpose is to facilitate the commercialization of technologies developed by one or more such institutions of higher education.

(B) Exception.—Subparagraph (A) shall not apply if any of the activities required to reduce to practice the subject matter of the claimed invention could not have been undertaken using funds provided by the Federal Government.

(f) Unreasonable assertion of defense.—If the defense under this section is pleaded by a person who is found to infringe the patent and who subsequently fails to demonstrate a reasonable basis for asserting the defense, the court shall find the case exceptional for the purpose of awarding attorney fees under section 285.

(g) Invalidity.—A patent shall not be deemed to be invalid under section 102 or 103 solely because a defense is raised or established under this section.

HISTORY:

(Nov. 29, 1999, P.L. 106-113, Div B, § 1000(a)(9), 113 Stat. 1536.)

(America Invents Act § 5(a))

CHAPTER 29. REMEDIES FOR INFRINGEMENT OF PATENT, AND OTHER ACTIONS

§ 281. Remedy for infringement of patent

A patentee shall have remedy by civil action for infringement of his patent.

HISTORY:

(July 19, 1952, ch 950, § 1, 66 Stat. 812.)

35 USC § 282

§ 282. Presumption of validity; defenses

~~A patent~~ (a) In general.—A patent shall be presumed valid. Each claim of a patent (whether in independent, dependent, or multiple dependent form) shall be presumed valid independently of the validity of other claims; dependent or multiple dependent claims shall be presumed valid even though dependent upon an invalid claim. ~~Notwithstanding the preceding sentence, if a claim to a composition of matter is held invalid and that claim was the basis of a determination of nonobviousness under section 103(b)(1) [35 USC § 103(b)(1)], the process shall no longer be considered nonobvious solely on the basis of section 103(b)(1) [35 USC § 103(b)(1)].~~ The burden of establishing invalidity of a patent or any claim thereof shall rest on the party asserting such invalidity.

~~The following~~ (b) Defenses.—The following shall be defenses in any action involving the validity or infringement of a patent and shall be pleaded:

(1) Noninfringement, absence of liability for infringement or ~~unenforceability,~~ unenforceability.

(2) Invalidity of the patent or any claim in suit on any ground specified in part II ~~of this title~~ [35 USC §§ 100 et seq.] as a condition for ~~patentability,~~ patentability.

~~(3) Invalidity of the patent or any claim in suit for failure to comply with any requirement of sections 112 or 251 of this title [35 USC §§ 112 or 251].~~

(3) Invalidity of the patent or any claim in suit for failure to comply with—

(A) any requirement of section 112, except that the failure to disclose the best mode shall not be a basis on which any claim of a patent may be canceled or held invalid or otherwise unenforceable; or

(B) any requirement of section 251.

(4) Any other fact or act made a defense by this title.

~~In actions involving the validity or infringement of a patent~~ (c) Notice of actions; actions during extension of patent term.—In an action involving the validity or infringement of a patent the party asserting invalidity or noninfringement shall give notice in the pleadings or otherwise in writing to the adverse party at least thirty days before the trial, of the country, number, date, and name of the patentee of any patent, the title, date, and page numbers of any publication to be relied upon as anticipation of the patent in suit or, except in actions in the United States ~~Claims Court~~ Court of Federal Claims, as showing the state of the art, and the name and address of any person who may be relied upon as the prior inventor or as having prior knowledge of or as having previously used or offered for sale the invention of the patent in suit. In the absence of such notice proof of the said matters may not be made at the trial except on such terms as the court requires. Invalidity of the extension of a patent term or any portion thereof under section 154(b) or 156 ~~of this title~~ [35 USC § 154(b) or 156] because of the material failure—

(1) by the applicant for the extension, or

(2) by the Director,

to comply with the requirements of such section shall be a defense in any action involving the infringement of a patent during the period of the extension of its term and shall be pleaded. A due diligence determination under section 156(d)(2) [35 USC § 156(d)(2)] is not subject to review in such an action.

HISTORY:

(July 19, 1952, ch 950, § 1, 66 Stat. 812; July 24, 1965, P.L. 89-83, § 10, 79 Stat. 261; Nov. 14, 1975, P.L. 94-131, § 10, 89 Stat. 692; April 2, 1982, P.L. 97-164, Title I, Part B, § 161 (7), 96 Stat. 49; Sept. 24, 1984, P.L. 98-417, Title II, § 203, 98 Stat. 1603; Nov. 1, 1995, P.L. 104-41, § 2, 109 Stat. 352; Nov. 29, 1999, P.L. 106-

113, Div B, § 1000(a)(9), 113 Stat. 1536; Nov. 2, 2002, P.L. 107-273, Div C, Title III, Subtitle B, § 13206(b)(1)(B), (4), 116 Stat. 1906.)

(America Invents Act §§ 15(a); 20(g)(1)(A)-(B), (2)(A)-(C), (3)(A)-(B),(j)(1).)

§ 283. Injunction

The several courts having jurisdiction of cases under this title [35 USC §§ 1 et seq.] may grant injunctions in accordance with the principles of equity to prevent the violation of any right secured by patent, on such terms as the court deems reasonable.

HISTORY:

(July 19, 1952, ch 950, § 1, 66 Stat. 812.)

§ 284. Damages

Upon finding for the claimant the court shall award the claimant damages adequate to compensate for the infringement, but in no event less than a reasonable royalty for the use made of the invention by the infringer, together with interest and costs as fixed by the court.

When the damages are not found by a jury, the court shall assess them. In either event the court may increase the damages up to three times the amount found or assessed. Increased damages under this paragraph shall not apply to provisional rights under section 154(d) ~~of this title~~ [35 USC § 154(d)].

The court may receive expert testimony as an aid to the determination of damages or of what royalty would be reasonable under the circumstances.

HISTORY:

(July 19, 1952, ch 950, § 1, 66 Stat. 813; Nov. 29, 1999, P.L. 106-113, Div B, § 1000(a)(9), 113 Stat. 1536.)

(America Invents Act § 20(j)(1).)

§ 285. Attorney fees

The court in exceptional cases may award reasonable attorney fees to the prevailing party.

HISTORY:

(July 19, 1952, ch 950, § 1, 66 Stat. 813.)

§ 286. Time limitation on damages

Except as otherwise provided by law, no recovery shall be had for any infringement committed more than six years prior to the filing of the complaint or counterclaim for infringement in the action.

In the case of claims against the United States Government for use of a patented invention, the period before bringing suit, up to six years, between the date of receipt of a written claim for compensation by the department or agency of the Government having authority to settle such claim, and the date of mailing by the Government of a notice to the claimant that his claim has been denied shall not be counted as part of the period referred to in the preceding paragraph.

HISTORY:

(July 19, 1952, ch 950, § 1, 66 Stat. 813.)

§ 287. Limitation on damages and other remedies; marking and notice

(a) Patentees, and persons making, offering for sale, or selling within the United States any patented article for or under them, or importing any patented article into the United States, may give notice to the public that the same is patented, either by fixing thereon the word "patent" or the abbreviation "pat.", together with the number of the patent, ~~or when,~~ or by fixing thereon the word "patent" or the abbreviation "pat." together with an address of

35 USC § 287

a posting on the Internet, accessible to the public without charge for accessing the address, that associates the patented article with the number of the patent, or when, from the character of the article, this can not be done, by fixing to it, or to the package wherein one or more of them is contained, a label containing a like notice. In the event of failure so to mark, no damages shall be recovered by the patentee in any action for infringement, except on proof that the infringer was notified of the infringement and continued to infringe thereafter, in which event damages may be recovered only for infringement occurring after such notice. Filing of an action for infringement shall constitute such notice.

(b)(1) An infringer under section 271(g) [35 USC § 271(g)] shall be subject to all the provisions of this title relating to damages and injunctions except to the extent those remedies are modified by this subsection or section 9006 of the Process Patent Amendments Act of 1988 [35 USC § 271 note]. The modifications of remedies provided in this subsection shall not be available to any person who—

(A) practiced the patented process;

(B) owns or controls, or is owned or controlled by, the person who practiced the patented process; or

(C) had knowledge before the infringement that a patented process was used to make the product the importation, use, offer for sale, or sale of which constitutes the infringement.

(2) No remedies for infringement under section 271(g) ~~of this title~~ [35 USC § 271(g)] shall be available with respect to any product in the possession of, or in transit to, the person subject to liability under such section before that person had notice of infringement with respect to that product. The person subject to liability shall bear the burden of proving any such possession or transit.

(3)(A) In making a determination with respect to the remedy in an action brought for infringement under section 271(g) [35 USC § 271(g)], the court shall consider—

(i) the good faith demonstrated by the defendant with respect to a request for disclosure,

(ii) the good faith demonstrated by the plaintiff with respect to a request for disclosure, and

(iii) the need to restore the exclusive rights secured by the patent.

(B) For purposes of subparagraph (A), the following are evidence of good faith:

(i) a request for disclosure made by the defendant;

(ii) a response within a reasonable time by the person receiving the request for disclosure; and

(iii) the submission of the response by the defendant to the manufacturer, or if the manufacturer is not known, to the supplier, of the product to be purchased by the defendant, together with a request for a written statement that the process claimed in any patent disclosed in the response is not used to produce such product.

The failure to perform any acts described in the preceding sentence is evidence of absence of good faith unless there are mitigating circumstances. Mitigating circumstances include the case in which, due to the nature of the product, the number of sources for the product, or like commercial circumstances, a request for disclosure is not necessary or practicable to avoid infringement.

(4)(A) For purposes of this subsection, a "request for disclosure" means a written request made to a person then engaged in the manufacture of a product to identify all process patents owned by or licensed to that person, as of the time of the request, that the person then reasonably believes could be asserted to be infringed under section 271(g) [35 USC § 271(g)] if that product were imported into, or sold, offered for sale, or used in, the United States by an unauthorized person. A request for disclosure is further limited to a request—

(i) which is made by a person regularly engaged in the United States in the sale of the same type of products as those manufactured by the person to whom the request is directed, or which includes facts showing that the person making the request plans to engage in the sale of such products in the United States;

(ii) which is made by such person before the person's first importation, use, offer for sale, or sale of units of the product produced by an infringing process and before the person had notice of infringement with respect to the product; and

(iii) which includes a representation by the person making the request that such person will promptly submit the patents identified pursuant to the request to the manufacturer, or if the manufacturer is not known, to the supplier, of the product to be purchased by the person making the request, and will request from that manufacturer or supplier a written statement that none of the processes claimed in those patents is used in the manufacture of the product.

(B) In the case of a request for disclosure received by a person to whom a patent is licensed, that person shall either identify the patent or promptly notify the licensor of the request for disclosure.

(C) A person who has marked, in the manner prescribed by subsection (a), the number of the process patent on all products made by the patented process which have been offered for sale or sold by that person in the United States, or imported by the person into the United States, before a request for disclosure is received is not required to respond to the request for disclosure. For purposes of the preceding sentence, the term "all products" does not include products made before the effective date of the Process Patent Amendments Act of 1988.

(5)(A) For purposes of this subsection, notice of infringement means actual knowledge, or receipt by a person of a written notification, or a combination thereof, of information sufficient to persuade a reasonable person that it is likely that a product was made by a process patented in the United States.

(B) A written notification from the patent holder charging a person with infringement shall specify the patented process alleged to have been used and the reasons for a good faith belief that such process was used. The patent holder shall include in the notification such information as is reasonably necessary to explain fairly the patent holder's belief, except that the patent holder is not required to disclose any trade secret information.

(C) A person who receives a written notification described in subparagraph (B) or a written response to a request for disclosure described in paragraph (4) shall be deemed to have notice of infringement with respect to any patent referred to in such written notification or response unless that person, absent mitigating circumstances—

(i) promptly transmits the written notification or response to the manufacturer or, if the manufacturer is not known, to the supplier, of the product purchased or to be purchased by that person; and

(ii) receives a written statement from the manufacturer or supplier which on its face sets forth a well grounded factual basis for a belief that the identified patents are not infringed.

(D) For purposes of this subsection, a person who obtains a product made by a process patented in the United States in a quantity which is abnormally large in relation to the volume of business of such person or an efficient inventory level shall be rebuttably presumed to have actual knowledge that the product was made by such patented process.

(6) A person who receives a response to a request for disclosure under this subsection shall pay to the person to whom the request was made a reasonable fee to cover actual costs incurred in complying with the request, which may not exceed the cost of a commercially available automated patent search of the matter involved, but in no case more than $ 500.

(c)(1) With respect to a medical practitioner's performance of a medical activity that constitutes an infringement under section 271(a) or (b) ~~of this title~~ [35 USC § 271(a) or (b)], the provisions of sections 281, 283, 284, and 285 ~~of this title~~ [35 USC §§ 281, 283, 284, and 285] shall not apply against the medical practitioner or against a related health care entity with respect to such medical activity.

(2) For the purposes of this subsection:

(A) the term "medical activity" means the performance of a medical or surgical procedure on a body, but shall not include (i) the use of a patented machine, manufacture, or composition of matter in violation of such patent, (ii) the practice of a patented use of a composition of matter in violation of such patent, or (iii) the practice of a process in violation of a biotechnology patent.

(B) the term "medical practitioner" means any natural person who is licensed by a State to provide the medical activity described in subsection (c)(1) or who is acting under the direction of such person in the performance of the medical activity.

(C) the term "related health care entity" shall mean an entity with which a medical practitioner has a professional affiliation under which the medical practitioner performs the medical activity, including but not limited to a nursing home, hospital, university, medical school, health maintenance organization, group medical practice, or a medical clinic.

(D) the term "professional affiliation" shall mean staff privileges, medical staff membership, employment or contractual relationship, partnership or ownership interest, academic appointment, or other affiliation under which a medical practitioner provides the medical activity on behalf of, or in association with, the health care entity.

(E) the term "body" shall mean a human body, organ or cadaver, or a nonhuman animal used in medical research or instruction directly relating to the treatment of humans.

(F) the term "patented use of a composition of matter" does not include a claim for a method of performing a medical or surgical procedure on a body that recites the use of a composition of matter where the use of that composition of matter does not directly contribute to achievement of the objective of the claimed method.

(G) the term "State" shall mean ~~any state~~ any State or territory of the United States, the District of Columbia, and the Commonwealth of Puerto Rico.

(3) This subsection does not apply to the activities of any person, or employee or agent of such person (regardless of whether such person is a tax exempt organization under section 501(c) of the Internal Revenue Code [26 USC § 501(c)]), who is engaged in the commercial development, manufacture, sale, importation, or distribution of a machine, manufacture, or composition of matter or the provision of pharmacy or clinical laboratory services (other than clinical laboratory services provided in a physician's office), where such activities are:

(A) directly related to the commercial development, manufacture, sale, importation, or distribution of a machine, manufacture, or composition of matter or the provision of pharmacy or clinical laboratory services (other than clinical laboratory services provided in a physician's office), and

(B) regulated under the Federal Food, Drug, and Cosmetic Act, the Public Health Service Act, or the Clinical Laboratories Improvement Act.

(4) This subsection shall not apply to any patent issued based on an application the earliest effective filing date of which is prior to which has an effective filing date before September 30, 1996.

HISTORY:

(July 19, 1952, ch 950, § 1, 66 Stat. 813; Aug. 23, 1988, P.L. 100-418, Title IX, Subtitle A, § 9004(a), 102 Stat. 1564; Dec. 8, 1994, P.L. 103-465, Title V, Subtitle C § 533(b)(5), 108 Stat. 4989; Sept. 30, 1996, P.L. 104-208, Div A, Title I, § 101(a) [Title VI, § 616], 110 Stat. 3009-67; Nov. 29, 1999, P.L. 106-113, Div B, § 1000(a)(9), 113 Stat. 1536.)

(America Invents Act §§ 3(g)(2); 16(a)(1); 20(i)(4), (j)(1))

§ 288. Action for infringement of a patent containing an invalid claim

Whenever, without deceptive intention, a claim of a patent is invalid, an action may be maintained for the infringement of a claim of the patent which may be valid. The patentee shall recover no costs unless a disclaimer of the invalid claim has been entered at the Patent and Trademark Office before the commencement of the suit.

HISTORY:

(July 19, 1952, ch 950, § 1, 66 Stat. 813; Jan. 2, 1975, P.L. 93-596, § 1, 88 Stat. 1949.)

(America Invents Act § 20(h).)

§ 289. Additional remedy for infringement of design patent

Whoever during the term of a patent for a design, without license of the owner, (1) applies the patented design, or any colorable imitation thereof, to any article of manufacture for the purpose of sale, or (2) sells or exposes for sale any article of manufacture to which such design or colorable imitation has been applied shall be liable to the owner to the extent of his total profit, but not less than $ 250, recoverable in any United States district court having jurisdiction of the parties.

Nothing in this section shall prevent, lessen, or impeach any other remedy which an owner of an infringed patent has under the provisions of this title [35 USC §§ 1 et seq.], but he shall not twice recover the profit made from the infringement.

HISTORY:

(July 19, 1952, ch 950, § 1, 66 Stat. 813.)

§ 290. Notice of patent suits

The clerks of the courts of the United States, within one month after the filing of an action under this title shall give notice thereof in writing to the Director, setting forth so far as known the names and addresses of the parties, name of the inventor, and the designating number of the patent upon which the action has been brought. If any other patent is subsequently included in the action he shall give like notice thereof. Within one month after the decision is rendered or a judgment issued the clerk of the court shall give notice thereof to the Director. The Director shall, on receipt of such notices, enter the same in the file of such patent.

HISTORY:

(July 19, 1952, ch 950, § 1, 66 Stat. 814; Nov. 29, 1999, P.L. 106-113, Div B, § 1000(a)(9), 113 Stat. 1536; Nov. 2, 2002, P.L. 107-273, Div C, Title III, Subtitle B, § 13206(b)(1)(B), 116 Stat. 1906.)

§ 291. Interfering patents

The owner of an interfering patent may have relief against the owner of another by civil action, and the court may adjudge the question of the validity of any of the interfering patents, in whole or in part. The provisions of the second paragraph of section 146 of this title [35 USC § 146] shall apply to actions brought under this section.

35 USC § 291

§ 291. Derived Patents

(a) In General.—The owner of a patent may have relief by civil action against the owner of another patent that claims the same invention and has an earlier effective filing date, if the invention claimed in such other patent was derived from the inventor of the invention claimed in the patent owned by the person seeking relief under this section.

(b) Filing Limitation.—An action under this section may be filed only before the end of the 1-year period beginning on the date of the issuance of the first patent containing a claim to the allegedly derived invention and naming an individual alleged to have derived such invention as the inventor or joint inventor.

HISTORY:

(July 19, 1952, ch 950, § 1, 66 Stat. 814.)

(America Invents Act § 3(h)(1).)

§ 292. False marking

(a) Whoever, without the consent of the patentee, marks upon, or affixes to, or uses in advertising in connection with anything made, used, offered for sale, or sold by such person within the United States, or imported by the person into the United States, the name or any imitation of the name of the patentee, the patent number, or the words "patent," "patentee," or the like, with the intent of counterfeiting or imitating the mark of the patentee, or of deceiving the public and inducing them to believe that the thing was made, offered for sale, sold, or imported into the United States by or with the consent of the patentee; or

Whoever marks upon, or affixes to, or uses in advertising in connection with any unpatented article, the word "patent" or any word or number importing that the same is patented, for the purpose of deceiving the public; or

Whoever marks upon, or affixes to, or uses in advertising in connection with any article, the words "patent applied for," "patent pending," or any word importing that an application for patent has been made, when no application for patent has been made, or if made, is not pending, for the purpose of deceiving the public—

Shall be fined not more than $ 500 for every such offense. Only the United States may sue for the penalty authorized by this subsection.

~~(b) Any person may sue for the penalty, in which event one-half shall go to the person suing and the other to the use of the United States.~~

(b) A person who has suffered a competitive injury as a result of a violation of this section may file a civil action in a district court of the United States for recovery of damages adequate to compensate for the injury.

(c) The marking of a product, in a manner described in subsection (a), with matter relating to a patent that covered that product but has expired is not a violation of this section.

HISTORY:

(July 19, 1952, ch 950, § 1, 66 Stat. 814; Dec. 8, 1994, P.L. 103-465, Title V, Subtitle C, § 533(b)(6), 108 Stat. 4990.)

(America Invents Act § 16(b)(1)-(3).)

§ 293. Nonresident patentee; service and notice

Every patentee not residing in the United States may file in the Patent and Trademark Office a written designation stating the name and address of a person residing within the United States on whom may be served process or notice of proceedings affecting the patent or rights thereunder. If the person designated cannot be found at the address given in the last designation, or if no person has been designated, the ~~United States District Court for the District of Columbia~~ United States District Court for the Eastern District of Virginia shall have jurisdiction and summons shall be served by publication or otherwise as the court directs. The court shall have the same jurisdiction to take any action respecting the patent or rights thereunder that it would have if the patentee were personally within the jurisdiction of the court.

HISTORY:

(July 19, 1952, ch 950, § 1, 66 Stat. 814; Jan. 2, 1975, P.L. 93-596, § 1, 88 Stat. 1949.)

(America Invents Act § 9(a).)

§ 294. Voluntary arbitration

(a) A contract involving a patent or any right under a patent may contain a provision requiring arbitration of any dispute relating to patent validity or infringement arising under the contract. In the absence of such a provision, the parties to an existing patent validity or infringement dispute may agree in writing to settle such dispute by arbitration. Any such provision or agreement shall be valid, irrevocable, and enforceable, except for any grounds that exist at law or in equity for revocation of a contract.

(b) Arbitration of such disputes, awards by arbitrators and confirmation of awards shall be governed by title 9, to the extent such title is not inconsistent with this section. In any such arbitration proceeding, the defenses provided for under section 282 ~~of this title~~ [35 USC § 282] shall be considered by the arbitrator if raised by any party to the proceeding.

(c) An award by an arbitrator shall be final and binding between the parties to the arbitration but shall have no force or effect on any other person. The parties to an arbitration may agree that in the event a patent which is the subject matter of an award is subsequently determined to be invalid or unenforceable in a judgment rendered by a court of competent jurisdiction from which no appeal can or has been taken, such award may be modified by any court of competent jurisdiction upon application by any party to the arbitration. Any such modification shall govern the rights and obligations between such parties from the date of such modification.

(d) When an award is made by an arbitrator, the patentee, his assignee or licensee shall give notice thereof in writing to the Director. There shall be a separate notice prepared for each patent involved in such proceeding. Such notice shall set forth the names and addresses of the parties, the name of the inventor, and the name of the patent owner, shall designate the number of the patent, and shall contain a copy of the award. If an award is modified by a court, the party requesting such modification shall give notice of such modification to the Director. The Director shall, upon receipt of either notice, enter the same in the record of the prosecution of such patent. If the required notice is not filed with the Director, any party to the proceeding may provide such notice to the Director.

(e) The award shall be unenforceable until the notice required by subsection (d) is received by the Director.

HISTORY:

(Added Aug. 27, 1982, P.L. 97-247, § 17(b)(1), 96 Stat. 322; Nov. 29, 1999, P.L. 106-113, Div B, § 1000(a)(9), 113 Stat. 1536; Nov. 2, 2002, P.L. 107-273, Div C, Title III, Subtitle B, § 13206(a)(19), (b)(1)(B), 116 Stat. 1905, 1906.)

(America Invents Act § 20(j)(1).)

§ 295. Presumption: Product made by patented process

In actions alleging infringement of a process patent based on the importation, sale, offer for sale, or use of a product which is made from a process patented in the United States, if the court finds—

(1) that a substantial likelihood exists that the product was made by the patented process, and

(2) that the plaintiff has made a reasonable effort to determine the process actually used in the production of the product and was unable to so determine,

the product shall be presumed to have been so made, and the burden of establishing that the product was not made by the process shall be on the party asserting that it was not so made.

HISTORY:

(Added Aug. 23, 1988, P.L. 100-418, Title IX, § 9005(a), 102 Stat. 1566; Dec. 8, 1994, P.L. 103-465, Title V, Subtitle C, § 533(b)(7), 108 Stat. 4990.)

§ 296. Liability of States, instrumentalities of States, and State officials for infringement of patents

(a) In general. Any State, any instrumentality of a State, and any officer or employee of a State or instrumentality of a State acting in his official capacity, shall not be immune, under the eleventh amendment of the Constitution of the United States or under any other doctrine of sovereign immunity, from suit in Federal court by any person, including any governmental or nongovernmental entity, for infringement of a patent under section 271 [35 USC § 271], or for any other violation under this title.

(b) Remedies. In a suit described in subsection (a) for a violation described in that subsection, remedies (including remedies both at law and in equity) are available for the violation to the same extent as such remedies are available for such a violation in a suit against any private entity. Such remedies include damages, interest, costs, and treble damages under section 284 [35 USC § 284], attorney fees under section 285 [35 USC § 285], and the additional remedy for infringement of design patents under section 289 [35 USC § 289].

HISTORY:

(Added Oct. 28, 1992, P.L. 102-560, § 2(a)(2), 106 Stat. 4230.)

§ 297. Improper and deceptive invention promotion

(a) In general. An invention promoter shall have a duty to disclose the following information to a customer in writing, prior to entering into a contract for invention promotion services:

(1) the total number of inventions evaluated by the invention promoter for commercial potential in the past 5 years, as well as the number of those inventions that received positive evaluations, and the number of those inventions that received negative evaluations;

(2) the total number of customers who have contracted with the invention promoter in the past 5 years, not including customers who have purchased trade show services, research, advertising, or other nonmarketing services from the invention promoter, or who have defaulted in their payment to the invention promoter;

(3) the total number of customers known by the invention promoter to have received a net financial profit as a direct result of the invention promotion services provided by such invention promoter;

(4) the total number of customers known by the invention promoter to have received license agreements for their inventions as a direct result of the invention promotion services provided by such invention promoter; and

(5) the names and addresses of all previous invention promotion companies with which the invention promoter or its officers have collectively or individually been affiliated in the previous 10 years.

(b) Civil action.

(1) Any customer who enters into a contract with an invention promoter and who is found by a court to have been injured by any material false or fraudulent statement or representation, or any omission of material fact, by that invention promoter (or any agent, employee, director, officer, partner, or independent contractor of such invention promoter), or by the failure of that invention promoter to disclose such information as required under subsection (a), may recover in a civil action against the invention promoter (or the officers, directors, or partners of such invention promoter), in addition to reasonable costs and attorneys' fees—

(A) the amount of actual damages incurred by the customer; or

(B) at the election of the customer at any time before final judgment is rendered, statutory damages in a sum of not more than $ 5,000, as the court considers just.

(2) Notwithstanding paragraph (1), in a case where the customer sustains the burden of proof, and the court finds, that the invention promoter intentionally misrepresented or omitted a material fact to such customer, or willfully failed to disclose such information as required under subsection (a), with the purpose of deceiving that customer, the court may increase damages to not more than three times the amount awarded, taking into account past complaints made against the invention promoter that resulted in regulatory sanctions or other corrective actions based on those records compiled by the Commissioner of Patents under subsection (d).

(c) **Definitions.** For purposes of this section—

(1) a "contract for invention promotion services" means a contract by which an invention promoter undertakes invention promotion services for a customer;

(2) a "customer" is any individual who enters into a contract with an invention promoter for invention promotion services;

(3) the term "invention promoter" means any person, firm, partnership, corporation, or other entity who offers to perform or performs invention promotion services for, or on behalf of, a customer, and who holds itself out through advertising in any mass media as providing such services, but does not include—

(A) any department or agency of the Federal Government or of a State or local government;

(B) any nonprofit, charitable, scientific, or educational organization, qualified under applicable State law or described under section 170(b)(1)(A) of the Internal Revenue Code of 1986 [26 USC § 170(b)(1)(A)];

(C) any person or entity involved in the evaluation to determine commercial potential of, or offering to license or sell, a utility patent or a previously filed nonprovisional utility patent application;

(D) any party participating in a transaction involving the sale of the stock or assets of a business; or

(E) any party who directly engages in the business of retail sales of products or the distribution of products; and

(4) the term "invention promotion services" means the procurement or attempted procurement for a customer of a firm, corporation, or other entity to develop and market products or services that include the invention of the customer.

(d) **Records of complaints.**

(1) **Release of complaints.** The Commissioner of Patents shall make all complaints received by the Patent and Trademark Office involving invention promoters publicly available, together with any response of the invention promoters. The Commissioner of Patents

shall notify the invention promoter of a complaint and provide a reasonable opportunity to reply prior to making such complaint publicly available.

(2) Request for complaints. The Commissioner of Patents may request complaints relating to invention promotion services from any Federal or State agency and include such complaints in the records maintained under paragraph (1), together with any response of the invention promoters.

§ 298. Advice of counsel

The failure of an infringer to obtain the advice of counsel with respect to any allegedly infringed patent, or the failure of the infringer to present such advice to the court or jury, may not be used to prove that the accused infringer willfully infringed the patent or that the infringer intended to induce infringement of the patent.

HISTORY:

(America Invents Act § 17(a).)

§ 299. Joinder of parties

(a) Joinder of accused infringers.—With respect to any civil action arising under any Act of Congress relating to patents, other than an action or trial in which an act of infringement under section 271(e)(2) has been pled, parties that are accused infringers may be joined in one action as defendants or counterclaim defendants, or have their actions consolidated for trial, or counterclaim defendants only if—

(1) any right to relief is asserted against the parties jointly, severally, or in the alternative with respect to or arising out of the same transaction, occurrence, or series of transactions or occurrences relating to the making, using, importing into the United States, offering for sale, or selling of the same accused product or process; and

(2) questions of fact common to all defendants or counterclaim defendants will arise in the action.

(b) Allegations insufficient for joinder.—For purposes of this subsection, accused infringers may not be joined in one action as defendants or counterclaim defendants, or have their actions consolidated for trial, based solely on allegations that they each have infringed the patent or patents in suit.

(c) Waiver.—A party that is an accused infringer may waive the limitations set forth in this section with respect to that party.

HISTORY:

(America Invents Act § 19(d)(1).)

CHAPTER 30. PRIOR ART CITATIONS TO OFFICE AND EX PARTE REEXAMINATION OF PATENTS

§ 301. Citation of prior art

~~Any person at any time may cite to the Office in writing prior art consisting of patents or printed publications which that person believes to have a bearing on the patentability of any claim of a particular patent. If the person explains in writing the pertinency and manner of applying such prior art to at least one claim of the patent, the citation of such prior art and the explanation thereof will become a part of the official file of the patent. At the written request of the person citing the prior art, his or her identity will be excluded from the patent file and kept confidential.~~

§ 301. Citation of prior art and written statements

(a) In General.—Any person at any time may cite to the Office in writing—

(1) prior art consisting of patents or printed publications which that person believes to have a bearing on the patentability of any claim of a particular patent; or

(2) statements of the patent owner filed in a proceeding before a Federal court or the Office in which the patent owner took a position on the scope of any claim of a particular patent.

(b) Official File.—If the person citing prior art or written statements pursuant to subsection (a) explains in writing the pertinence and manner of applying the prior art or written statements to at least 1 claim of the patent, the citation of the prior art or written statements and the explanation thereof shall become a part of the official file of the patent.

(c) Additional Information.—A party that submits a written statement pursuant to subsection (a)(2) shall include any other documents, pleadings, or evidence from the proceeding in which the statement was filed that addresses the written statement.

(d) Limitations.—A written statement submitted pursuant to subsection (a)(2), and additional information submitted pursuant to subsection (c), shall not be considered by the Office for any purpose other than to determine the proper meaning of a patent claim in a proceeding that is ordered or instituted pursuant to section 304, 314, or 324. If any such written statement or additional information is subject to an applicable protective order, such statement or information shall be redacted to exclude information that is subject to that order.

(e) Confidentiality.—Upon the written request of the person citing prior art or written statements pursuant to subsection (a), that person's identity shall be excluded from the patent file and kept confidential.

HISTORY:

(Added Dec. 12, 1980, P.L. 96-517, § 1, 94 Stat. 3015.)

(America Invents Act § 6(g)(1).)

§ 302. Request for reexamination

Any person at any time may file a request for reexamination by the Office of any claim of a patent on the basis of any prior art cited under the provisions of section 301 ~~of this title~~ [35 USC § 301]. The request must be in writing and must be accompanied by payment of a reexamination fee established by the Director pursuant to the provisions of section 41 ~~of this title~~ [35 USC § 41]. The request must set forth the pertinency and manner of applying cited prior art to every claim for which reexamination is requested. Unless the requesting person is the owner of the patent, the Director promptly will send a copy of the request to the owner of record of the patent.

HISTORY:

(Added Dec. 12, 1980, P.L. 96-517, § 1, 94 Stat. 3015; Nov. 29, 1999, P.L. 106-113, Div B, § 1000(a)(9), 113 Stat. 1536; Nov. 2, 2002, P.L. 107-273, Div C, Title III, Subtitle B, § 13206(b)(1)(B), 116 Stat. 1906.)

(America Invents Act § 20(j)(1).)

§ 303. Determination of issue by Director

(a) Within three months following the filing of a request for reexamination under the provisions of section 302 ~~of this title~~ [35 USC § 302], the Director will determine whether a substantial new question of patentability affecting any claim of the patent concerned is raised by the request, with or without consideration of other patents or printed publications. On his own initiative, and any time, the Director may determine whether a substantial new question of patentability is raised by patents and publications discovered by him or cited under the provisions of ~~section 301 of this title [35 USC § 301]~~ section 301 or 302. The existence of a substantial new question of patentability is not precluded by the fact that a patent or printed publication was previously cited by or to the Office or considered by the Office.

35 USC § 303

(b) A record of the Director's determination under subsection (a) of this section will be placed in the official file of the patent, and a copy promptly will be given or mailed to the owner of record of the patent and to the person requesting reexamination, if any.

(c) A determination by the Director pursuant to subsection (a) of this section that no substantial new question of patentability has been raised will be final and nonappealable. Upon such a determination, the Director may refund a portion of the reexamination fee required under section 302 ~~of this title~~ [35 USC § 302].

HISTORY:

(Added Dec. 12, 1980, P.L. 96-517, § 1, 94 Stat. 3015; Nov. 29, 1999, P.L. 106-113, Div B, § 1000(a)(9), 113 Stat. 1536; Nov. 2, 2002, P.L. 107-273, Div C, Title III, Subtitle A, § 13105(a), Subtitle B, § 13206(b)(1) (A), (B), 116 Stat. 1900, 1905.).)

(America Invents Act §§ 6(h)(1)(A); 20(j)(1).)

§ 304. Reexamination order by Director

If, in a determination made under the provisions of subsection 303(a) ~~of this title~~, the Director finds that a substantial new question of patentability affecting any claim of a patent is raised, the determination will include an order for reexamination of the patent for resolution of the question. The patent owner will be given a reasonable period, not less than two months from the date a copy of the determination is given or mailed to him, within which he may file a statement on such question, including any amendment to his patent and new claim or claims he may wish to propose, for consideration in the reexamination. If the patent owner files such a statement, he promptly will serve a copy of it on the person who has requested reexamination under the provisions of section 302 ~~of this title~~ [35 USC § 302]. Within a period of two months from the date of service, that person may file and have considered in the reexamination a reply to any statement filed by the patent owner. That person promptly will serve on the patent owner a copy of any reply filed.

HISTORY:

(Added Dec. 12, 1980, P.L. 96-517, § 1, 94 Stat. 3016; Nov. 29, 1999, P.L. 106-113, Div B, § 1000(a)(9), 113 Stat. 1536; Nov. 2, 2002, P.L. 107-273, Div C, Title III, Subtitle B, § 13206(b)(1)(B), 116 Stat. 1906.)

(America Invents Act § 20(j)(1).)

§ 305. Conduct of reexamination proceedings

After the times for filing the statement and reply provided for by section 304 ~~of this title~~ [35 USC § 304] have expired, reexamination will be conducted according to the procedures established for initial examination under the provisions of sections 132 and 133 ~~of this title~~ [35 USC §§ 132 and 133]. In any reexamination proceeding under this chapter [35 USC §§ 301 et seq.], the patent owner will be permitted to propose any amendment to his patent and a new claim or claims thereto, in order to distinguish the invention as claimed from the prior art cited under the provisions of section 301 ~~of this title~~ [35 USC § 301], or in response to a decision adverse to the patentability of a claim of a patent. No proposed amended or new claim enlarging the scope of a claim of the patent will be permitted in a reexamination proceeding under this chapter [35 USC §§ 301 et seq.]. All reexamination proceedings under this section, including any appeal to the ~~Board of Patent Appeals and Interferences~~ Patent Trial and Appeal Board, will be conducted with special dispatch within the Office.

HISTORY:

(Added Dec. 12, 1980, P.L. 96-517, § 1, 94 Stat. 3016; Nov. 8, 1984, P.L. 98-622, Title II, § 204(c), 98 Stat. 3388.)

(America Invents Act §§ 3(j)(1); 20(j)(1).)

§ 306. Appeal

The patent owner involved in a reexamination proceeding under this chapter [35 USC §§ 301 et seq.] may appeal under the provisions of section 134 ~~of this title~~ [35 USC § 134], and may seek court review under the provisions of sections 141 to ~~145~~ 144 ~~of this title~~ [35 USC §§ 141 to 144], with respect to any decision adverse to the patentability of any original or proposed amended or new claim of the patent.

HISTORY:

(Added Dec. 12, 1980, P.L. 96-517, § 1, 94 Stat. 3016.)

(America Invents Act §§ 6(h)(2)(A); 20(j)(1).)

§ 307. Certificate of patentability, unpatentability, and claim cancellation

(a) In a reexamination proceeding under this chapter [35 USC §§ 301 et seq.], when the time for appeal has expired or any appeal proceeding has terminated, the Director will issue and publish a certificate canceling any claim of the patent finally determined to be unpatentable, confirming any claim of the patent determined to be patentable, and incorporating in the patent any proposed amended or new claim determined to be patentable.

(b) Any proposed amended or new claim determined to be patentable and incorporated into a patent following a reexamination proceeding will have the same effect as that specified in section 252 ~~of this title~~ [35 USC § 252] for reissued patents on the right of any person who made, purchased, or used within the United States, or imported into the United States, anything patented by such proposed amended or new claim, or who made substantial preparation for the same, prior to issuance of a certificate under the provisions of subsection (a) of this section.

HISTORY:

(Added Dec. 12, 1980, P.L. 96-517, § 1, 94 Stat. 3016; Dec. 8, 1994, P.L. 103-465, Title V, Subtitle C, § 533(b)(8), 108 Stat. 4990; Nov. 29, 1999, P.L. 106-113, Div B, § 1000(a)(9), 113 Stat. 1536; Nov. 2, 2002, P.L. 107-273, Div C, Title III, Subtitle B, § 13206(b)(1)(B), 116 Stat. 1906.)

(America Invents Act § 20(j)(1).)

~~CHAPTER 31. OPTIONAL INTER PARTES REEXAMINATION PROCEDURES~~

CHAPTER 31—INTER PARTES REVIEW

§ 311. Request for inter partes reexamination

~~(a) In general. Any third-party requester at any time may file a request for inter partes reexamination by the Office of a patent on the basis of any prior art cited under the provisions of section 301 [35 USC § 301].~~

~~(b) Requirements. The request shall —~~

~~(1) be in writing, include the identity of the real party in interest, and be accompanied by payment of an inter partes reexamination fee established by the Director under section 41 [35 USC § 41]; and~~

~~(2) set forth the pertinency and manner of applying cited prior art to every claim for which reexamination is requested.~~

~~(c) Copy. The Director promptly shall send a copy of the request to the owner of record of the patent.~~

§ 311. Inter partes review

(a) In General.—Subject to the provisions of this chapter, a person who is not the owner of a patent may file with the Office a petition to institute an inter partes review of the patent. The Director shall establish, by regulation, fees to be paid by the person requesting the review, in such amounts as the Director determines to be reasonable, considering the aggregate costs of the review.

(b) Scope.—A petitioner in an inter partes review may request to cancel as unpatentable 1 or more claims of a patent only on a ground that could be raised under section 102 or 103 and only on the basis of prior art consisting of patents or printed publications.

(c) Filing Deadline.—A petition for inter partes review shall be filed after the later of either—

(1) the date that is 9 months after the grant of a patent or issuance of a reissue of a patent; or

(2) if a post-grant review is instituted under chapter 32, the date of the termination of such post-grant review.

HISTORY:

(Added Nov. 29, 1999, P.L. 106-113, Div B, § 1000(a)(9), 113 Stat. 1536; Nov. 2, 2002, P.L. 107-273, Div C, Title III, Subtitle B, § 13202(a)(1), (c)(1), 116 Stat. 1901, 1902.)

(America Invents Act § 6(a).)

§ 312. Determination of issue by Director

(a) Reexamination. Not later than 3 months after the filing of a request for inter partes reexamination under section 311 [35 USC § 311], the Director shall determine whether a substantial new question of patentability affecting any claim of the patent concerned is raised by the request, with or without consideration of other patents or printed publications. The existence of a substantial new question of patentability is not precluded by the fact that a patent or printed publication was previously cited by or to the Office or considered by the Office.

(b) Record. A record of the Director's determination under subsection (a) shall be placed in the official file of the patent, and a copy shall be promptly given or mailed to the owner of record of the patent and to the third-party requester.

(c) Final decision. A determination by the Director under subsection (a) shall be final and non-appealable. Upon a determination that no substantial new question of patentability has been raised, the Director may refund a portion of the inter partes reexamination fee required under section 311 [35 USC § 311].

§ 312. Petitions

(a) Requirements of Petition.—A petition filed under section 311 may be considered only if—

(1) the petition is accompanied by payment of the fee established by the Director under section 311;

(2) the petition identifies all real parties in interest;

(3) the petition identifies, in writing and with particularity, each claim challenged, the grounds on which the challenge to each claim is based, and the evidence that supports the grounds for the challenge to each claim, including—

(A) copies of patents and printed publications that the petitioner relies upon in support of the petition; and

(B) affidavits or declarations of supporting evidence and opinions, if the petitioner relies on expert opinions;

(4) the petition provides such other information as the Director may require by regulation; and

(5) the petitioner provides copies of any of the documents required under paragraphs (2), (3), and (4) to the patent owner or, if applicable, the designated representative of the patent owner.

(b) Public Availability.—As soon as practicable after the receipt of a petition under section 311, the Director shall make the petition available to the public.

HISTORY:

(Added Nov. 29, 1999, P.L. 106-113, Div B, § 1000(a)(9), 113 Stat. 1536; Nov. 2, 2002, P.L. 107-273, Div B, Title V, Subtitle A, § 13105(a), Subtitle B, § 13202(a)(2), (c)(1), 116 Stat. 1900, 1901, 1902.)

(America Invents Act § 6(a).)

§ 312. Determination of issue by Director [Transitional Provision]

(a) Reexamination. Not later than 3 months after the filing of a request for inter partes reexamination under section 311 [35 USC § 311], the Director shall determine whether ~~a substantial new question of patentability affecting any claim of the patent concerned is raised by the request,~~ the information presented in the request shows that there is a reasonable likelihood that the requester would prevail with respect to at least 1 of the claims challenged in the request, with or without consideration of other patents or printed publications. ~~The existence of a substantial new question of patentability~~ A showing that there is a reasonable likelihood that the requester would prevail with respect to at least 1 of the claims challenged in the request is not precluded by the fact that a patent or printed publication was previously cited by or to the Office or considered by the Office.

(b) Record. A record of the Director's determination under subsection (a) shall be placed in the official file of the patent, and a copy shall be promptly given or mailed to the owner of record of the patent and to the third-party requester.

(c) Final decision. A determination by the Director under subsection (a) shall be final and non-appealable. Upon a determination that ~~no substantial new question of patentability has been raised,~~ the showing required by subsection (a) has not been made, the Director may refund a portion of the inter partes reexamination fee required under section 311 [35 USC § 311].

HISTORY:

(Added Nov. 29, 1999, P.L. 106-113, Div B, § 1000(a)(9), 113 Stat. 1536; Nov. 2, 2002, P.L. 107-273, Div B, Title V, Subtitle A, § 13105(a), Subtitle B, § 13202(a)(2), (c)(1), 116 Stat. 1900, 1901, 1902.)

(America Invents Act §§ 6(c)(3)(A)(i)(I)(aa)-(bb), (II).)

~~§ 313. Inter partes reexamination order by Director~~

~~If, in a determination made under section 312(a) [35 USC § 312(a)], the Director finds that a substantial new question of patentability affecting a claim of a patent is raised, the determination shall include an order for inter partes reexamination of the patent for resolution of the question. The order may be accompanied by the initial action of the Patent and Trademark Office on the merits of the inter partes reexamination conducted in accordance with section 314 [35 USC § 314].~~

§ 313. Preliminary response to petition

If an inter partes review petition is filed under section 311, the patent owner shall have the right to file a preliminary response to the petition, within a time period set by the Director, that sets forth reasons why no inter partes review should be instituted based upon the failure of the petition to meet any requirement of this chapter.

HISTORY:

(Added Nov. 29, 1999, P.L. 106-113, Div B, § 1000(a)(9), 113 Stat. 1536; Nov. 2, 2002, P.L. 107-273, Div C, Title III, Subtitle B, § 13202(c)(1), 116 Stat. 1902.)

(America Invents Act § 6(a).)

§ 313. Inter partes reexamination order by Director [Transitional Provision]

If, in a determination made under section 312(a) [35 USC § 312(a)], the Director finds that a substantial new question of patentability affecting a claim of a patent is raised it has been shown that there is a reasonable likelihood that the requester would prevail with respect to at least 1 of the claims challenged in the request, the determination shall include an order for inter partes reexamination of the patent for resolution of the question. The order may be accompanied by the initial action of the Patent and Trademark Office on the merits of the inter partes reexamination conducted in accordance with section 314 [35 USC § 314].

HISTORY:

(Added Nov. 29, 1999, P.L. 106-113, Div B, § 1000(a)(9), 113 Stat. 1536; Nov. 2, 2002, P.L. 107-273, Div C, Title III, Subtitle B, § 13202(c)(1), 116 Stat. 1902.)

(America Invents Act § 6(c)(3)(A)(ii).)

§ 314. Conduct of inter partes reexamination proceedings

(a) In general. Except as otherwise provided in this section, reexamination shall be conducted according to the procedures established for initial examination under the provisions of sections 132 and 133 [35 USC §§ 132 and 133]. In any inter partes reexamination proceeding under this chapter [35 USC §§ 311 et seq.], the patent owner shall be permitted to propose any amendment to the patent and a new claim or claims, except that no proposed amended or new claim enlarging the scope of the claims of the patent shall be permitted.

(b) Response.

(1) With the exception of the inter partes reexamination request, any document filed by either the patent owner or the third-party requester shall be served on the other party. In addition, the Office shall send to the third-party requester a copy of any communication sent by the Office to the patent owner concerning the patent subject to the inter partes reexamination proceeding.

(2) Each time that the patent owner files a response to an action on the merits from the Patent and Trademark Office, the third-party requester shall have one opportunity to file written comments addressing issues raised by the action of the Office or the patent owner's response thereto, if those written comments are received by the Office within 30 days after the date of service of the patent owner's response.

(3) [Redesignated]

(c) Special dispatch. Unless otherwise provided by the Director for good cause, all inter partes reexamination proceedings under this section, including any appeal to the Board of Patent Appeals and Interferences, shall be conducted with special dispatch within the Office.

§ 314. Institution of inter partes review

(a) Threshold.—The Director may not authorize an inter partes review to be instituted unless the Director determines that the information presented in the petition filed under section 311 and any response filed under section 313 shows that there is a reasonable likelihood that the petitioner would prevail with respect to at least 1 of the claims challenged in the petition.

(b) Timing.—The Director shall determine whether to institute an inter partes review under this chapter pursuant to a petition filed under section 311 within 3 months after—

    (1) receiving a preliminary response to the petition under section 313; or

    (2) if no such preliminary response is filed, the last date on which such response may be filed.

    (c) Notice.—The Director shall notify the petitioner and patent owner, in writing, of the Director's determination under subsection (a), and shall make such notice available to the public as soon as is practicable. Such notice shall include the date on which the review shall commence.

    (d) No Appeal.—The determination by the Director whether to institute an inter partes review under this section shall be final and nonappealable.

HISTORY:

(Added Nov. 29, 1999, P.L. 106-113, Div B, § 1000(a)(9), 113 Stat. 1536; Nov. 2, 2002, P.L. 107-273, Div C, Title III, Subtitle B, § 13202(a)(3), (c)(1), 116 Stat. 1901, 1902.)

(America Invents Act § 6(a).)

§ 315. Appeal

    (a) Patent owner. The patent owner involved in an inter partes reexamination proceeding under this chapter [35 USC §§ 311 et seq.]—

    (1) may appeal under the provisions of section 134 and may appeal under the provisions of sections 141 through 144 [35 USC §§ 141 through 144], with respect to any decision adverse to the patentability of any original or proposed amended or new claim of the patent; and

    (2) may be a party to any appeal taken by a third-party requester under subsection (b).

    (b) Third-party requester. A third-party requester—

    (1) may appeal under the provisions of section 134, and may appeal under the provisions of sections 141 through 144 [35 USC § 141 through 144], with respect to any final decision favorable to the patentability of any original or proposed amended or new claim of the patent; and

    (2) may, subject to subsection (c), be a party to any appeal taken by the patent owner under the provisions of section 134 [35 USC § 134] or sections 141 through 144 [35 USC § 141 through 144].

    (c) Civil action. A third-party requester whose request for an inter partes reexamination results in an order under section 313 [35 USC § 313] is estopped from asserting at a later time, in any civil action arising in whole or in part under section 1338 of title 28, the invalidity of any claim finally determined to be valid and patentable on any ground which the third-party requester raised or could have raised during the inter partes reexamination proceedings. This subsection does not prevent the assertion of invalidity based on newly discovered prior art unavailable to the third-party requester and the Patent and Trademark Office at the time of the inter partes reexamination proceedings.

§ 315. Relation to other proceedings or actions

    (a) Infringer's civil action.—

    (1) Inter partes review barred by civil action.—An inter partes review may not be instituted if, before the date on which the petition for such a review is filed, the petitioner or real party in interest filed a civil action challenging the validity of a claim of the patent.

    (2) Stay of civil action.—If the petitioner or real party in interest files a civil action challenging the validity of a claim of the patent on or after the date on which the petitioner files a petition for inter partes review of the patent, that civil action shall be automatically stayed until either—

    (A) the patent owner moves the court to lift the stay;

    (B) the patent owner files a civil action or counterclaim alleging that the petitioner or real party in interest has infringed the patent; or

    (C) the petitioner or real party in interest moves the court to dismiss the civil action.

    (3) Treatment of counterclaim.—A counterclaim challenging the validity of a claim of a patent does not constitute a civil action challenging the validity of a claim of a patent for purposes of this subsection.

    (b) Patent Owner's Action.—An inter partes review may not be instituted if the petition requesting the proceeding is filed more than 1 year after the date on which the petitioner, real party in interest, or privy of the petitioner is served with a complaint alleging infringement of the patent. The time limitation set forth in the preceding sentence shall not apply to a request for joinder under subsection (c).

    (c) Joinder.—If the Director institutes an inter partes review, the Director, in his or her discretion, may join as a party to that inter partes review any person who properly files a petition under section 311 that the Director, after receiving a preliminary response under section 313 or the expiration of the time for filing such a response, determines warrants the institution of an inter partes review under section 314.

    (d) Multiple Proceedings.—Notwithstanding sections 135(a), 251, and 252, and chapter 30, during the pendency of an inter partes review, if another proceeding or matter involving the patent is before the Office, the Director may determine the manner in which the inter partes review or other proceeding or matter may proceed, including providing for stay, transfer, consolidation, or termination of any such matter or proceeding.

    (e) Estoppel.—

    (1) Proceedings before the office.—The petitioner in an inter partes review of a claim in a patent under this chapter that results in a final written decision under section 318(a), or the real party in interest or privy of the petitioner, may not request or maintain a proceeding before the Office with respect to that claim on any ground that the petitioner raised or reasonably could have raised during that inter partes review.

    (2) Civil actions and other proceedings.—The petitioner in an inter partes review of a claim in a patent under this chapter that results in a final written decision under section 318(a), or the real party in interest or privy of the petitioner, may not assert either in a civil action arising in whole or in part under section 1338 of title 28 or in a proceeding before the International Trade Commission under section 337 of the Tariff Act of 1930 that the claim is invalid on any ground that the petitioner raised or reasonably could have raised during that inter partes review.

HISTORY:

(Added Nov. 29, 1999, P.L. 106-113, Div B, § 1000(a)(9), 113 Stat. 1536; Nov. 2, 2002, P.L. 107-273, Div C, Title III, Subtitle A, § 13106(a), Subtitle B, § 13202(a)(4), (c)(1), 116 Stat. 1900, 1901, 1902.)

(America Invents Act § 6(a).)

§ 316. ~~Certificate of patentability, unpatentability, and claim cancellation~~

~~(a) In general. In an inter partes reexamination proceeding under this chapter [35 USC §§ 311 et seq.], when the time for appeal has expired or any appeal proceeding has terminated, the Director shall issue and publish a certificate canceling any claim of the patent finally~~

~~determined to be unpatentable, confirming any claim of the patent determined to be patent-~~
~~able, and incorporating in the patent any proposed amended or new claim determined to be~~
~~patentable.~~

~~**(b) Amended or new claim.** Any proposed amended or new claim determined to be pat-~~
~~entable and incorporated into a patent following an inter partes reexamination proceeding~~
~~shall have the same effect as that specified in section 252 of this title [35 USC § 252] for~~
~~reissued patents on the right of any person who made, purchased, or used within the United~~
~~States, or imported into the United States, anything patented by such proposed amended or~~
~~new claim, or who made substantial preparation therefor, prior to issuance of a certificate~~
~~under the provisions of subsection (a) of this section.~~

§ 316. Conduct of inter partes review

(a) **Regulations.**—The Director shall prescribe regulations—

(1) providing that the file of any proceeding under this chapter shall be made available to the public, except that any petition or document filed with the intent that it be sealed shall, if accompanied by a motion to seal, be treated as sealed pending the outcome of the ruling on the motion;

(2) setting forth the standards for the showing of sufficient grounds to institute a review under section 314(a);

(3) establishing procedures for the submission of supplemental information after the petition is filed;

(4) establishing and governing inter partes review under this chapter and the relationship of such review to other proceedings under this title;

(5) setting forth standards and procedures for discovery of relevant evidence, including that such discovery shall be limited to—

(A) the deposition of witnesses submitting affidavits or declarations; and

(B) what is otherwise necessary in the interest of justice;

(6) prescribing sanctions for abuse of discovery, abuse of process, or any other improper use of the proceeding, such as to harass or to cause unnecessary delay or an unnecessary increase in the cost of the proceeding;

(7) providing for protective orders governing the exchange and submission of confidential information;

(8) providing for the filing by the patent owner of a response to the petition under section 313 after an inter partes review has been instituted, and requiring that the patent owner file with such response, through affidavits or declarations, any additional factual evidence and expert opinions on which the patent owner relies in support of the response;

(9) setting forth standards and procedures for allowing the patent owner to move to amend the patent under subsection (d) to cancel a challenged claim or propose a reasonable number of substitute claims, and ensuring that any information submitted by the patent owner in support of any amendment entered under subsection (d) is made available to the public as part of the prosecution history of the patent;

(10) providing either party with the right to an oral hearing as part of the proceeding;

(11) requiring that the final determination in an inter partes review be issued not later than 1 year after the date on which the Director notices the institution of a review under this chapter, except that the Director may, for good cause shown, extend the 1-year period by not more than 6 months, and may adjust the time periods in this paragraph in the case of joinder under section 315(c);

(12) setting a time period for requesting joinder under section 315(c); and

(13) providing the petitioner with at least 1 opportunity to file written comments within a time period established by the Director.

(b) Considerations.—In prescribing regulations under this section, the Director shall consider the effect of any such regulation on the economy, the integrity of the patent system, the efficient administration of the Office, and the ability of the Office to timely complete proceedings instituted under this chapter.

(c) Patent Trial and Appeal Board.—The Patent Trial and Appeal Board shall, in accordance with section 6, conduct each inter partes review instituted under this chapter.

(d) Amendment of the Patent.—

(1) In general.—During an inter partes review instituted under this chapter, the patent owner may file 1 motion to amend the patent in 1 or more of the following ways:

(A) Cancel any challenged patent claim.

(B) For each challenged claim, propose a reasonable number of substitute claims.

(2) Additional motions.—Additional motions to amend may be permitted upon the joint request of the petitioner and the patent owner to materially advance the settlement of a proceeding under section 317, or as permitted by regulations prescribed by the Director.

(3) Scope of claims.—An amendment under this subsection may not enlarge the scope of the claims of the patent or introduce new matter.

(e) Evidentiary Standards.—In an inter partes review instituted under this chapter, the petitioner shall have the burden of proving a proposition of unpatentability by a preponderance of the evidence.

HISTORY:

(Added Nov. 29, 1999, P.L. 106-113, Div B, § 1000(a)(9), 113 Stat. 1536; Nov. 2, 2002, P.L. 107-273, Div C, Title III, Subtitle B, § 13202(c)(1), 116 Stat. 1902.)

(America Invents Act § 6(a).)

~~§ 317. Inter partes reexamination prohibited~~

~~**(a) Order for reexamination.** Notwithstanding any provision of this chapter [35 USC §§ 311 et seq.], once an order for inter partes reexamination of a patent has been issued under section 313 [35 USC § 313], neither the third-party requester nor its privies[,] may file a subsequent request for inter partes reexamination of the patent until an inter partes reexamination certificate is issued and published under section 316 [35 USC § 316], unless authorized by the Director.~~

~~**(b) Final decision.** Once a final decision has been entered against a party in a civil action arising in whole or in part under section 1338 of title 28, that the party has not sustained its burden of proving the invalidity of any patent claim in suit or if a final decision in an inter partes reexamination proceeding instituted by a third-party requester is favorable to the patentability of any original or proposed amended or new claim of the patent, then neither that party nor its privies may thereafter request an inter partes reexamination of any such patent claim on the basis of issues which that party or its privies raised or could have raised in such civil action or inter partes reexamination proceeding, and an inter partes reexamination requested by that party or its privies on the basis of such issues may not thereafter be maintained by the Office, notwithstanding any other provision of this chapter [35 USC §§ 311 et seq.]. This subsection does not prevent the assertion of invalidity based on newly discovered prior art unavailable to the third-party requester and the Patent and Trademark Office at the time of the inter partes reexamination proceedings.~~

§ 317. Settlement

(a) **In General.**—An inter partes review instituted under this chapter shall be terminated with respect to any petitioner upon the joint request of the petitioner and the patent owner, unless the Office has decided the merits of the proceeding before the request for termination is filed. If the inter partes review is terminated with respect to a petitioner under this section, no estoppel under section 315(e) shall attach to the petitioner, or to the real party in interest or privy of the petitioner, on the basis of that petitioner's institution of that inter partes review. If no petitioner remains in the inter partes review, the Office may terminate the review or proceed to a final written decision under section 318(a).

(b) **Agreements in Writing.**—Any agreement or understanding between the patent owner and a petitioner, including any collateral agreements referred to in such agreement or understanding, made in connection with, or in contemplation of, the termination of an inter partes review under this section shall be in writing and a true copy of such agreement or understanding shall be filed in the Office before the termination of the inter partes review as between the parties. At the request of a party to the proceeding, the agreement or understanding shall be treated as business confidential information, shall be kept separate from the file of the involved patents, and shall be made available only to Federal Government agencies on written request, or to any person on a showing of good cause.

HISTORY:

(Added Nov. 29, 1999, P.L. 106-113, Div B, § 1000(a)(9), 113 Stat. 1536; Nov. 2, 2002, P.L. 107-273, Div C, Title III, Subtitle B, § 13202(a)(5), (c)(1), 116 Stat. 1901, 1902.)

(America Invents Act § 6(a).)

§ 318. Stay of litigation

~~Once an order for inter partes reexamination of a patent has been issued under section 313 [35 USC § 313], the patent owner may obtain a stay of any pending litigation which involves an issue of patentability of any claims of the patent which are the subject of the inter partes reexamination order, unless the court before which such litigation is pending determines that a stay would not serve the interests of justice.~~

§ 318. Decision of the Board

(a) **Final Written Decision.**—If an inter partes review is instituted and not dismissed under this chapter, the Patent Trial and Appeal Board shall issue a final written decision with respect to the patentability of any patent claim challenged by the petitioner and any new claim added under section 316(d).

(b) **Certificate.**—If the Patent Trial and Appeal Board issues a final written decision under subsection (a) and the time for appeal has expired or any appeal has terminated, the Director shall issue and publish a certificate canceling any claim of the patent finally determined to be unpatentable, confirming any claim of the patent determined to be patentable, and incorporating in the patent by operation of the certificate any new or amended claim determined to be patentable.

(c) **Intervening Rights.**—Any proposed amended or new claim determined to be patentable and incorporated into a patent following an inter partes review under this chapter shall have the same effect as that specified in section 252 for reissued patents on the right of any person who made, purchased, or used within the United States, or imported into the United States, anything patented by such proposed amended or new claim, or who made substantial preparation therefor, before the issuance of a certificate under subsection (b).

(d) Data on Length of Review.—The Office shall make available to the public data describing the length of time between the institution of, and the issuance of a final written decision under subsection (a) for, each inter partes review.

HISTORY:

(Added Nov. 29, 1999, P.L. 106-113, Div B, § 1000(a)(9), 113 Stat. 1536; Nov. 2, 2002, P.L. 107-273, Div C, Title III, Subtitle B, § 13202(c)(1), 116 Stat. 1902.)

(America Invents Act § 6(a).)

§ 319. Appeal

A party dissatisfied with the final written decision of the Patent Trial and Appeal Board under section 318(a) may appeal the decision pursuant to sections 141 through 144. Any party to the inter partes review shall have the right to be a party to the appeal.

HISTORY:

(America Invents Act § 6(a).)

CHAPTER 32—POST-GRANT REVIEW

§ 321. Post-grant review

(a) In General.—Subject to the provisions of this chapter, a person who is not the owner of a patent may file with the Office a petition to institute a post-grant review of the patent. The Director shall establish, by regulation, fees to be paid by the person requesting the review, in such amounts as the Director determines to be reasonable, considering the aggregate costs of the post-grant review.

(b) Scope.—A petitioner in a post-grant review may request to cancel as unpatentable 1 or more claims of a patent on any ground that could be raised under paragraph (2) or (3) of section 282(b) (relating to invalidity of the patent or any claim).

(c) Filing Deadline.—A petition for a post-grant review may only be filed not later than the date that is 9 months after the date of the grant of the patent or of the issuance of a reissue patent (as the case may be).

HISTORY:

(America Invents Act § 6(d).)

§ 322. Petitions

(a) Requirements of Petition.—A petition filed under section 321 may be considered only if—

(1) the petition is accompanied by payment of the fee established by the Director under section 321;

(2) the petition identifies all real parties in interest;

(3) the petition identifies, in writing and with particularity, each claim challenged, the grounds on which the challenge to each claim is based, and the evidence that supports the grounds for the challenge to each claim, including—

(A) copies of patents and printed publications that the petitioner relies upon in support of the petition; and

(B) affidavits or declarations of supporting evidence and opinions, if the petitioner relies on other factual evidence or on expert opinions;

(4) the petition provides such other information as the Director may require by regulation; and

(5) the petitioner provides copies of any of the documents required under paragraphs

(2), (3), and (4) to the patent owner or, if applicable, the designated representative of the patent owner.

(b) Public Availability.—As soon as practicable after the receipt of a petition under section 321, the Director shall make the petition available to the public.

HISTORY:

(America Invents Act § 6(d).)

§ 323. Preliminary response to petition

If a post-grant review petition is filed under section 321, the patent owner shall have the right to file a preliminary response to the petition, within a time period set by the Director, that sets forth reasons why no post-grant review should be instituted based upon the failure of the petition to meet any requirement of this chapter.

HISTORY:

(America Invents Act § 6(d).)

§ 324. Institution of post-grant review

(a) Threshold.—The Director may not authorize a post-grant review to be instituted unless the Director determines that the information presented in the petition filed under section 321, if such information is not rebutted, would demonstrate that it is more likely than not that at least 1 of the claims challenged in the petition is unpatentable.

(b) Additional Grounds.—The determination required under subsection (a) may also be satisfied by a showing that the petition raises a novel or unsettled legal question that is important to other patents or patent applications.

(c) Timing.—The Director shall determine whether to institute a post-grant review under this chapter pursuant to a petition filed under section 321 within 3 months after—

(1) receiving a preliminary response to the petition under section 323; or

(2) if no such preliminary response is filed, the last date on which such response may be filed.

(d) Notice.—The Director shall notify the petitioner and patent owner, in writing, of the Director's determination under subsection (a) or (b), and shall make such notice available to the public as soon as is practicable. Such notice shall include the date on which the review shall commence.

(e) No Appeal.—The determination by the Director whether to institute a post-grant review under this section shall be final and nonappealable.

HISTORY:

(America Invents Act § 6(d).)

§ 325. Relation to other proceedings or actions

(a) Infringer's civil action.—

(1) Post-grant review barred by civil action.—A post-grant review may not be instituted under this chapter if, before the date on which the petition for such a review is filed, the petitioner or real party in interest filed a civil action challenging the validity of a claim of the patent.

(2) Stay of civil action.—If the petitioner or real party in interest files a civil action challenging the validity of a claim of the patent on or after the date on which the petitioner files a petition for post-grant review of the patent, that civil action shall be automatically stayed until either—

(A) the patent owner moves the court to lift the stay;

(B) the patent owner files a civil action or counterclaim alleging that the petitioner or real party in interest has infringed the patent; or

(C) the petitioner or real party in interest moves the court to dismiss the civil action.

(3) Treatment of counterclaim.—A counterclaim challenging the validity of a claim of a patent does not constitute a civil action challenging the validity of a claim of a patent for purposes of this subsection.

(b) Preliminary Injunctions.—If a civil action alleging infringement of a patent is filed within 3 months after the date on which the patent is granted, the court may not stay its consideration of the patent owner's motion for a preliminary injunction against infringement of the patent on the basis that a petition for post-grant review has been filed under this chapter or that such a post-grant review has been instituted under this chapter.

(c) Joinder.—If more than 1 petition for a post-grant review under this chapter is properly filed against the same patent and the Director determines that more than 1 of these petitions warrants the institution of a post-grant review under section 324, the Director may consolidate such reviews into a single post-grant review.

(d) Multiple Proceedings.—Notwithstanding sections 135(a), 251, and 252, and chapter 30, during the pendency of any post-grant review under this chapter, if another proceeding or matter involving the patent is before the Office, the Director may determine the manner in which the post-grant review or other proceeding or matter may proceed, including providing for the stay, transfer, consolidation, or termination of any such matter or proceeding. In determining whether to institute or order a proceeding under this chapter, chapter 30, or chapter 31, the Director may take into account whether, and reject the petition or request because, the same or substantially the same prior art or arguments previously were presented to the Office.

(e) Estoppel.—

(1) Proceedings before the office.—The petitioner in a post-grant review of a claim in a patent under this chapter that results in a final written decision under section 328(a), or the real party in interest or privy of the petitioner, may not request or maintain a proceeding before the Office with respect to that claim on any ground that the petitioner raised or reasonably could have raised during that post-grant review.

(2) Civil actions and other proceedings.—The petitioner in a post-grant review of a claim in a patent under this chapter that results in a final written decision under section 328(a), or the real party in interest or privy of the petitioner, may not assert either in a civil action arising in whole or in part under section 1338 of title 28 or in a proceeding before the International Trade Commission under section 337 of the Tariff Act of 1930 that the claim is invalid on any ground that the petitioner raised or reasonably could have raised during that post-grant review.

(f) Reissue Patents.—A post-grant review may not be instituted under this chapter if the petition requests cancellation of a claim in a reissue patent that is identical to or narrower than a claim in the original patent from which the reissue patent was issued, and the time limitations in section 321(c) would bar filing a petition for a post-grant review for such original patent.

HISTORY:

(America Invents Act § 6(d).)

§ 326. Conduct of post-grant review

(a) Regulations.—The Director shall prescribe regulations—

(1) providing that the file of any proceeding under this chapter shall be made available

to the public, except that any petition or document filed with the intent that it be sealed shall, if accompanied by a motion to seal, be treated as sealed pending the outcome of the ruling on the motion;

(2) setting forth the standards for the showing of sufficient grounds to institute a review under subsections (a) and (b) of section 324;

(3) establishing procedures for the submission of supplemental information after the petition is filed;

(4) establishing and governing a post-grant review under this chapter and the relationship of such review to other proceedings under this title;

(5) setting forth standards and procedures for discovery of relevant evidence, including that such discovery shall be limited to evidence directly related to factual assertions advanced by either party in the proceeding;

(6) prescribing sanctions for abuse of discovery, abuse of process, or any other improper use of the proceeding, such as to harass or to cause unnecessary delay or an unnecessary increase in the cost of the proceeding;

(7) providing for protective orders governing the exchange and submission of confidential information;

(8) providing for the filing by the patent owner of a response to the petition under section 323 after a post-grant review has been instituted, and requiring that the patent owner file with such response, through affidavits or declarations, any additional factual evidence and expert opinions on which the patent owner relies in support of the response;

(9) setting forth standards and procedures for allowing the patent owner to move to amend the patent under subsection (d) to cancel a challenged claim or propose a reasonable number of substitute claims, and ensuring that any information submitted by the patent owner in support of any amendment entered under subsection (d) is made available to the public as part of the prosecution history of the patent;

(10) providing either party with the right to an oral hearing as part of the proceeding;

(11) requiring that the final determination in any post-grant review be issued not later than 1 year after the date on which the Director notices the institution of a proceeding under this chapter, except that the Director may, for good cause shown, extend the 1-year period by not more than 6 months, and may adjust the time periods in this paragraph in the case of joinder under section 325(c); and

(12) providing the petitioner with at least 1 opportunity to file written comments within a time period established by the Director.

(b) Considerations.—In prescribing regulations under this section, the Director shall consider the effect of any such regulation on the economy, the integrity of the patent system, the efficient administration of the Office, and the ability of the Office to timely complete proceedings instituted under this chapter.

(c) Patent Trial and Appeal Board.—The Patent Trial and Appeal Board shall, in accordance with section 6, conduct each post-grant review instituted under this chapter.

(d) Amendment of the Patent.—

(1) In general.—During a post-grant review instituted under this chapter, the patent owner may file 1 motion to amend the patent in 1 or more of the following ways:

(A) Cancel any challenged patent claim.

(B) For each challenged claim, propose a reasonable number of substitute claims.

(2) Additional motions.—Additional motions to amend may be permitted upon the joint request of the petitioner and the patent owner to materially advance the settlement

of a proceeding under section 327, or upon the request of the patent owner for good cause shown.

(3) Scope of claims.—An amendment under this subsection may not enlarge the scope of the claims of the patent or introduce new matter.

(e) Evidentiary Standards.—In a post-grant review instituted under this chapter, the petitioner shall have the burden of proving a proposition of unpatentability by a preponderance of the evidence.

HISTORY:

(America Invents Act § 6(d).)

§ 327. Settlement

(a) In General.—A post-grant review instituted under this chapter shall be terminated with respect to any petitioner upon the joint request of the petitioner and the patent owner, unless the Office has decided the merits of the proceeding before the request for termination is filed. If the post-grant review is terminated with respect to a petitioner under this section, no estoppel under section 325(e) shall attach to the petitioner, or to the real party in interest or privy of the petitioner, on the basis of that petitioner's institution of that post-grant review. If no petitioner remains in the post-grant review, the Office may terminate the post-grant review or proceed to a final written decision under section 328(a).

(b) Agreements in Writing.—Any agreement or understanding between the patent owner and a petitioner, including any collateral agreements referred to in such agreement or understanding, made in connection with, or in contemplation of, the termination of a post-grant review under this section shall be in writing, and a true copy of such agreement or understanding shall be filed in the Office before the termination of the post-grant review as between the parties. At the request of a party to the proceeding, the agreement or understanding shall be treated as business confidential information, shall be kept separate from the file of the involved patents, and shall be made available only to Federal Government agencies on written request, or to any person on a showing of good cause.

HISTORY:

(America Invents Act § 6(d).)

§ 328. Decision of the Board

(a) Final Written Decision.—If a post-grant review is instituted and not dismissed under this chapter, the Patent Trial and Appeal Board shall issue a final written decision with respect to the patentability of any patent claim challenged by the petitioner and any new claim added under section 326(d).

(b) Certificate.—If the Patent Trial and Appeal Board issues a final written decision under subsection (a) and the time for appeal has expired or any appeal has terminated, the Director shall issue and publish a certificate canceling any claim of the patent finally determined to be unpatentable, confirming any claim of the patent determined to be patentable, and incorporating in the patent by operation of the certificate any new or amended claim determined to be patentable.

(c) Intervening Rights.—Any proposed amended or new claim determined to be patentable and incorporated into a patent following a post-grant review under this chapter shall have the same effect as that specified in section 252 of this title for reissued patents on the right of any person who made, purchased, or used within the United States, or imported into the United States, anything patented by such proposed amended or new claim, or who made substantial preparation therefor, before the issuance of a certificate under subsection (b).

(d) Data on Length of Review.—The Office shall make available to the public data describing the length of time between the institution of, and the issuance of a final written decision under subsection (a) for, each post-grant review.

HISTORY:

(America Invents Act § 6(d).)

§ 329. Appeal

A party dissatisfied with the final written decision of the Patent Trial and Appeal Board under section 328(a) may appeal the decision pursuant to sections 141 through 144. Any party to the post-grant review shall have the right to be a party to the appeal.

HISTORY:

(America Invents Act § 6(d).)

PART IV. PATENT COOPERATION TREATY

CHAPTER 35. DEFINITIONS

§ 351. Definitions

When used in this part [35 USC §§ 351 et seq.] unless the context otherwise indicates—

(a) The term "treaty" means the Patent Cooperation Treaty done at Washington, on June 19, 1970.

(b) The term "Regulations", when capitalized, means the Regulations under the treaty, done at Washington on the same date as the treaty. The term "regulations", when not capitalized, means the regulations established by the Director under this title.

(c) The term "international application" means an application filed under the treaty.

(d) The term "international application originating in the United States" means an international application filed in the Patent and Trademark Office when it is acting as a Receiving Office under the treaty, irrespective of whether or not the United States has been designated in that international application.

(e) The term "international application designating the United States" means an international application specifying the United States as a country in which a patent is sought, regardless where such international application is filed.

(f) The term "Receiving Office" means a national patent office or intergovernmental organization which receives and processes international applications as prescribed by the treaty and the Regulations.

(g) The terms "International Searching Authority" and "International Preliminary Examining Authority" mean a national patent office or intergovernmental organization as appointed under the treaty which processes international applications as prescribed by the treaty and the Regulations.

(h) The term "International Bureau" means the international intergovernmental organization which is recognized as the coordinating body under the treaty and the Regulations.

(i) Terms and expressions not defined in this part are to be taken in the sense indicated by the treaty and the Regulations.

HISTORY:

(Added Nov. 14, 1975, P.L. 94-131, § 1, 89 Stat. 685; Nov. 8, 1984, P.L. 98-622, Title IV, § 403(a) in part, 98 Stat. 3392; Nov. 6, 1986, P.L. 99-616, § 2(a)-(c), 100 Stat. 3485; Nov. 29, 1999, P.L. 106-113, Div B, § 1000(a)(9), 113 Stat. 1536; Nov. 2, 2002, P.L. 107-273, Div C, Title III, Subtitle B, § 13206(b)(1)(B), 116 Stat. 1906.)

§ 361. Receiving Office

(a) The Patent and Trademark Office shall act as a Receiving Office for international applications filed by nationals or residents of the United States. In accordance with any agreement made between the United States and another country, the Patent and Trademark Office may also act as a Receiving Office for international applications filed by residents or nationals of such country who are entitled to file international applications.

(b) The Patent and Trademark Office shall perform all acts connected with the discharge of duties required of a Receiving Office, including the collection of international fees and their transmittal to the International Bureau.

(c) International applications filed in the Patent and Trademark Office shall be in the English language.

(d) The international fee, and the transmittal and search fees prescribed under section 376(a) of this part [35 USC § 376(a)], shall either be paid on filing of an international application or within such later time as may be fixed by the Director.

HISTORY:

(Added Nov. 14, 1975, P.L. 94-131, § 1, 89 Stat. 686; Nov. 8, 1984, P.L. 98-622, Title IV, §§ 401(a), 403(a) in part, 98 Stat. 3391, 3392; Nov. 6, 1986, P.L. 99-616, § 2(d), 100 Stat. 3485; Nov. 29, 1999, P.L. 106-113, Div B, § 1000(a)(9), 113 Stat. 1536; Nov. 2, 2002, P.L. 107-273, Div C, Title III, Subtitle B, § 13206(b)(1)(B), 116 Stat. 1906.)

§ 362. International Searching Authority and International Preliminary Examining Authority

(a) The Patent and Trademark Office may act as an International Searching Authority and International Preliminary Examining Authority with respect to international applications in accordance with the terms and conditions of an agreement which may be concluded with the International Bureau, and may discharge all duties required of such Authorities, including the collection of handling fees and their transmittal to the International Bureau.

(b) The handling fee, preliminary examination fee, and any additional fees due for international preliminary examination shall be paid within such time as may be fixed by the Director.

HISTORY:

(Added Nov. 14, 1975, P.L. 94-131, § 1, 89 Stat. 686; Nov. 8, 1984, P.L. 98-622, Title IV, § 403(a) in part, 98 Stat. 3392; Nov. 6, 1986, P.L. 99-616, § 4, 100 Stat. 3485; Nov. 29, 1999, P.L. 106-113, Div B, § 1000(a) (9), 113 Stat. 1536; Nov. 2, 2002, P.L. 107-273, Div C, Title III, Subtitle B, § 13206(b)(1)(B), 116 Stat. 1906.)

§ 363. International application designating the United States: Effect

An international application designating the United States shall have the effect, from its international filing date under article 11 of the treaty, of a national application for patent regularly filed in the Patent and Trademark Office except as otherwise provided in section 102(e) of this title [35 USC § 102(e)].

HISTORY:

(Added Nov. 14, 1975, P.L. 94-131, P.L. 94-131, § 1, 89 Stat. 686; Nov. 8, 1984, P.L. 98-622, Title IV, § 403(a), 98 Stat. 3392.)

(America Invents Act § 3(g)(3).)

§ 364. International stage: Procedure

(a) International applications shall be processed by the Patent and Trademark Office when acting as a Receiving Office, International Searching Authority, or International Preliminary Examining Authority in accordance with the applicable provisions of the treaty, the Regulations, and this title.

(b) An applicant's failure to act within prescribed time limits in connection with requirements pertaining to a pending international application may be excused upon a showing satisfactory to the Director of unavoidable delay, to the extent not precluded by the treaty and the Regulations, and provided the conditions imposed by the treaty and the Regulations regarding the excuse of such failure to act are complied with.

HISTORY:

(Added Nov. 14, 1975, P.L. 94-131, § 1, 89 Stat. 686; Nov. 8, 1984, P.L. 98-622, Title IV, § 403(a) in part, 98 Stat. 3392; Nov. 6, 1986, P.L. 99-616, § 5, 100 Stat. 3485; Nov. 29, 1999, P.L. 106-113, Div B, § 1000(a) (9), 113 Stat. 1536; Nov. 2, 2002, P.L. 107-273, Div C, Title III, Subtitle B, § 13206(b)(1)(B), 116 Stat. 1906.)

§ 365. Right of priority; benefit of the filing date of a prior application

(a) In accordance with the conditions and requirements of subsections (a) through (d) of section 119 of this title [35 USC § 119], a national application shall be entitled to the right of priority based on a prior filed international application which designated at least one country other than the United States.

(b) In accordance with the conditions and requirement of section 119(a) of this title [35 USC § 119(a)] and the treaty and the Regulations, an international application designating the United States shall be entitled to the right of priority based on a prior foreign application, or a prior international application designating at least one country other than the United States.

(c) In accordance with the conditions and requirements of section 120 of this title [35 USC § 120], an international application designating the United States shall be entitled to the benefit of the filing date of a prior national application or a prior international application designating the United States, and a national application shall be entitled to the benefit of the filing date of a prior international application designating the United States. If any claim for the benefit of an earlier filing date is based on a prior international application which designated but did not originate in the United States, the Director may require the filing in the Patent and Trademark Office of a certified copy of such application together with a translation thereof into the English language, if it was filed in another language.

HISTORY:

(Added Nov. 14, 1975, P.L. 94-131, § 1, 89 Stat. 686; Nov. 8, 1984, P.L. 98-622, Title IV, § 403(a) in part, 98 Stat. 3392; Dec. 8, 1994, P.L. 103-465, Title V, Subtitle C, § 532(c)(4), 108 Stat. 4987; Nov. 29, 1999, P.L. 106-113, Div B, § 1000(a)(9), 113 Stat. 1536; Nov. 2, 2002, P.L. 107-273, Div C, Title III, Subtitle B, § 13206(b) (1)(B), 116 Stat. 1906.)

(America Invents Act § 20(j)(1).)

§ 366. Withdrawn international application

Subject to section 367 of this part [35 USC § 367], if an international application designating the United States is withdrawn or considered withdrawn, either generally or as to the United States, under the conditions of the treaty and the Regulations, before the applicant has complied with the applicable requirements prescribed by section 371(c) of this part [35 USC § 371(c)], the designation of the United States shall have no effect after the date of withdrawal, and shall be considered as not having been made, unless a claim for the benefit of a prior filing date under section 365(c) of this part [35 USC § 365(c)] was made in a national application, or an international application designating the United States, filed before the date of such withdrawal. However, such withdrawn international application may serve as the basis for a claim of priority under section 365(a) and (b) of this part [35 USC § 365(a), (b)], if it designated a country other than the United States.

HISTORY:

(Added Nov. 14, 1975, P.L. 94-131, § 1, 89 Stat. 687; Nov. 8, 1984, P.L. 98-622, Title IV, § 401(b), 98 Stat. 3391.)

§ 367. Actions of other authorities: Review

(a) Where a Receiving Office other than the Patent and Trademark Office has refused to accord an international filing date to an international application designating the United States or where it has held such application to be withdrawn either generally or as to the United States, the applicant may request review of the matter by the Director, on compliance with the requirements of and within the time limits specified by the treaty and the Regulations. Such review may result in a determination that such application be considered as pending in the national stage.

(b) The review under subsection (a) of this section, subject to the same requirements and conditions, may also be requested in those instances where an international application designating the United States is considered withdrawn due to a finding by the International Bureau under article 12(3) of the treaty.

HISTORY:

(Added Nov. 14, 1975, P.L. 94-131, § 1, 89 Stat. 687; Nov. 8, 1984, P.L. 98-622, Title IV, § 403(a) in part, 98 Stat. 3392; Nov. 29, 1999, P.L. 106-113, Div B, § 1000(a)(9), 113 Stat. 1536; Nov. 2, 2002, P.L. 107-273, Div C, Title III, Subtitle B, § 13206(b)(1)(B), 116 Stat. 1906.)

§ 368. Secrecy of certain inventions; filing international applications in foreign countries

(a) International applications filed in the Patent and Trademark Office shall be subject to the provisions of chapter 17 of this title [35 USC §§ 181 et seq.].

(b) In accordance with article 27(8) of the treaty, the filing of an international application in a country other than the United States on the invention made in this country shall be considered to constitute the filing of an application in a foreign country within the meaning of chapter 17 of this title [35 USC §§ 181 et seq.], whether or not the United States is designated in that international application.

(c) If a license to file in a foreign country is refused or if an international application is ordered to be kept secret and a permit refused, the Patent and Trademark Office when acting as a Receiving Office, International Searching Authority, or International Preliminary Examining Authority, may not disclose the contents of such application to anyone not authorized to receive such disclosure.

HISTORY:

(Added Nov. 14, 1975, P.L. 94-131, § 1, 89 Stat. 687; Nov. 8, 1984, P.L. 98-622, Title IV, § 403(a) in part, 98 Stat. 3392; Nov. 6, 1986, P.L. 99-616, § 6, 100 Stat. 3486.)

(America Invents Act § 20(j)(1).)

CHAPTER 37. NATIONAL STAGE

§ 371. National stage: Commencement

(a) Receipt from the International Bureau of copies of international applications with any amendments to the claims, international search reports, and international preliminary examination reports including any annexes thereto may be required in the case of international applications designating or electing the United States.

(b) Subject to subsection (f) of this section, the national stage shall commence with the expiration of the applicable time limit under article 22(1) or (2), or under article 39(1)(a) ~~of the treaty~~ of the treaty.

(c) The applicant shall file in the Patent and Trademark Office—

(1) the national fee provided in section 41(a) ~~of this title~~ [35 USC § 41(a)];

(2) a copy of the international application, unless not required under subsection (a) of this section or already communicated by the International Bureau, and a translation into the English language of the international application, if it was filed in another language;

(3) amendments, if any, to the claims in the international application, made under article 19 of the treaty, unless such amendments have been communicated to the Patent and Trademark Office by the International Bureau, and a translation into the English language if such amendments were made in another language;

(4) an oath or declaration of the inventor (or other person authorized under chapter 11 ~~of this title~~ [35 USC §§ 111 et seq.]) complying with the requirements of section 115 ~~of this title~~ [35 USC § 115] and with regulations prescribed for oaths or declarations of applicants;

(5) a translation into the English language of any annexes to the international preliminary examination report, if such annexes were made in another language.

(d) The requirements with respect to the national fee referred to in subsection (c)(1), the translation referred to in subsection (c)(2), and the oath or declaration referred to in subsection (c)(4) of this section shall be complied with by the date of the commencement of the national stage or by such later time as may be fixed by the Director. The copy of the international application referred to in subsection (c)(2) shall be submitted by the date of the commencement of the national stage. Failure to comply with these requirements shall be regarded as abandonment of the application by the parties thereof, unless it be shown to the satisfaction of the Director that such failure to comply was unavoidable. The payment of a surcharge may be required as a condition of accepting the national fee referred to in subsection (c)(1) or the oath or declaration referred to in subsection (c)(4) of this section if these requirements are not met by the date of the commencement of the national stage. The requirements of subsection (c)(3) of this section shall be complied with by the date of the commencement of the national stage, and failure to do so shall be regarded as a cancellation of the amendments to the claim in the international application made under article 19 of the treaty. The requirement of subsection (c)(5) shall be complied with at such time as may be fixed by the Director and failure to do so shall be regarded as cancellation of the amendments made under article 34(2)(b) of the treaty.

(e) After an international application has entered the national stage, no patent may be granted or refused thereon before the expiration of the applicable time limit under article 28 or article 41 of the treaty, except with the express consent of the applicant. The applicant may present amendments to the specification, claims, and drawings of the application after the national stage has commenced.

(f) At the express request of the applicant, the national stage of processing may be commenced at any time at which the application is in order for such purpose and the applicable requirements of subsection (c) of this section have been complied with.

HISTORY:

(Added Nov. 14, 1975, P.L. 94-131, § 1, 89 Stat. 688; Nov. 8, 1984, P.L. 98-622, Title IV, §§ 402(a)-(d), 403(a) in part, 98 Stat. 3391, 3392; Nov. 6, 1986, P.L. 99-616, § 7, 100 Stat. 3486; Dec. 10, 1991, P.L. 102-204, § 5(g)(2), 105 Stat. 1641; Nov. 29, 1999, P.L. 106-113, Div B, § 1000(a)(9), 113 Stat. 1536; Nov. 2, 2002, P.L. 107-273, Div C, Title III, Subtitle B, § 13206(a)(20), (b)(1)(B), 116 Stat. 1905, 1906.)

(America Invents Act §§ 20(i)(5), (j)(1).)

§ 372. National stage: Requirements and procedure

(a) All questions of substance and, within the scope of the requirements of the treaty and Regulations, procedure in an international application designating the United States shall be determined as in the case of national applications regularly filed in the Patent and Trademark Office.

(b) In case of international applications designating but not originating in, the United States—

(1) the Director may cause to be reexamined questions relating to form and contents of the application in accordance with the requirements of the treaty and the Regulations;

(2) the Director may cause the question of unity of invention to be reexamined under section 121 ~~of this title~~ [35 USC § 121], within the scope of the requirements of the treaty and the Regulations; and

(3) the Director may require a verification of the translation of the international application or any other document pertaining to the application if the application or other document was filed in a language other than English.

HISTORY:

(Added Nov. 14, 1975, P.L. 94-131, § 1, 89 Stat. 689; Nov. 8, 1984, P.L. 98-622, Title IV, §§ 402(e), (f), 403(a) in part, 98 Stat. 3392; Nov. 29, 1999, P.L. 106-113, Div B, § 1000(a)(9), 113 Stat. 1536; Nov. 2, 2002, P.L. 107-273, Div C, Title III, Subtitle B, § 13206(b)(1)(B), 116 Stat. 1906.)

(America Invents Act § 20(j)(1).)

§ 373. Improper applicant

An international application designating the United States, shall not be accepted by the Patent and Trademark Office for the national stage if it was filed by anyone not qualified under chapter 11 ~~of this title~~ [35 USC §§ 111 et seq.] to be an applicant for the purpose of filing a national application in the United States. Such international applications shall not serve as the basis for the benefit of an earlier filing date under section 120 ~~of this title~~ [35 USC § 120] in a subsequently filed application, but may serve as the basis for a claim of the right of priority under subsections (a) through (d) of section 119 ~~of this title~~ [35 USC § 119], if the United States was not the sole country designated in such international application.

HISTORY:

(Added Nov. 14, 1975, P.L. 94-131, § 1, 89 Stat. 689; Nov. 8, 1984, P.L. 98-622, Title IV, § 403(a) in part, 98 Stat. 3392; Dec. 8, 1994, P.L. 103-465, Title V, Subtitle C, § 532(c)(5), 108 Stat. 4987.)

(America Invents Act § 20(j)(1).)

§ 374. Publication of international application

The publication under the treaty defined in section 351(a) ~~of this title~~ [35 USC § 351(a)], of an international application designating the United States shall be deemed a publication under section 122(b) [35 USC § 122(b)], except as provided in ~~sections 102(e) and 154(d) of this title [35 USC §§ 102(e) and 154(d)]~~ section 154(d).

HISTORY:

(Added Nov. 14, 1975, P.L. 94-131, § 1, 89 Stat. 689; Nov. 29, 1999, P.L. 106-113, Div B, § 1000(a)(9), 113 Stat. 1536; Nov. 2, 2002, P.L. 107-273, Div C, Title III, Subtitle B, § 13205(2)(E), 116 Stat. 1903.)

(America Invents Act § 3(g)(4); 20(j)(1).)

§ 375. Patent issued on international application: Effect

(a) A patent may be issued by the Director based on an international application designating the United States, in accordance with the provisions of this title. ~~Subject to section 102(e)~~

~~of this title [35 USC § 102(e)], such~~ Such patent shall have the force and effect of a patent issued on a national application filed under the provisions of chapter 11 ~~of this title~~ [35 USC §§ 111 et seq.].

(b) Where due to an incorrect translation the scope of a patent granted on an international application designating the United States, which was not originally filed in the English language, exceeds the scope of the international application in its original language, a court of competent jurisdiction may retroactively limit the scope of the patent, by declaring it unenforceable to the extent that it exceeds the scope of the international application in its original language.

HISTORY:

(Added Nov. 14, 1975, P.L. 94-131, § 1, 89 Stat. 689; Nov. 29, 1999, P.L. 106-113, Div B, § 1000(a)(9), 113 Stat. 1536; Nov. 2, 2002, P.L. 107-273, Div C, Title III, Subtitle B, § 13206(b)(1)(B), 116 Stat. 1906.)

(America Invents Act §§ 3(g)(5); 20(j)(1).)

§ 376. Fees

(a) The required payment of the international fee and the handling fee, which amounts are specified in the Regulations, shall be paid in United States currency. The Patent and Trademark Office shall charge a national fee as provided in section 41(a) [35 USC § 41(a)], and may also charge the following fees:

(1) A transmittal fee (see section 361(d) [35 USC § 361(d)]).

(2) A search fee (see section 361(d) [35 USC § 361(d)]).

(3) A supplemental search fee (to be paid when required).

(4) A preliminary examination fee and any additional fees (see section 362(b) [35 USC § 362(b)]).

(5) Such other fees as established by the Director.

(b) The amounts of fees specified in subsection (a) of this section, except the international fee, and the handling fee shall be prescribed by the Director. He may refund any sum paid by mistake or in excess of the fees so specified, or if required under the treaty and the Regulations. The Director may also refund any part of the search fee, the national fee, the preliminary examination fee, and any additional fees, where he determines such refund to be warranted.

HISTORY:

(Added Nov. 14, 1975, P.L. 94-131, § 1, 89 Stat. 690; Nov. 8, 1984, P.L. 98-622, Title IV, §§ 402(g), 403(a) in part, 98 Stat. 3392; Nov. 6, 1986, P.L. 99-616, § 8, 100 Stat. 3486; Dec. 10, 1991, P.L. 102-204, § 5(g)(1), 105 Stat. 1640; Nov. 29, 1999, P.L. 106-113, Div B, § 1000(a)(9), 113 Stat. 1536; Nov. 2, 2002, P.L. 107-273, Div C, Title III, Subtitle B, § 13206(a)(21), (b)(1)(B), 116 Stat. 1905, 1906.)

SELECTED PROVISIONS OF TITLE 28

Table of Sections

CHAPTER 83—COURTS OF APPEALS

1295. Jurisdiction of the United States Court of Appeals for the Federal Circuit

(a) The United States Court of Appeals for the Federal Circuit shall have exclusive jurisdiction –

~~(1) of an appeal from a final decision of a district court of the United States, the United States District Court for the District of the Canal Zone, the District Court of Guam, the District Court of the Virgin Islands, or the District Court for the Northern Mariana Islands, if the jurisdiction of that court was based, in whole or in part, on section 1338 of this title, except that a case involving a claim arising under any Act of Congress relating to copyrights, exclusive rights in mask works, or trademarks and no other claims under section 1338(a) shall be governed by sections 1291, 1292, and 1294 of this title;~~

<u>(1)</u> of an appeal from a final decision of a district court of the United States, the District Court of Guam, the District Court of the Virgin Islands, or the District Court of the Northern Mariana Islands, in any civil action arising under, or in any civil action in which a party has asserted a compulsory counterclaim arising under, any Act of Congress relating to patents or plant variety protection;

(2) of an appeal from a final decision of a district court of the United States, the United States District Court for the District of the Canal Zone, the District Court of Guam, the District Court of the Virgin Islands, or the District Court for the Northern Mariana Islands, if the jurisdiction of that court was based, in whole or in part, on section 1346 of this title, except that jurisdiction of an appeal in a case brought in a district court under section 1346(a)(1), 1346(b), 1346(e), or 1346(f) of this title or under section 1346(a)(2) when the claim is founded upon an Act of Congress or a regulation of an executive department providing for internal revenue shall be governed by sections 1291, 1292, and 1294 of this title;

(3) of an appeal from a final decision of the United States Court of Federal Claims;

(4) of an appeal from a decision of –

28 USC § 1295

(A) the Board of Patent Appeals and Interferences of the United States Patent and ~~Trademark Office with respect to patent applications and interferences, at the instance of~~ ~~an applicant for a patent or any party to a patent interference, and any such appeal shall~~ ~~waive the right of such applicant or party to proceed under section 145 or 146 of title 35;~~

(A) the Patent Trial and Appeal Board of the United States Patent and Trademark Office with respect to a patent application, derivation proceeding, reexamination, post-grant review, or inter partes review under title 35, at the instance of a party who exercised that party's right to participate in the applicable proceeding before or appeal to the Board, except that an applicant or a party to a derivation proceeding may also have remedy by civil action pursuant to section 145 or 146 of title 35; an appeal under this subparagraph of a decision of the Board with respect to an application or derivation proceeding shall waive the right of such applicant or party to proceed under section 145 or 146 of title 35;

(B) the Under Secretary of Commerce for Intellectual Property and Director of the United States Patent and Trademark Office or the Trademark Trial and Appeal Board with respect to applications for registration of marks and other proceedings as provided in section 21 of the Trademark Act of 1946 (15 U.S.C. 1071); or

(C) a district court to which a case was directed pursuant to section 145, 146, or 154(b) of title 35;

(5) of an appeal from a final decision of the United States Court of International Trade;

(6) to review the final determinations of the United States International Trade Commission relating to unfair practices in import trade, made under section 337 of the Tariff Act of 1930 (19 U.S.C. 1337);

(7) to review, by appeal on questions of law only, findings of the Secretary of Commerce under U.S. note 6 to subchapter X of chapter 98 of the Harmonized Tariff Schedule of the United States (relating to importation of instruments or apparatus);

(8) of an appeal under section 71 of the Plant Variety Protection Act (7 U.S.C. 2461);

(9) of an appeal from a final order or final decision of the Merit Systems Protection Board, pursuant to sections 7703(b)(1) and 7703(d) of title 5;

(10) of an appeal from a final decision of an agency board of contract appeals pursuant to section 7107(a)(1) of title 41;

(11) of an appeal under section 211 of the Economic Stabilization Act of 1970;

(12) of an appeal under section 5 of the Emergency Petroleum Allocation Act of 1973;

(13) of an appeal under section 506(c) of the Natural Gas Policy Act of 1978; and

(14) of an appeal under section 523 of the Energy Policy and Conservation Act.

(b) The head of any executive department or agency may, with the approval of the Attorney General, refer to the Court of Appeals for the Federal Circuit for judicial review any final decision rendered by a board of contract appeals pursuant to the terms of any contract with the United States awarded by that department or agency which the head of such department or agency has concluded is not entitled to finality pursuant to the review standards specified in section 7107(b) of title 41. The head of each executive department or agency shall make any referral under this section within one hundred and twenty days after the receipt of a copy of the final appeal decision.

(c) The Court of Appeals for the Federal Circuit shall review the matter referred in accordance with the standards specified in section 7107(b) of title 41. The court shall proceed with judicial review on the administrative record made before the board of contract appeals on matters so referred as in other cases pending in such court, shall determine the issue of

28 USC § 1295

finality of the appeal decision, and shall, if appropriate, render judgment thereon, or remand the matter to any administrative or executive body or official with such direction as it may deem proper and just.

-SOURCE- (Added Pub. L. 97-164, title I, Sec. 127(a), Apr. 2, 1982, 96 Stat. 37; amended Pub. L. 98-622, title II, Sec. 205(a), Nov. 8, 1984, 98 Stat. 3388; Pub. L. 100-418, title I, Sec. 1214(a)(3), Aug. 23, 1988, 102 Stat. 1156; Pub. L. 100-702, title X, Sec. 1020(a)(3), Nov. 19, 1988, 102 Stat. 4671; Pub. L. 102-572, title I, Sec. 102(c), title IX, Sec. 902(b)(1), Oct. 29, 1992, 106 Stat. 4507, 4516; Pub. L. 106-113, div. B, Sec. 1000(a) (9) [title IV, Secs. 4402(b)(2), 4732(b)(14)], Nov. 29, 1999, 113 Stat. 1536, 1501A-560, 1501A-584; Pub. L. 111-350, Sec. 5(g)(5), Jan. 4, 2011, 124 Stat. 3848.)

(America Invents Act §§ 7(c)(2); 19(b).)

CHAPTER 85—DISTRICT COURTS; JURISDICTION

§ 1338. Patents, plant variety protection, copyrights, mask works, designs, trademarks, and unfair competition

(a) The district courts shall have original jurisdiction of any civil action arising under any Act of Congress relating to patents, plant variety protection, copyrights and trademarks. ~~Such jurisdiction shall be exclusive of the courts of the states in patent, plant variety protection and copyright cases.~~ No State court shall have jurisdiction over any claim for relief arising under any Act of Congress relating to patents, plant variety protection, or copyrights. For purposes of this subsection, the term 'State' includes any State of the United States, the District of Columbia, the Commonwealth of Puerto Rico, the United States Virgin Islands, American Samoa, Guam, and the Northern Mariana Islands.

(b) The district courts shall have original jurisdiction of any civil action asserting a claim of unfair competition when joined with a substantial and related claim under the copyright, patent, plant variety protection or trademark laws.

(c) Subsections (a) and (b) apply to exclusive rights in mask works under chapter 9 of title 17, and to exclusive rights in designs under chapter 13 of title 17, to the same extent as such subsections apply to copyrights.

(June 25, 1948, ch. 646, 62 Stat. 931; Pub. L. 91-577, title III, Sec. 143(b), Dec. 24, 1970, 84 Stat. 1559; Pub. L. 100-702, title X, Sec. 1020(a)(4), Nov. 19, 1988, 102 Stat. 4671; Pub. L. 105-304, title V, Sec. 503(b)(1), (2) (A), Oct. 28, 1998, 112 Stat. 2917; Pub. L. 106-113, div. B, Sec. 1000(a)(9) [title III, Sec. 3009(1)], Nov. 29, 1999, 113 Stat. 1536, 1501A-551.)

(America Invents Act § 19(a).)

CHAPTER 87—DISTRICT COURTS; VENUE

§ 1400. Patents and copyrights, mask works and designs

(a) Civil actions, suits, or proceedings arising under any Act of Congress relating to copyrights or exclusive rights in mask works or designs may be instituted in the district in which the defendant or his agent resides or may be found.

(b) Any civil action for patent infringement may be brought in the judicial district where the defendant resides, or where the defendant has committed acts of infringement and has a regular and established place of business.

(June 25, 1948, ch. 646, 62 Stat. 936; Pub. L. 100-702, title X, Sec. 1020(a)(5), Nov. 19, 1988, 102 Stat. 4671; Pub. L. 105-304, title V, Sec. 503(c)(1), (2), Oct. 28, 1998, 112 Stat. 2917; Pub. L. 106-44, Sec. 2(a), Aug. 5, 1999, 113 Stat. 223.)

CHAPTER 89—DISTRICT COURTS; REMOVAL OF CASES
FROM STATE COURTS

§ 1454. Patent, plant variety protection, and copyright cases

(a) In general.—A civil action in which any party asserts a claim for relief arising under any Act of Congress relating to patents, plant variety protection, or copyrights may be removed to the district court of the United States for the district and division embracing the place where the action is pending.

(b) Special rules.—The removal of an action under this section shall be made in accordance with section 1446, except that if the removal is based solely on this section—

(1) the action may be removed by any party; and

(2) the time limitations contained in section 1446(b) may be extended at any time for cause shown.

(c) Clarification of jurisdiction in certain cases.—The court to which a civil action is removed under this section is not precluded from hearing and determining any claim in the civil action because the State court from which the civil action is removed did not have jurisdiction over that claim.

(d) Remand.—If a civil action is removed solely under this section, the district court—

(1) shall remand all claims that are neither a basis for removal under subsection (a) nor within the original or supplemental jurisdiction of the district court under any Act of Congress; and

(2) may, under the circumstances specified in section 1367(c), remand any claims within the supplemental jurisdiction of the district court under section 1367.

(America Invents Act § 19(c)(1).)

Committee Report 112-98

Excerpt from the House Judiciary Committee Report on the America Invents Act

(Rept. 112-98, June 1, 2011)

Purpose and Summary

[Publisher's Note: Subsequent to this Report, H.R. 1249 was amended by the House of Representatives. These amendments are summarized in the end note following this Report.]

The Constitution explicitly grants Congress the power to "promote the progress of science and useful arts, by securing for limited times to . . . inventors the exclusive right to their respective . . . discoveries."[1] Congress has responded by authorizing patents to issue to inventors of new and useful inventions or improvements on inventions.[2] The patent law thus accomplishes two objectives, consistent with the authorization granted by the Constitution: first, it encourages inventors by granting them limited, but exclusive rights to their inventions; second, in exchange for the grant of those exclusive rights, the patent law requires disclosure of the invention and terminates the monopoly after a period of years.[3] This disclosure and limited time benefits both society and future inventors by making the details of the invention available to the public immediately, and the right to make use of that invention after the expiration of 20 years from the date the patent application was filed.

Congress has not enacted comprehensive patent law reform in nearly 60 years.[4] The object of the patent law today must remain true to the constitutional command, but its form needs to change, both to correct flaws in the system that have become unbearable, and to accommodate changes in the economy and the litigation practices in the patent realm. The need to update our patent laws has been meticulously documented in 15 hearings before the Committee or its Subcommittee on Courts, the Internet, and Intellectual Property, as well as eight hearings before the United States Senate Committee on the Judiciary. In addition, these legislative findings are augmented by the Federal Trade Commission and the National Academy of Sciences,[5] both of which published authoritative reports on patent reform, and a plethora of academic commentary.[6]

While Congress has considered patent reform legislation over the last four Congresses, the need to modernize our patent laws has found expression in the courts, as well. The Supreme

---

1 U.S. Const. Art. 1, § 8.

2 See 35 U.S.C. § 101.

3 See Perspectives on Patents: Post-Grant Review Procedures and Other Litigation Reforms:Hearing before the Subcomm. on Intellectual Prop. of the Senate Comm. on the Judiciary, 109th Cong. (2006) (statement of Nathan P. Myhrvold, Chief Executive Officer, Intellectual Ventures); Perspectives on Patents: Hearing before the Subcomm. on Intellectual Prop. of the Senate Comm. on the Judiciary, 109th Cong. (2005) (statement of Dean Kamen, President, DEKA Research and Development Corp.).

4 The last major revision of the patent laws was the Patent Act of 1952, P.L. 82–593.

5 The National Academy of Sciences (NAS), and the Federal Trade Commission (FTC) conducted multi-year studies on the patent system and its need for reform. See National Research Council of the National Academies, A Patent System for the 21st Century (2004) (hereinafter "NAS Report"); and Federal Trade Comm'n, To Promote Innovation: The Proper Balance of Competition and Patent Law and Policy (2003) (hereinafter "FTC Report").

6 See, e.g., Mark A. Lemley and Carl Shapiro, Patent Holdup and Royalty Stacking, 85 Tex. L. Rev. 1991 (2007); Donald S. Chisum, Reforming Patent Law Reform, 4 J. Marshall Rev. Intell. Prop. L. 336 (2005); Gerald J. Mossinghoff, The First-to-Invent Rule in the U.S. Patent System has Provided no Advantage to Small Entities, 87 JPTOS 514 (2005); Joseph Farrell & Robert P. Merges, Incentives to Challenge and Defend Patents: Why Litigation Won't Reliably Fix Patent Office Errors and Why Administrative Patent Review Might Help, 19 Berkeley Tech. L.J. 943,958 (2004); see also Adam B. Jaffe & Josh Lerner, Innovation and Its Discontents: How Our Broken Patent System is Endangering Innovation and Progress, and What to Do About It (2004); Kevin G. Rivette & David Kline, Rembrandts in the Attic, Unlocking the Hidden Value of Patents (2000).

Court has reversed the Federal Circuit in six of the patent-related cases that it has heard since the beginning of the 109th Congress.[7] The Court's decisions have moved in the direction of improving patent quality and making the determination of patent validity more efficient. The decisions reflect a growing sense that questionable patents are too easily obtained and are too difficult to challenge.[8] Recent decisions by the Federal Circuit reflect a similar trend in response to these concerns.[9] But the courts are constrained in their decisions by the text of the statutes at issue. It is time for Congress to act.

The voices heard during the debate over changes to the patent law have been diverse and their proposals have been far from uniform. They have focused the Committee's attention on the value of harmonizing our system for granting patents with the best parts of other major patent systems throughout the industrialized world for the benefit of U.S. patent holders; improving patent quality and providing a more efficient system for challenging patents that should not have issued; and reducing unwarranted litigation costs and inconsistent damage awards.

The purpose of the "America Invents Act," as reported by the Committee on the Judiciary, is to ensure that the patent system in the 21st century reflects the constitutional imperative. Congress must promote innovation by granting inventors temporally limited monopolies on their inventions in a manner that ultimately benefits the public through the disclosure of the invention to the public. The legislation is designed to establish a more efficient and streamlined patent system that will improve patent quality and limit unnecessary and counterproductive litigation costs.

If the United States is to maintain its competitive edge in the global economy, it needs a system that will support and reward all innovators with high quality patents. The Committee has taken testimony from and its members have held meetings with interested parties that have different and often conflicting perspectives on the patent system. The Committee has taken all of those views into consideration, and drafted and then amended the "America Invents Act" to balance the competing interests. The legislation ordered reported by the Committee on a vote of 32–3 is a consensus approach that will modernize the United States patent system in significant respects.

Background and Need for the Legislation

First Inventor to File

The "America Invents Act" creates a new "first-inventor-to-file" system. Every industri-

---

7 See Bilski v. Kappos,lll U.S. ll, 130 S.Ct. 3218 (2010) (reversing the Federal Circuit and holding that the machine-or-transformation test is not the sole test for determining the patent eligibility of a process); Quanta Computer, Inc. v. LG Elecs. Inc., 553 U.S. 617 (2008) (reversing the Federal Circuit and holding that patent exhaustion applies to method patents when the essential or inventive feature of the invention is embodied in the product); Microsoft Corp. v. AT&T Corp., 550 U.S. 437 (2007) (reversing the Federal Circuit and limiting the extraterritorial reach of section 271(f), which imposes liability on a party which supplies from the U.S. components of a patented invention for combination outside the U.S.); KSR Int'l Co. v. Teleflex Inc., 550 U.S. 398 (2007) (reversing the Federal Circuit and strengthening the standard for determining when an invention is obvious under section 103); MedImmune, Inc. v. Genentech, Inc., 549 U.S. 118 (2007) (reversing the Federal Circuit and holding that the threat of a private enforcement action is sufficient to confirm standing under the Constitution); eBay Inc. v. MercExchange, L.L.C., 547 U.S. 388 (2006) (reversing the Federal Circuit and holding that the generally applicable four-factor test for injunctive relief applies to disputes in patent cases).

8 See generally Patent Reform in the 111th Congress: Legislation and Recent Court Decisions, Senate Judiciary Committee, 111th Cong. (2009) (statement of Professor Mark A. Lemley, Stanford Law School).

9 See, e.g., In re Seagate Tech., LLC, 497 F.3d 1360 (Fed. Cir. 2007) (holding that willful infringement requires at least a demonstration of objectively reckless behavior and removing any affirmative obligation to obtain an opinion of counsel letter to combat an allegation of willful infringement).

alized nation other than the United States uses a patent priority system commonly referred to as "first-to-file." In a first-to-file system, when more than one application claiming the same invention is filed, the priority of a right to a patent is based on the earlier-filed application. The United States, by contrast, currently uses a "first-to-invent" system, in which priority is established through a proceeding to determine which applicant actually invented the claimed invention first. Differences between the two systems arise in large part from the date that is most relevant to each respective system. In a first-to-file system, the filing date of the application is most relevant;[10] the filing date of an application is an objective date, simple to determine, for it is listed on the face of the patent. In contrast, in a first-to-invent system, the date the invention claimed in the application was actually invented is the determinative date. Unlike the objective date of filing, the date someone invents something is often uncertain, and, when disputed, typically requires corroborating evidence as part of an adjudication.

There are significant, practical differences between the two systems. Among them is the ease of determining the right to a claimed invention in the instance in which two different people file patent applications for the same invention. In a first-to-file system, the application with the earlier filing date prevails and will be awarded the patent, if one issues. In the first-to-invent system, a lengthy, complex and costly administrative proceeding (called an "interference proceeding") must be conducted at the United States Patent and Trademark Office ("USPTO") to determine who actually invented first.[11] Interference proceedings can take years to complete (even if there is no appeal to the United States Court of Appeals for the Federal Circuit), cost hundreds of thousands of dollars, and require extensive discovery.[12] In addition, because it is always possible that an applicant could be involved in an interference proceeding, companies must maintain extensive recording and document retention systems in case they are later required to prove the date they invented the claimed invention.

Another important difference between the two systems is that in some first-to-file systems, prior art can include the inventor's own disclosure of his invention prior to the filing date of his application. Such systems do not provide the inventor any grace period during which time he is allowed to publish his invention without fear of its later being used against him as prior art. The Committee heard from universities and small inventors, in particular, about the importance of maintaining that grace period in our system.[13] They argued that the grace period affords the necessary time to prepare and file applications, and in some instances, to obtain the necessary funding that enables the inventor to prepare adequately the application. In addition, the grace period benefits the public by encouraging early disclosure of new inventions, regardless of whether an application may later be filed for a patent on it.

Numerous organizations, institutions, and companies have advocated that the U.S. adopt a first-to-file system similar to those used in the rest of the world.[14] The National Academy

---

10   When the term "filing date" is used herein, it is also meant to include, when appropriate, the effective filing date, i.e., the earliest date the claim in an application-claims priority.

11   See 35 U.S.C. § 135.

12   See, e.g., Robert W. Pritchard, The Future is Now—The Case for Patent Harmonization, 20 N.C. J. Int'l L. & Com. Reg. 291, 313 (1995).

13   See, e.g., Perspectives on Patents: Harmonization and Other Matters: Hearing Before the Subcomm. on Intellectual Prop. of the Senate Comm. on the Judiciary, 109th Cong. (2005) (statement of Charles E. Phelps, Provost, University of Rochester, on behalf of the Association of American Universities); Patent Law Reform: Injunctions and Damages: Hearing Before the Subcomm. on Intellectual Prop. of the Senate Comm. on the Judiciary, 109th Cong. (2005) (statement of Carl Gulbrandsen, Managing Director, Wisconsin Alumni Research Foundation (WARF)); Perspective on Patents: Hearing Before the Subcomm. on Intellectual Prop. of the Senate Comm. on the Judiciary, 109th Cong. (2005) (statement of William Parker, Diffraction, Ltd.).

14   See, e.g., Perspectives on Patents: Harmonization and Other Matters: Hearing Before the Subcomm. on Intel-

of Sciences made a similar recommendation after an extensive study of the patent system.[15] When the United States patent system was first adopted, inventors did not typically file in other countries. It is now common for inventors and companies to file for protection in several countries at the same time.[16] Thus, United States applicants, who also want to file abroad, are forced to follow and comply with two different filing systems. Maintaining a filing system so different from the rest of the world disadvantages United States applicants who, in most instances, also file in other countries.[17] A change is long overdue.[18]

Drawing on the best aspects of the two existing systems, the America Invents Act creates a new "first-inventor-to-file" system. This new system provides patent applicants in the United States the efficiency benefits of the first-to-file systems used in the rest of the world by moving the U.S. system much closer to a first-to-file system and making the filing date that which is most relevant in determining whether an application is patentable. The new system continues, however, to provide inventors the benefit of the 1-year grace period. As part of the transition to a simpler, more efficient first-inventor-to-file system, this provision eliminates costly, complex interference proceedings, because priority will be based on the first application. A new administrative proceeding—called a "derivation" proceeding—is created to ensure that the first person to file the application is actually a true inventor. This new proceeding will ensure that a person will not be able to obtain a patent for the invention that he did not actually invent. If a dispute arises as to which of two applicants is a true inventor (as opposed to who invented it first), it will be resolved through an administrative proceeding by the Patent Board. The Act also simplifies how prior art is determined, provides more certainty, and reduces the cost associated with filing and litigating patents.

lectual Prop. of the Senate Comm. on the Judiciary, 109th Cong. (2005) (statement of Gerald J. Mossinghoff, Former Assistant Secretary of Commerce and Commissioner of Patents and Trademarks); Perspectives on Patents: Harmonization and Other Matters: Hearing Before the Subcomm. on Intellectual Prop. of the Senate Comm. on the Judiciary, 109th Cong. (2005) (statement of Q. Todd Dickinson, Former Under Secretary of Commerce for Intellectual Property and Director of the United States Patent and Trademark Office); Patent Law Reform: Injunctions and Damages: Hearing Before the Subcomm. on Intellectual Prop. of the Senate Comm. on the Judiciary, 109th Cong. (2005) (statement of Jeffrey P. Kushan, Partner, Sidley Austin Brown & Wood, LLP); Patent Law Reform: Injunctions and Damages: Hearing Before the Subcomm. on Intellectual Prop. of the Senate Comm. on the Judiciary, 109th Cong. (2005) (statement of Mark A. Lemley, Professor, Stanford Law School); Perspectives on Patents: Hearing Before the Subcomm. on Intellectual Prop. of the Senate Comm. on the Judiciary, 109th Cong. (2005) (statement of Robert A. Armitage, Senior Vice President and General Patent Counsel, Eli Lilly and Company); Perspectives on Patents: Hearing Before the Subcomm. on Intellectual Prop. of the Senate Comm. on the Judiciary, 109th Cong. (2005) (statement of Michael K. Kirk, Executive Director, American Intellectual Property Law Association).

15 See NAS Report at 124; see also Perspectives on Patents: Hearing Before the Subcomm. on Intellectual Prop. of the Senate Comm. on the Judiciary, 109th Cong. (2005) (statement of Richard C. Levin, Yale University).

16 See Perspectives on Patents: Harmonization and Other Matters: Hearing Before the Subcomm. on Intellectual Prop. of the Senate Comm. on the Judiciary, 109th Cong. (2005) (statement of Gerald J. Mossinghoff, Former Assistant Secretary of Commerce and Commissioner of Patents and Trademarks) .

17 See Perspectives on Patents: Hearing Before the Subcomm. on Intellectual Prop. of the Senate Comm. on the Judiciary, 109th Cong. (2005) (statement of Richard C. Levin, President, Yale University, and Mark B. Meyers, Visiting Executive Professor, Management Department at the Wharton Business School, University of Pennsylvania), estimating that it costs as much as $750,000 to $1 million to obtain worldwide patent protection on an important invention, and the lack of harmonization regarding filing systems adds unnecessary cost and delay.

18 The NAS recommended changing the U.S. to a first-to-file system, while maintaining a grace period. See NAS Report at 124–27. See also Patent Reform in the 111th Congress: Legislation and Recent Court Decisions: Hearing Before the Senate Comm. on the Judiciary, 111th Cong. (2009) (statement of Steven Appleton, Chairman and Chief Executive Officer, Micron Technologies, Inc.); Patent Reform in the 111th Congress: Legislation and Recent Court Decisions: Hearing Before the Senate Comm. on the Judiciary, 111th Cong. (2009) (statement of Philip S. Johnson, Chief Patent Counsel, Johnson & Johnson); Patent Reform in the 111th Congress: Legislation and Recent Court Decisions: Hearing Before the Senate Comm. on the Judiciary, 111th Cong. (2009) (statement of Herbert C. Wamsley, Executive Director, Intellectual Property Owners Association); Patent Reform in the 111th Congress: Legislation and Recent Court Decisions: Hearing Before the Senate Comm. on the Judiciary, 111th Cong. (2009) (statement of Mark A. Lemley, Professor, Stanford Law School).

Committee Report 112-98

The Act maintains a 1-year grace period for U.S. applicants. Applicants' own publication or disclosure that occurs within 1 year prior to filing will not act as prior art against their applications. Similarly, disclosure by others during that time based on information obtained (directly or indirectly) from the inventor will not constitute prior art. This 1-year grace period should continue to give U.S. applicants the time they need to prepare and file their applications.

This provision also, and necessarily, modifies the prior-art sections of the patent law. Prior art will be measured from the filing date of the application and will typically include all art that publicly exists prior to the filing date, other than disclosures by the inventor within 1 year of filing. Prior art also will no longer have any geographic limitations. Thus, in section 102 the "in this country" limitation as applied to "public use" and "on sale" is removed, and the phrase "available to the public" is added to clarify the broad scope of relevant prior art, as well as to emphasize the fact that it must be publicly accessible. Prior art based on earlier-filed United States applications is maintained,[19] as is current law's grace period, which will apply to all actions by the patent owner during the year prior to filing that would otherwise create § 102(a) prior art.[20] Sections (and subsections) of the existing statute are renumbered, modified, or deleted consistent with converting to a first-inventor-to-file system.[21] Finally, the intent behind the CREATE Act to promote joint research activities is preserved by including a prior art exception for subject matter invented by parties to a joint research agreement. The Act also provides that its enactment of new section 102(c) of title 35 is done with the same intent to promote joint research activities that was expressed in the Cooperative Research and Technology Enhancement Act of 2004 (Public Law 108–453), and that section 102(c) shall be administered in a manner consistent with such intent.

Inventor's oath or declaration

The U.S. patent system, when first adopted in 1790, contemplated that individual inventors would file their own patent applications, or would have a patent practitioner do so on their behalf. It has become increasingly common for patent applications to be assigned to corporate entities, most commonly the employer of the inventor.[22] In fact, many employment contracts require employees to assign their inventions to their employer.[23]

Current law still reflects the antiquated notion that it is the inventor who files the application, not the company-assignee. For example, every inventor must sign an oath as part of the patent application stating that the inventor believes he or she is the true inventor of the invention claimed in the application.[24] By the time an application is eventually filed, however, the applicant filing as an assignee may have difficulty locating and obtaining every inventor's signature for the statutorily required oath. Although the USPTO has adopted certain regulations to allow filing of an application when the inventor's signature is unobtainable,[25] many

---

19   Compare current § 102(e) with new § 102(a)(2).
20   See generally 157 Cong. Rec. S.1496–97 (daily ed. March 9, 2011), S. 1370–71 (daily ed. March 8, 2011).
21   The Committee does not intend a substantive change by replacing the word "negatived" in section 103 of title 35 with "negated."
22   See John R. Allison & Mark A. Lemley, The Growing Complexity of the United States Patent System, 82 B.U. L. Rev. 77, 97 (2002) (study showing that approximately 85% of the patents issued between 1996–98 were assigned by inventors to corporations; an increase from 79% during the period between 1976–78).
23   See Jerry C. Liu, Overview of Patent Ownership Considerations in Joint Technology Development, 2005 Syracuse Sci. & Tech. L. Rep. 1 (2005).
24   35 U.S.C. § 115.
25   See 37 C.F.R. § 1.47, which permits an applicant to petition the Director of the USPTO to have the application accepted without every inventor's signature in limited circumstances, e.g., when the inventor cannot be found or refuses to participate in the application.

have advocated that the statute be modernized to facilitate the filing of applications by assignees.[26]

The Act updates the patent system by facilitating the process by which an assignee may file and prosecute patent applications. It provides similar flexibility for a person to whom the inventor is obligated to assign, but has not assigned, rights to the invention (the "obligated assignee").

Section 115 of title 35 is amended to allow a substitute statement to be submitted in lieu of an inventor's oath when either the inventor (i) is unable to submit an oath, or (ii) is both unwilling to do so and under an obligation to assign the invention. If an error is discovered, the statement may later be corrected. A savings clause is included to prevent an invalidity or unenforceability challenge to the patent based on failure to comply with these requirements, provided that any error has been remedied. Willful false statements remain punishable, however, under Federal criminal laws.[27]

Section 118 of title 35 is also amended to make it easier for an assignee to file a patent application. The amendment now allows obligated assignees—entities to which the inventor is obligated to assign the application—to file applications, as well. It also allows a person who has a sufficient proprietary interest in the invention to file an application to preserve that person's rights and those of the inventor.

Defense to infringement based on earlier inventor

Under current law, "prior user rights" may offer a defense to patent infringement when the patent in question is a "business method patent" [28] and its inventor uses the invention, but never files a patent application for it.[29] If the same invention is later patented by another party, the prior user may not be liable for infringement to the new patent holder, although all others may be.

Many counties [sic, probably should be "countries"] include a more expansive prior-user rights regime within their first-to-file system. In the United States, this is particularly important to high-tech businesses that prefer not to patent every process or method that is part of their commercial operations. The Act responds to this point by revising US law as follows: First, the prior-use defense may be asserted against any patent (not just method patents), provided the person asserting the defense reduced the subject matter of the patent to practice and commercially used the subject matter at least 1 year before the effective filing date of the patent. Second, the defense cannot be asserted if the subject matter was derived from the patent holder or persons in privity with the patent holder. And third, the defense cannot be asserted unless the prior user both reduced the subject matter of the patent to practice and commercially used it at least 1 year before the effective filing date of the patent or the date that the patentee publicly disclosed the invention and invoked the § 102(b) grace period, whichever is earlier.

This narrow expansion of prior-user rights balances the interests of patent holders, including universities, against the legitimate concerns of businesses that want to avoid infringement suits relating to processes that they developed and used prior to another party acquiring related patents.

---

26 See Perspectives on Patents: Harmonization and Other Matters: Hearing Before the Subcomm. on Intellectual Prop. of the Senate Comm. on the Judiciary, 109th Cong. (2005) (statement of David Beier, Senior Vice President of Global Government Affairs, Amgen).

27 See 18 U.S.C. § 1001.

28 35 U.S.C. § 273(a)(3) states: "The term 'method' means a method of doing or conducting business."

29 See 35 U.S.C. § 273.

Committee Report 112-98

Post-grant review proceedings

The Act amends ex parte and inter partes reexamination and establishes a new post-grant review procedure. Under current law, there are two ways to challenge the validity and enforceability of a patent that has issued. The patent may be challenged in district court litigation or in a reexamination at the USPTO.

Nearly 30 years ago, Congress created the administrative "reexamination" process, through which the USPTO could review the validity of already-issued patents on the request of either the patent holder or a third party,[30] in the expectation that it would serve as an effective and efficient alternative to often costly and protracted district court litigation.[31] Reexamination requires the USPTO to review the patent in light of a substantial new question of patentability not presented during the original examination.[32] The initial reexamination statute had several limitations that later proved to make it a less viable alternative to litigation for evaluating patent validity than Congress intended. First, a reexamination request could only be based on prior art, and could not be based on prior public use or prior sales. Moreover, the requestor could not raise any challenge based on § 101 (utility, eligibility) or § 112 (indefiniteness, enablement, written description, best mode). A third party alleging a patent is invalid, therefore, had fewer challenges it could raise in the proceeding and, therefore, may instead opt to risk infringement and litigate the validity of the patent in court. Second, in the original reexamination system, the third-party challenger had no role once the proceeding was initiated, while the patent holder had significant input throughout the entire process. Third, a challenger that lost at the USPTO under reexamination had no right to appeal an examiner's, or the Patent Board's, decision either administratively or in court. Restrictions such as these made reexamination a much less favored avenue to challenge questionable patents than litigation. Reexamination proceedings are also often costly, taking several years to complete,[33] and are first conducted by examiners and, if the patent is rejected, then by Patent Board judges. Thus, many patents must go through two rounds of administrative review (one by the examiner, and a second by the Patent Board) adding to the length of the proceeding.[34]

---

30 See 35 U.S.C. §§ 301–307. A patent holder will typically request reexamination to bolster the patent in view of new prior art. A third party may request reexamination to challenge, and ultimately invalidate, the patent.

31 "Reexamination will permit efficient resolution of questions about the validity of issued patents without recourse to expensive and lengthy infringement litigation.... The reexamination of issued patents could be conducted with a fraction of the time and cost of formal legal proceedings and would help restore confidence in the effectiveness of our patent system.... It is anticipated that these measures provide a useful and necessary alternative for challengers and for patent owners to test the validity of united states patents in an efficient and relatively inexpensive manner." See H.R. Rep. No. 96–1307(I) at 3 (1980), reprinted in 1980 U.S.C.C.A.N.6460, 6462–63.

32 See 35 U.S.C. § 303.

33 See Perspectives on Patents: Hearing Before the Subcomm. on Intellectual Prop. of the Senate Comm. on the Judiciary, 109th Cong. (2005) (statement of Jon W. Dudas, Undersecretary of Commerce for Intellectual Property, Director of the U.S. Patent and Trademark Office), explaining that "a large number of reexamination proceedings have been pending before the USPTO for more than 4 years," and questioning whether this amount of time is consistent with the statutory requirement that "[a]ll reexamination proceedings . . . will be conducted with special dispatch within the Office." See also 35 U.S.C. § 305.

34 For several years, the standard practice at the USPTO was to assign the reexamination to the patent examiner who had originally examined that patent. In addition, the same third-party requester could file multiple, serial reexaminations based on the same "substantial new question of patentability," so long as the initial reexamination was not complete. More recently, the USPTO ended some of these procedures, and now reexaminations are handled by a Central Reexamination Unit (CRU), and subsequent serial reexamination, based on the same "substantial new question of patentability," is no longer permitted. See, e.g., Manual of Patent Examining Procedure (MPEP) §§ 2236 and 2240 (August 2006).

Congress has responded several times to criticisms of the reexamination system by making amendments to the process.[35] In 1999, Congress created a second reexamination procedure—called inter partes reexamination—that gave third-party challengers greater input throughout the proceeding by permitting them to respond to every pleading submitted by the patent holder.[36] Congress also eventually gave third-party challengers the right to appeal adverse decisions.[37]

As part of the 1999 improvements to reexamination, Congress directed the USPTO to submit a report to Congress evaluating the inter partes reexamination process and making any recommendations for changes.[38] Initially, the USPTO projected that in the first year after the creation of inter partes reexamination, it would receive 400 such requests and it projected that by 2004 it would receive nearly 600.[39] No inter partes reexamination requests were actually filed in 2000 and only 27 such requests had been filed by 2004.[40] Over the 5-year period studied by the USPTO, it issued 900,000 patents and received only 53 requests for inter partes reexamination.[41]

The Act expands the category of documents that may be cited in a reexamination proceeding to include written statements of the patent owner that have been filed in a proceeding before a Federal court or the USPTO regarding the scope of claims. This addition will counteract the ability of patent owners to offer differing interpretations of prior art in different proceedings. These written statements, which include documents, pleadings or evidence from proceedings that address the patent owner's statements, shall not be considered for any purpose other than to determine the proper meaning of the claims that are the subject of the request in a proceeding. Specifically, the Committee does not intend these statements to be a basis for the institution of a reexamination proceeding. Reexaminations will continue to be available only on the basis of "patents or printed publications." [42]

The Act also amends the ex parte reexamination procedure to allow the Director to institute a reexamination on the Director's own initiative if a substantial new question of patentability is raised by patents or publications.

The Act converts inter partes reexamination from an examinational to an adjudicative proceeding, and renames the proceeding "inter partes review." The Act also makes the following improvements to this proceeding:

- **"Reasonable likelihood of success"** for instituting inter partes review. The threshold for initiating an inter partes review is elevated from "significant new question of patentability"—a standard that currently allows 95% of all requests to be granted— to a standard requiring petitioners to present information showing that their challenge has a reasonable likelihood of success. Satisfaction of the new threshold will

35 See e.g., 21st Century Dep't of Justice Appropriations Authorization Act, Pub. L. No. 107–273, §§ 13105–06, 13202, 116 Stat. 1758, 1761 (2002) (effective Nov. 2, 2002); American Inventors Protection Act, Pub.L. 106–113, 113 Stat. 1536, § 1501A et seq. (1999) (creating inter partes reexamination) (hereafter referred to as the "AIPA").
36 See 35 U.S.C. §§ 311–318.
37 See 35 U.S.C. § 315(b).
38 AIPA, Pub. L. 106–113, § 4606.
39 See United States Patent and Trademark Office, Report to Congress on Inter Partes Reexamination (2004) (hereinafter referred to as "Report on Inter Partes Reexamination"), at 4.
40 Id. at 5.
41 Id.
42 The scope of "patent and printed publication" prior art in the amended section 301 is intended to be coextensive with these terms in current section 102 of the title 35. Further, amendments made by Section 2 of the Act, which expand and contract the definition of certain other forms of prior art, are not intended to change the particular "patent or printed publication" prior art, which will continue to be the sole basis for initiating reexamination proceedings.

be assessed based on the information presented both in the petition for the proceeding and in the patent owner's response to the petition.

- **"Reasonably could have raised" estoppel applied to subsequent administrative proceedings.** A party that uses inter partes review is estopped from raising in a subsequent PTO proceeding (such as an ex parte reexam or inter partes review) any issue that it raised or reasonably could have raised in the inter partes review.

- **Repeal of the 1999 limit.** The limit on challenging patents issued before 1999 in inter partes reexamination is eliminated; all patents can be challenged in inter partes review.

- **Preponderance burden.** Petitioners bear the burden of proving that a patent is invalid by a preponderance of the evidence in inter partes review.

- **Time limits during litigation.** Parties who want to use inter partes review during litigation are required to seek a proceeding within 12 months of being served with a complaint alleging infringement of the patent, and are barred from seeking or maintaining an inter partes review if they file an action for a declaratory judgment that the patent is invalid.

- **Discovery.** Parties may depose witnesses submitting affidavits or declarations and seek such discovery as the Patent Office determines is otherwise necessary in the interest of justice.

- **12- to 18-month deadline.** Inter partes review must be completed within 1 year of when the proceeding is instituted, except that the Office can extend this deadline by 6 months for good cause.

- **Oral hearing.** Each party has the right to request an oral hearing as part of an inter partes review.

- **Three-judge panels.** Inter partes reviews will be conducted before a panel of three APJs. Decisions will be appealed directly to the Federal Circuit.

The Act also creates a new post-grant opposition procedure that can be utilized during the first 12 months after the grant of a patent or issue of a reissue patent. Unlike reexamination proceedings, which provide only a limited basis on which to consider whether a patent should have issued, the post-grant review proceeding permits a challenge on any ground related to invalidity under section 282. The intent of the post-grant review process is to enable early challenges to patents, while still protecting the rights of inventors and patent owners against new patent challenges unbounded in time and scope. The Committee believes that this new, early-stage process for challenging patent validity and its clear procedures for submission of art will make the patent system more efficient and improve the quality of patents and the patent system. This new, but time-limited, post-grant review procedure will provide a meaningful opportunity to improve patent quality and restore confidence in the presumption of validity that comes with issued patents in court.

In utilizing the post-grant review process, petitioners, real parties in interest, and their privies are precluded from improperly mounting multiple challenges to a patent or initiating challenges after filing a civil action challenging the validity a claim in the patent. Further, a final decision in a post-grant review process will prevent the petitioner, a real party in interest, or its privy from challenging any patent claim on a ground that was raised in the post-grant review process. The post-grant review procedure is not intended, however, to inhibit patent owners from pursuing the various avenues of enforcement of their rights under a patent, and the amendment makes clear that the filing or institution of a post-grant review proceeding does not limit a patent owner from commencing such actions.

The Committee recognizes the importance of quiet title to patent owners to ensure continued investment resources. While this amendment is intended to remove current disincentives to current administrative processes, the changes made by it are not to be used as tools for harassment or a means to prevent market entry through repeated litigation and administrative attacks on the validity of a patent. Doing so would frustrate the purpose of the section as providing quick and cost effective alternatives to litigation. Further, such activity would divert resources from the research and development of inventions. As such, the Committee intends for the USPTO to address potential abuses and current inefficiencies under its expanded procedural authority.

Patent Trial and Appeal Board.

The Act renames the Patent Board the "Patent Trial and Appeal Board" and sets forth its duties, which are expanded to include jurisdiction over the new post-grant review and derivation proceedings. This section strikes references to proceedings eliminated by the Act, including interference proceedings, and updates the various appeals statutes.

Preissuance submissions by third parties

After an application is published, members of the public—most likely, a competitor or someone else familiar with the patented invention's field—may realize they have information relevant to a pending application. The relevant information may include prior art that would prohibit the pending application from issuing as a patent. Current USPTO rules permit the submission of such prior art by third parties only if it is in the form of a patent or publication,[43] but the submitter is precluded from explaining why the prior art was submitted or what its relevancy to the application might be.[44] Such restrictions decrease the value of the information to the examiner and may, as a result, deter such submissions.[45]

The Act improves the process by which third parties submit relevant information to the UPSTO by permitting those third parties to make statements concerning the relevance of the patents, patent applications, and other printed publications that they bring to the USPTO's attention.

Venue

In 1999, as part of the American Inventors Protection Act (AIPA), Congress established that as a general matter the venue of the USPTO is the district where it resides.[46] The USPTO currently resides in the Eastern District of Virginia. However, Congress inadvertently failed to make this change uniformly throughout the entire patent statute. As a result, certain sections of the patent statute (and one section of the trademark statute) continue to allow challenges to USPTO decisions to be brought in the District of Columbia, a place where the USPTO has not resided in decades.

---

43   See 35 C.F.R. § 1.99.
44   See 35 C.F.R. § 1.99(d) ("A submission under this section shall not include any explanation of the patents or publications, or any other information.").
45   See Perspectives on Patents: Hearing Before the Subcomm. on Intellectual Prop. of the Senate Comm. on the Judiciary, 109th Cong. (2005) (statement of David Simon, Chief Patent Counsel, Intel Corporation).
46   See 35 U.S.C. § 1(b).

Committee Report 112-98

Because the USPTO no longer resides in the District of Columbia, the sections that authorize venue for litigation against the USPTO are consistently changed to reflect the venue where the USPTO currently resides.

Fee-setting authority

a) Agency fee setting authority

Although the USPTO has had the ability to set certain fees by regulation, most fees (e.g., filing fee, issuance fee, maintenance fees) are set by Congress.[47] History has shown that such a scheme does not allow the USPTO to respond promptly to the challenges that confront it. The USPTO has argued for years that it must have fee-setting authority to administer properly the agency and its growing workload.

The Act allows the USPTO to set or adjust all of its fees, including those related to patents and trademarks, so long as they do no more than reasonably compensate the USPTO for the services performed. Prior to setting such fees, the Director must give notice to, and receive input from, the Patent or Trademark Public Advisory Committee (PPAC or TPAC). The Director may also reduce fees for any given fiscal year, but only after consultation with the PPAC or TPAC. The Act details the procedures for how the Director shall consult with the PPAC and TPAC, including providing for public hearings and the dissemination to the public of any recommendations made by either Committee. Fees shall be prescribed by rule. Any proposed fee change shall be published in the Federal Register and include the specific rationale and purpose for the proposed change. The Director must seek public comments for no less than 45 days. The Director must also notify Congress of any final decision regarding proposed fees. Congress shall have no more than 45 days to consider and comment on any proposed fee, but no proposed fee shall be effective prior to the expiration of this 45-day period.

b) "Micro entity" defined

As part of the ongoing effort to nurture U.S. innovation, Congress has long recognized that certain groups, including independent inventors, small business concerns, and non-profit organizations (collectively referred to as "small business entities") should not bear the same financial burden for filing patent applications as larger corporate interests. The current statute provides for a significant reduction in certain fees for small business entities.[48] The Committee was made aware, however, that there is likely a benefit to describing—and then accommodating—a group of inventors who are even smaller, in order to ensure that the USPTO can tailor its requirements, and its assistance, to the people with very little capital, and just a few inventions, as they are starting out.

This section of the Act defines this even smaller group—the micro-entity—that includes only truly independent inventors. The Committee expects that the USPTO will make accommodations under its authority in recognition of the special status of micro-entities.

Supplemental examination

Patents are unenforceable and invalid if they are obtained through fraud. This concept is addressed in the "inequitable conduct" defense, which allows a defendant in an infringement suit to plead that the plaintiff patent-holder would not have received a patent but for misrepresentations made to the USPTO. Inequitable conduct requires proof of materiality as well as intent to deceive. These standards require courts and litigants to invest time and

---

47 See, e.g., 35 U.S.C. § 41.
48 See 35 U.S.C. § 41(h).

resources in determining the patent-holder's state of mind or intent when developing the invention and submitting the application. Critics of the inequitable conduct defense, including the National Academies and the Federal Trade Commission, argue that our patent system is hampered by provisions that require courts to divine the difficult-to-prove subjective intent of individuals in patent disputes. And most defendants reflexively plead inequitable conduct as a defense to infringement, prompting the Federal Circuit to label the practice a "plague" on the patent system.

The Act addresses the inequitable conduct doctrine by authorizing supplemental examination of a patent to correct errors or omissions in proceedings before the Office. Under this new procedure, information that was not considered or was inadequately considered or was incorrect can be presented to the Office. If the Office determines that the information does not present a substantial new question of patentability or that the patent is still valid, that information cannot later be used to hold the patent unenforceable or invalid on the basis for an inequitable-conduct attack in civil litigation.

Funding agreements

The Patent and Trademark Amendments Act of 1980 (commonly referred to as the Bayh-Dole Act)[49] granted universities, other non-profit organizations, and small businesses the right to title to inventions developed using Federal funds. In 1984, Congress amended the law to ensure that universities and small businesses operating at Government facilities (GO-COs) reaped the benefits of Bayh-Dole by giving them the right to elect title to a subject invention.[50] The 1984 Act permitted GOCOs to retain the balance of any royalties or income earned from licensing inventions, up to 5 percent of the annual budget of the facility, for further research, development, and related activities. If the balance exceeds 5 percent of the facility's annual budget, however, 75 percent of the excess is re-couped by the Government, with the remaining 25 percent of the excess also retained by the GOCO for further research, development, and related activities.[51]

The Senate Judiciary Committee considered testimony that the requirement to repay the government 75 percent of the excess on royalty payments may be causing a disincentive for universities and small business operating under the GOCO provisions to commercialize products.[52] Based on these concerns, the Act maintains the essence of the agreement GOCOs made with the taxpayers when they received funding that they would reimburse the taxpayer if they are sufficiently successful in commercializing a product invented with taxpayer dollars, but which reduces the burden on universities and small businesses, thereby encouraging commercialization. Pursuant to the Act, instead of reimbursing 75% of the excess to the Government, the GOCO will retain 85 percent for further research, development, and related activities and reimburse the Government 15 percent.

Tax strategies deemed within the prior art

In recent years, the numbers of patents on tax-strategies have increased. Critics assert that it is not fair to permit patents on techniques used to satisfy a government mandate, such as compliance with the Internal Revenue Code.

---

49 P.L. 96–517.
50 P.L. 98–620, § 501.
51 35 U.S.C. § 202(c)(7).
52 See The Role of Federally-Funded University Research in the Patent System: Hearing Before the Senate Comm. on the Judiciary, 110th Cong. (2008) (statement of Dr. Elizabeth Hoffman, Executive Vice President and Provost, Iowa State University).

Committee Report 112-98

Tax preparers, lawyers, and planners have a long history of sharing their knowledge regarding how to file returns, plan estates, and advise clients. The ability to interpret the tax law and implement such interpretations should remain in the public domain, available to all taxpayers and their advisors.

The Act mandates that tax strategies are deemed "insufficient to differentiate a claimed invention from the prior art." In other words, any future tax strategy will be considered indistinguishable from all other publicly available information that is relevant to a patent's claim of originality. Under the Act, however, protection (an exclusion) is made available for software that enables individuals to file their income tax returns or that assists them with managing their finances. The exclusion does not apply to that part of the software related to a tax strategy.

Best mode requirement

The Act amends § 282(b) to eliminate as a defense to patent infringement the patentee's failure to comply with the best mode requirement of § 112. An applicant for a patent must disclose: (1) a written description of the invention; (2) a written description of the manner of making and using the invention, sufficient to enable one skilled in the art to make and use it (known as the "enablement requirement"); and (3) the best mode contemplated by the inventor of carrying out the invention.[53] The disclosures required of an applicant are part of the important tradeoff that underlies the patent laws: the grant of a limited-term monopoly in exchange for disclosure of the invention.

Under current law, the defense of patent invalidity is available for failure to comply with any requirement of § 112 (specification) or § 251 (reissued patents). Further, a defendant in patent litigation may also allege an intentional nondisclosure of the best mode, with intent to deceive the Office, as a basis for an unenforceability defense. Many have argued in recent years that the best mode requirement, which is unique to American patent law, is counterproductive.[54] They argue that challenges to patents based on best mode are inherently subjective and not relevant by the time the patent is in litigation, because the best mode contemplated at the time of the invention may not be the best mode for practicing or using the invention years later.

In response to these concerns, the Act includes a provision that eliminates best mode as a basis for both invalidity and unenforceability defenses under § 282; other defenses are unaffected.

Marking

a) Virtual Marking

In general, for patented "articles," a patent holder must give an alleged infringer notice of the claimed infringement, and the infringer must continue to infringe, before the patent holder may succeed in a suit for damages.[55] Actual notice requires the affirmative communication of infringement to the defendant, which may include the filing of a lawsuit. Constructive notice is possible by "marking" any patented article that the patent holder (or its licensee)

---

53 35 U.S.C. § 112. Section 112 also requires an applicant to disclose a written description of the invention and a written description of the manner of making and using the invention, sufficient to enable one skilled in the art to make and use it.

54 Among those who have so argued are the National Academy of Sciences, the Biotechnology Industry Organization, the American Intellectual Property Law Association, the Intellectual Property Owners Association, and Pharmaceutical Research and Manufacturers of America.

55 See 35 U.S.C. § 287.

makes, uses, sells or imports.[56] Failure to appropriately mark an article can preclude the recovery of damages until notice is effective.

The Act permits patent holders to "virtually mark" a product by providing the address of a publicly available website that associates the patented article with the number of the patent. The burden will remain on the patent holder to demonstrate that the marking was effective. This amendment will save costs for producers of products that include technology on which a patent issues after the product is on the market, and will facilitate effective marking on smaller products.

b) False marking

The Federal Circuit's recent decision in Forest Group, Inc. v. Bon Tool Co., 590 F.3d 1295 (Fed. Cir. 2009), which held that section 292's $500 fine is assessed for each product that is falsely marked, has created a surge in false-marking qui tam litigation. Though one might assume that section 292 actions are targeted at parties that assert fictitious patents in order to deter competitors, such a scenario is almost wholly unknown to false-marking litigation. False-marking suits are almost always based on allegations that a valid patent that did cover the product has expired, but the manufacturer continued to sell products stamped with the patent; or that an existing patent used to mark products is invalid or unenforceable; or that an existing and valid patent's claims should not be construed to cover the product in question.

Indeed, a recent survey of such suits found that a large majority involved valid patents that covered the products in question but had simply expired. For many products, it is difficult and expensive to change a mold or other means by which a product is marked as patented, and marked products continue to circulate in commerce for some period after the patent expires. It is doubtful that the Congress that originally enacted this section anticipated that it would force manufacturers to immediately remove marked products from commerce once the patent expired, given that the expense to manufacturers of doing so will generally greatly outweigh any conceivable harm of allowing such products to continue to circulate in commerce.

To address the recent surge in litigation, the bill replaces the qui tam remedy for false marking with a new action that allows a party that has suffered a competitive injury as a result of such marking to seek compensatory damages. The United States would be allowed to seek the $500-per-article fine, and competitors may recover in relation to actual injuries that they have suffered as a result of false marking, but the bill would eliminate litigation brought by unrelated, private third parties.

Advice of Counsel

The Act includes a new provision that bars courts and juries from drawing an adverse inference from an accused infringer's failure to obtain opinion of counsel as to infringement or his failure to waive privilege and disclose such an opinion. Section 298 of title 35 is designed to protect attorney-client privilege and to reduce pressure on accused infringers to obtain opinions of counsel for litigation purposes. It reflects a policy choice that the probative value of this type of evidence is outweighed by the harm that coercing a waiver of attorney-client privilege inflicts on the attorney-client relationship. Section 298 applies to findings of both willfulness and intent to induce infringement—and thus legislatively abrogates the Federal Circuit's decision in Broadcom Corp. v. Qualcomm Inc., 543 F.3d 683, 699 (Fed. Cir. 2008).

---

56   See id.

Committee Report 112-98

Transitional program for covered business method patents

A number of patent observers believe the issuance of poor business-method patents during the late 1990's through the early 2000's led to the patent "troll" lawsuits that compelled the Committee to launch the patent reform project 6 years ago. At the time, the USPTO lacked a sufficient number of examiners with expertise in the relevant art area. Compounding this problem, there was a dearth of available prior art to assist examiners as they reviewed business method applications. Critics also note that most countries do not grant patents for business methods.

The Act responds to the problem by creating a transitional program 1 year after enactment of the bill to implement a provisional post-grant proceeding for review of the validity of any business method patent. In contrast to the era of the late 1990's-early 2000's, examiners will review the best prior art available. A petition to initiate a review will not be granted unless the petitioner is first sued for infringement or is accused of infringement. The program otherwise generally functions on the same terms as other post-grant proceedings initiated pursuant to the bill. Any party may request a stay of a civil action if a related post-grant proceeding is granted. The program sunsets after 10 years, which ensures that patent holders cannot delay filing a lawsuit over a shorter time period to avoid reevaluation under the transitional program.

Jurisdictional and procedural matters

a) State court jurisdiction and the US Court of Appeals for the Federal Circuit

The US district courts area [sic] given original jurisdiction to hear patent cases,[57] while the US Court of Appeals for the Federal Circuit adjudicates all patent appeals.[58] The Supreme Court ruled in 2002,[59] however, that patent counterclaims do not give the Federal Circuit appellate jurisdiction over a case.

The Act clarifies the jurisdiction of the US district courts and stipulates that the US Court of Appeals for the Federal Circuit has jurisdiction over appeals involving compulsory patent counterclaims. The legislative history of this provision, which we reaffirm and adopt as our own, appears in the Committee Report accompanying H.R. 2955 from the 109th Congress,[60] which the Committee reported favorably to the House on April 5, 2006.

b) Joinder

The Act also addresses problems occasioned by the joinder of defendants (sometimes numbering in the dozens) who have tenuous connections to the underlying disputes in patent infringement suits.

The Act amends chapter 29 of the Patent Act by creating a new § 299 that addresses joinder under Rule 20 and consolidation of trials under Rule 42. Pursuant to the provision, parties who are accused infringers in most patent suits may be joined as defendants or counterclaim defendants only if: (1) relief is asserted against the parties, jointly, severally, or in the alternative, arising out of the same transaction regarding the manufacture, use, or importation of the accused product or process; and (2) questions of fact common to all of the defendants will arise in the action. New § 299 also clarifies that joinder will not be available if it based solely on allegations that a defendant has infringed the patent(s) in question.[61]

---

57 28 USC § 1338.
58 28 USC § 1295.
59 Holmes Group, Inc., v. Vornado Air Circulation Systems, Inc. 535 U.S. 826 (2002).
60 H. Rep. 109–405.
61 Section 299 legislatively abrogates the construction of Rule 20(a) adopted in MyMail, Ltd. v. America Online,

Committee Report 112-98

Technical amendments

The Act contains technical amendments to improve the organization of the patent statute.

Travel expenses and payment of administrative judges

The USPTO Director is authorized to conduct programs or exchanges pertaining to intellectual property law and protection "domestically and throughout the world." The House bill clarifies that this authority includes expending funds to cover the subsistence and travel expenses of non-Federal employees who attend these programs.

The House bill also clarifies that the Director may fix the pay for administrative patent judges and administrative trademark judges under the new Patent Trial and Appeal Board set forth in Section 6 of the bill.

Patent and Trademark Office funding

The USPTO is a fee-funded agency. The revenue it collects from fees imposed on inventors and trademark filers is deposited in a special USPTO appropriations account in the Treasury. To obtain funding for its operations, the agency must request the revenue back from congressional appropriators. Since the early 1990's, however, more than $800 million has been diverted from the agency and spent on non-USPTO initiatives.

The Committee believes the USPTO could operate more efficiently and productively if the agency had full access to all of its fee-generated revenue. The House bill therefore creates a USPTO revolving fund within the Treasury that allows the agency to keep all of the funds it raises until expended.

The provision also requires the Director to submit an annual spending plan as well as an annual year-end report to the House and Senate Appropriations and Judiciary Committees.

Satellite offices

The USPTO is conducting a pilot to create and operate a new satellite office located in Detroit. The bill requires the Director to establish three other satellite offices within a 3-year window, subject to available resources. The legislation includes criteria that must be invoked when selecting the new sites.

Designation of Detroit satellite office

The House and Senate bills contain a provision that designates the PTO satellite office in Detroit as the "Elijah J. McCoy United States Patent and Trademark Office." Elijah McCoy was an African-Canadian inventor who spent much of his life in Michigan and earned 57 US patents. His work on an automatic lubricator to oil railroad steam engines gave rise to the expression, "the real McCoy."

Patent Ombudsman Program for small business concerns

The Act requires the USPTO Director to establish a Patent Ombudsman Program to provide support and services regarding patent filings to small business concerns. The authorization is subject to available resources.

Inc., 223 F.R.D. 455 (E.D. Tex. 2004); Sprint Communications Co. v. Theglobe.com, Inc., 233 F.R.D. 615 (D. Kan. 2006); Adrain v. Genetec Inc., 2009 WL3063414 (E.D. Tex. September 22, 2009); Better Educ. Inc. v. Einstruction Corp., 2010 WL 918307 (E.D. Tex. March 10, 2010); Mannatech, Inc. v. Country Life, LLC, 2010 WL 2944574 (N.D. Tex. July 26, 2010); Alford Safety Services, Inc., v. Hot-Hed, Inc., 2010 WL 3418233 (E.D. La. August 24, 2010); and Eolas Technologies, Inc. v. Adobe Systems, Inc., 2010 WL 3835762 (E.D. Tex. September 28, 2010)—effectively conforming these courts' jurisprudence to that followed by a majority of jurisdictions. See generally Rudd v. Lux Products Corp., 2011 WL 148052 (N.D. Ill. January 12, 2011).

155

Committee Report 112-98

Priority examination for technologies important to American competitiveness

The Act stipulates that the USPTO may promulgate regulations, not inconsistent with law, that prioritize examination of applications for products, processes, or technologies that are important to the national economy or national competitiveness. This may be done without recovering the aggregate extra cost of providing the prioritization.

Calculation of 60-day period for application of patent term extension

The USPTO has inconsistently applied "counting" rules that are imposed on patent holders who must submit documents to the agency within statutory time periods for consideration of additional patent term under § 156 of the Patent Act. The Act clarifies that the agency should impose a "business-day" construction for application to § 156, consistent with recent case law on the matter [62].

Study on implementation

The Act requires the USPTO Director to conduct a study regarding the implementation of the legislation and on such other aspects of Federal patent policies and practices with respect to patent rights, innovation in the United States, competitiveness of US markets, access by small business to capital and investment, and such other issues as the Director deems appropriate. The study must be completed within 4 years and the results submitted to the House and Senate Committees on the Judiciary.

Pro bono program

The Committee acknowledges the importance of individuals and small businesses to the patent system and our national culture of innovation. Consistent with this sentiment, the Act requires the USPTO Director to support intellectual property law associations across the United States to establish pro bono programs to assist under-resourced independent inventors and businesses.

Effective date

Except as otherwise provided, the provisions of the bill take effect 1 year following the date of enactment and shall apply to any patent issued on or after that date.

Budgetary effects

The House bill retains a Senate provision that references a CBO PAYGO score in The Congressional Record.

Hearings

The Committee's Subcommittee on Intellectual Property, Competition, and the Internet held 1 day of hearings on H.R. 1249. The hearing took place on March 30, 2011. Testimony was received from the Honorable David Kappos, Under Secretary of Commerce for Intellectual Property and Director of the United States Patent and Trademark Office; Steve Bartlett, President and CEO of The Financial Services Roundtable; Steven Miller, President and General Counsel (Intellectual Property) for Procter & Gamble; Mark Chandler, Senior Vice President, General Counsel, and Secretary for Cisco; and John Vaughn, Executive Vice President of the Association of American Universities.

---

62 The Medicines Co. v. Kappos, et. al., 10–CV–286 (E.D. Va. August 3, 2010).

The Subcommittee also conducted three separate but related hearings on January 25, 2011 ("How an Improved US Patent and Trademark Office Can Create Jobs," Serial No. 112–6), February 11, 2011 ("Crossing the Finish Line on Patent Reform—What Can and Should be Done," Serial No. 112–8), and March 10, 2011 ("Review of Recent Judicial Decisions on Patent Law," Serial No. 112– 20).

Given that the bill is a 6-year work in progress, the legislative record should also reflect that the Subcommittee conducted related hearings on patent reform in the 109th through 111th Congresses. These hearings include the following: "H.R. 2795, the 'Patent Reform Act of 2005'" (June 19, 2005); "Committee Print Regarding Patent Quality Improvement (Part I)" (April 20, 2005, Serial No. 109–11); "Committee Print Regarding Patent Quality Improvement (Part II)" (April 28, 2005, Serial No. 109–11); "Review of US Patent and Trademark Office Operations" (September 8, 2005, Serial No. 109–48); "Patent Quality Enhancement in the Information-Based Economy" (April 5, 2006, Serial No. 109–99); "Patent Harmonization" (April 26, 2006, Serial No. 109–100); "Patent Trolls: Fact or Fiction?" (June 15, 2006, Serial No. 109–104); "Oversight Hearing on the US Patent and Trademark Office" (February 27, 2008, Serial No. 110–115); "The 'Patent Reform Act of 2007'" (April 26, 2007, Serial No. 110–65); "H.R. 1260, The 'Patent Reform Act of 2009'" (April 30, 2009, Serial No. 111–92); and "The US Patent and Trademark Office" (May 5, 2010, Serial No. 111–135).

Finally, the United States Senate Committee on the Judiciary devoted substantial process to patent reform over the same time period. Beginning in 2005, the Senate Judiciary Committee conducted eight hearings on the subject and reported separate bills in the 110th (S. 1145), 111th (S. 515), and 112th (S. 23) Congresses. The full Senate passed S. 23 on March 8, 2011, by a vote of 95– 5. H.R. 1249 is substantially similar to S. 23.

Committee Consideration

On April 14, 2011, the Committee met in open session and ordered the bill H.R. 1249 favorably reported with an amendment, by a roll call vote of 32 to 3, a quorum being present.

Publisher's End Note: Subsequent to this report, the following amendments to H.R. 1249 were approved by the House of Representatives on June 23, 2011: H.AMDT.491 (Manager's amendment makes numerous technical and clarifying changes to the bill); H.AMDT.494 (Amendment allows the United States Patent Trade Office to develop methods for ways to track the diversity of patent applicants); H.AMDT.495 (Amendment expresses the sense of Congress that "the patent system should promote industries to continue to develop new technologies that spur growth and create jobs across the country"); H.AMDT.496 (Amendment lists criteria that the Patent Trade Office Director must take into account when selecting satellite offices in the United States); H.AMDT.497 (Amendment mandates a United States Patent Trade Office led study with the Small Business Administration on how to better utilize existing government resources for education and technical assistance to help small businesses with international patent protection); H.AMDT.499 (Amendment clarifies the deadline for filing patent term extension applications covering drug products that must be approved by the FDA); H.AMDT.500 (Amendment requires the United States Patent Trade Office to provide rules for the exchange of relevant information during the derivation proceedings).